WATSON'S

THEOLOGICAL INSTITUTES

DEFENDED;

THE TEACHINGS OF TRANSCENDENTAL PHILOSOPHY SHOWN TO BE AT VARIANCE WITH SCRIPTURE AND MATTER OF FACT;

AND

THE BIBLE PROVED TO BE COMPLETE IN ITSELF, BOTH IN TEACHING AND EVIDENCE.

BY

REV. JOHN LEVINGTON.

"The world by wisdom [σοφιας] knew not God."—1 Cor. i, 21.
"The entrance of thy word giveth light."—Psalm cxix, 130.

FOR SALE BY
T. K. ADAMS, 90 WOODWARD AVENUE, DETROIT.
BARNES & BURR, NEW YORK.
1863.

JOHN F. TROW,
PRINTER, STEREOTYPER, AND ELECTROTYPER,
46, 48, & 50 Greene Street,
New York.

PREFACE.

When we read in the Quarterly Review the article which finally moved us to write the following pages, we confidently expected to see replies from strong men occupying the position of watchmen upon the walls of our Zion; but our expectations have been entirely disappointed; for although nearly twelve months have passed away since its appearing, nothing has appeared save notices of approval, and some of these from men of high standing in our Church. These approving notices on the part of some, and entire silence on the part of all others, sufficiently indicate the prevalence of the sentiments therein contained, and to which we have felt it our duty to object. We are fully aware, too, that the teachings here opposed are far more congenial with the popular sentiment of the day, than are the teachings which we oppose to them. Nor are we ignorant of the fact, that they are multitudinous who recognize no authority but *reason*, and no God but *nature*, which of course, are defined to be anything, and everything, according to the whims of their worshippers. From this class it is not at all likely that our little performance will have many admirers; though we still indulge the hope that it may be useful to some of them. Everything considered, we confess we are forcibly reminded of the well-known proverb, *Athanasius contra mundum*. But while the opposition in each case may be similar, the parties opposed are very different; yet, even this does not discourage us when we remember *that* truth, "God hath chosen the weak things of this world to confound the things which are mighty." Resting here, and merely claiming credit for sincerity of belief and honesty of purpose, and simply desiring a candid criticism, we commit the following thoughts to the wide, wide world of mind, trusting that by the blessing of God, to whose care we commend them, they will battle successfully with error, and exert a salutary influence on that world of mind in all time to come.

To those with whom I have felt it my duty to join issue, I have the kindest feeling, and cheerfully concede to them what I claim for myself, sincerity of belief and honesty of purpose.

In view of the variety and difficulty of the subjects discussed in the following pages, it would be folly to claim, or expect, that there is no mistake; but whether the mistakes be many or few, we have as yet failed to discover them. To mere fault-finders we have nothing to say: they are a class of people of whom no one has a high opinion, and their mere fault-finding is utterly unworthy of notice.

To those who are not acquainted with Watson's Theological Institutes, and who do not feel particularly interested in their defence, a few of the following pages may not be very interesting; with this exception, however, the subjects discussed are so various and important that their discussion cannot fail to be interesting to all.

It is quite evident that most of the views opposed in the following pages are becoming increasingly popular; and it is equally evident that they are utterly irreconcilable with those views hitherto denominated orthodox; therefore, whichever side is right, the sooner the issue is joined the better.

We have already mentioned "Fleming's Vocabulary of Philosophy," and will here acknowledge our indebtedness to that excellent little volume, both for thoughts and definitions.

JOHN LEVINGTON.

SALINE, *March* 27, 1863.

WATSON'S THEOLOGICAL INSTITUTES AND THE BIBLE DEFENDED.

CHAPTER I.

THE first article in the *Methodist Quarterly Review* for April, 1862, is entitled "Metaphysics of Watson's Institutes." This title would indicate that Watson's Metaphysics *only*, are involved in the discussion; but this is not the case, for his theological teachings are deeply involved, as we shall soon see. It is not this article alone that moves us to write this defence; certainly we would not make such an effort merely to refute the views of an individual. The teachings to which we object are, in the main, and claim to be, those of a certain school of philosophy, and are presented to us as some of the last and best discoveries of philosophical research. These views are, and always have been popular with the sceptical classes of society; but of late, if we mistake not, they are becoming more and more popular amongst other and very different classes of society. These, and other facts which will be called forth in the course of our investigations, are not only sufficient to justify us in attempting this defence, but will, we trust, secure the deep attention of every lover of truth, on whatever side the truth may be supposed to lie, seeing we take the ground that the teachings which we oppose are at variance with Scripture and matter of fact, and that to a very serious extent, as we expect to show.

The author of the article under consideration, after some preliminary remarks, proceeds thus:

"That we may clearly apprehend the philosophical views of Mr. Watson, and fairly estimate their influence on his theology, it will be necessary that we glance at the systems of philosophy which were prevalent and influential in his day. There are two schools of philosophy which may be said to have divided and given direction to the philosophic thought of the last century: the Sensational, or Empirical, and the Transcendental, or Rational. Their representatives respectively may be found in Locke and Kant: Locke at the head of the Sensational, Kant at the head of the Transcendental School."

After some remarks upon the prevailing and distinguishing tenets of those schools, which tenets will be noticed in due time, our reviewer reaches his first conclusion thus: "So much being premised, we have now no difficulty in determining Mr. Watson's relations to the prevailing schools of philosophy. Unquestionably he attaches himself to the system of Locke; he was a disciple of the Empirical School."

Now we decidedly object to this mode of procedure; we hold that Watson's Institutes should be tried upon their own merits; it is a review of "Watson's Metaphysics" that is undertaken, not the philosophic schools of his day. Moreover, it is doing Watson a gross injustice to represent him, in the entire absence of evidence, as being led by Locke, or by any other man or number of men; and it is calculated even to prejudice the reviewer and his readers against Watson, at the very commencement of the investigation. The deep-thinking, lofty-minded, self-made Watson, is the last man that we should suspect of being led, even by "the over-towering and all-pervading philosophy of Locke." So far from this, it seems quite evident that one special object of his mission was to rescue the great principles of religion out of the hands of bold, vain, speculative, and sceptical philosophers, a work for which he was admirably adapted, and in which he was gloriously successful. Nor is his work done; we have strong confidence that his Institutes will do in this country and age what they did in his own. And so far was he from being led by Locke, that he joined issue with him on the subject of government, which that philosopher and his followers called "the social compact." This idea of the man whose "imperial name ruled supreme in the English Universities and schools of learning," Mr. Watson boldly pronounced "a pure fiction." He quotes this same philosopher approvingly in the following instances, viz., as to his definition of moral good and evil; as to the necessity of divine authority to enforce moral precepts; and as to his statement that the bulk of mankind have neither leisure nor capacity for close, consecutive reasoning and demonstration. More than this we do not find that he quotes this great man at all. Why then is it asserted, "unquestionably he attaches himself to the system of Locke." He did with the teaching of Locke just what he did with that of all other men: he indorsed what he thought was right, and rejected what he thought was wrong. In proof of this we adduce a single fact just here. Having examined the Institutes with reference to this very thing, we find, if we count right, that he quotes from as many as three hundred leading systems, schools, and individuals; giving us their leading philosophical and theological views, or principles, and, at the same time, rejecting or indorsing according as he approves or disapproves; and giving us his reasons for so doing. The systems, schools, and persons thus quoted, flourished in different countries, and at different times, from the earliest period of history to his own times; nor does he hesitate to dissent from those whom he esteemed and loved most, as will be seen by all who carefully read his "Institutes," "Expositions," and published sermons.

But having declared Watson to be "a sensationalist, a disciple of the empirical school," he is made accountable for the teachings of that school, and of every individual belonging to it; hence it is quite an easy matter to make out a bill of charges. The appellation itself, too, will assist very much in making out such a bill. *Empiric:* Latin, *empiricus;* Greek, *empeirikos*, that is, one who makes experiments; a quack, who, being destitute of scientific skill, merely experimentizes. Hence this school, according to our reviewer (Review, p. 182), "Holds that all simple ideas existing in the human mind are the direct and only result of sensation, and that all our knowledge is derived from experience. Not only the *matter* of our ideas, but also their *form;* not merely the *occasion* of our ideas, but their *cause* is from without. The mind itself does not supply one element of truth. It has no standards of truth within itself. Nor does it, of itself, affirm any first principles, any primitive cognitions, judgments, or beliefs which are necessary to the attainment of truth. The human mind is an empty vessel, into which our sensations—a heterogeneous mixture—are poured from the external world, upon which the mind itself exerts no modifying influence, does not even give a color to the liquid, but simply retains it in memory until it shall crystallize into the classifications of science. Or, to employ the favorite figure of Locke himself, the mind is a 'tabula rasa,' a blank sheet of paper, void of all characters, and without any ideas, on which the external world, by a species of photography, writes its own images, and those which bear a strong resemblance naturally blend so as to form species and genera, the highest generalization becoming the apex of all science. *Man, therefore, has no ideas of right and wrong, of duty, of accountability, of retribution, of immortality, or of God, except as derived from without.* This school of philosophy landed, as indeed it must inevitably land, in pure materialism, and numbers among its disciples, or, more properly, its high priests, such writers as Hartley, Priestley, Combe, and Aug. Comte." Such was the school of which Watson was a disciple. Such were his fellow disciples and high priests, and such the tendency of the whole "that it landed, as indeed it must inevitably land, in pure materialism." The reviewer, however, very kindly apologizes for Watson thus: "It would ill become us to complain that Mr. Watson should have entertained these views. They were the prevailing opinions of his country and age. They were entertained by Locke, Ellis, Leland, Horsley, and other equally distinguished and honored names. Watson has, at least, this advantage—he stands amid illustrious men. Yet we can ill conceal our regrets. His design was noble and praiseworthy. He sought to prove the *necessity* of oral revelation, and vindicate for it the honor of furnishing all our knowledge of God, duty, and immortality; but in thus attempting to build up a strong presumption in favor of revealed religion by rejecting the intuitions of the human mind, and casting doubt upon the veracity of our faculties, the foundations of all truth are loosened and unsettled; yea, the very fundamental truths upon which we must plant our argument in demonstrating the truth of a revelation from God; and the inquiring mind is cast afloat upon an open sea of doubt." Poor Watson! he meant well, but, alas! by his teachings "the foundations of all truth are loosened and unsettled; yea, the very fundamental truths (I had supposed that these were included in *all truth*); and the inquiring mind is cast afloat upon an open sea of doubt." (P. 186.)

Now, on the part of the reviewer, this apology may be very kind, but we respectfully decline its acceptance; not only because the charges are utterly untrue, and, consequently, the apology uncalled for, but because we consider it little, if anything, better than an insult. Mr. Watson is prejudged, condemned, and apologized for, even before his case is examined. A certain school and certain men are represented as holding certain views, which we do not here pause to pronounce right or wrong, and Watson and those men are declared to be disciples of this school, and empirics and sensationalists, whose principles are erroneous in the last degree, so much so that the whole "landed, as indeed it must inevitably land, in pure materialism." Thus Watson is placed in company with these men, simply, it would seem, that with them he may be condemned.

It is necessary just here, we think, to give some attention to *appellations* and *terms*, in the use of which the reviewer is very faulty. He assumes, for instance, that the appellations *sensationalist* and *empiric* are interchangeable, as being of synonymous import. Hence the school to which he assumes Watson attaches himself, he denominates "the sensational or empirical," and is indifferent, consequently, as to which of the appellations he applies to Watson. He should know that these appellations are not synonymous and, consequently, not interchangeable. Empiricism is based on *experience*, and sensationalism on *sen-*

sation alone: the latter is what Fichte calls "the dirt philosophy." "The empirical philosophers," says Bacon, "are like pismires, they only lay up and use their store. The rationalists are like the spiders, they spin all out of their own bowels. But give me a philosopher, who, like the bee, hath a middle faculty, gathering from abroad, but digesting that which is gathered by his own virtue." How much Watson resembles the bee in the particulars here specified may be seen in the facts which we have already stated, and will be seen still more clearly in facts to be stated in the course of our investigations; so that in these particulars, at least, Watson is one of those philosophers whom Bacon so much admired. Mr. C. is also at fault in using certain terms as though their meaning were fixed and agreed upon by philosophers generally, whereas this is very far from being the fact. Hence Mr. C. has no right to conclude Mr. W.'s views merely from his rejecting or indorsing those terms; it is necessary to specify the sense in which he understands the terms indorsed or rejected, seeing different philosophers use them with different latitudes of meaning.

Intuition, for instance, is a word which conveys different ideas, as used by different philosophers. As it is used by some, neither Locke nor Watson would object to it; while they utterly reject it in the sense in which others use it. In his "Essay on the Human Understanding," Locke says: "Sometimes the mind perceives the agreement or disagreement of two ideas immediately by themselves, without the intervention of any other; and this, I think, we may call *intuitive* knowledge." He gives other instances of what he thinks may be called the intuitive; yet Mr. C. represents both Locke and Watson as denying all "intuitive beliefs." Taylor, in his "Elements of Thought," says: "What we know or comprehend, as soon as we perceive or attend to it, we are said to know by *intuition;* things which we know by *intuition* cannot be made more certain by arguments than they are at first. We know by *intuition* that all the parts of a thing together are equal to the whole of it. Axioms are propositions known by *intuition*."

"*Intuition* has been applied by Dr. Beattie and others, not only to the power by which we perceive the truth of the axioms of geometry, but to that by which we recognize the authority of the fundamental laws of belief, when we hear them enunciated in language. My only objection to this use of the word is, that it is a departure from common practice; according to which, if I be not mistaken, the proper objects of *intuition* are propositions analogous to the axioms prefixed to Euclid's Elements. In some other respects this innovation might perhaps be regarded as an improvement on the very limited and imperfect vocabulary of which we are able to avail ourselves in our present discussion." (Stewart's "Elements.")

"Perception is singular, incomplex, and immediate, i. e., is *intuition*. When I see a star, or hear the tones of a harp, the perceptions are immediate, incomplex, and *intuitive*. This is the good old logical meaning of the word *intuition*. In our philosophic writings, however, *intuitive* and *intuition* have come to be applied solely to propositions; it is here extended to the first elements of perception, whence such propositions spring. Again, *intuition*, in English, is restricted to perceptions *à priori;* but the established logical use and wont applies the word to every incomplex representation whatever; and it is left for further and more deep inquiry to ascertain what intuitions are founded on observation and experience, and what arise from *à priori* sources." (Semple, "Introduction to Metaphys. of Ethics.") According to this philosopher there are "*intuitions*" which "are founded on observation and experience," but it requires "further and more deep inquiry" to distinguish them and such as "arise from *à priori* sources."

"Besides its original and proper meaning (as a visual perception)," says Sir William Hamilton, "it has been employed to denote a kind of *apprehension* and a kind of *judgment*."

"*Intuition*," says Mansel, "is used in the extent of the German Anschauung, to include all the products of the perceptive (external or internal) and imaginative faculties; every act of consciousness, in short, of which the immediate is an *individual*, thing, state, or act of mind, presented under the condition of distinct existence in space or time."

Such are some of the definitions and explanations which different philosophers give us of that thing called *intuition*, the meaning of which Mr. C. assumes to be fixed and agreed upon by the philosophers who use it, but with what reason the above quotations will show; and, what is not less marvellous, he is not only confident in the use of it himself, but is quite out of patience with Watson, because the views of that writer do not exactly quadrate with his own in reference to the use of a term to which philosophers attach so many shades of meaning. Ignoring all this, together with the fact that Locke himself specifies what he says may be called "intuitive knowledge," Mr. C. assures us that Mr. Watson teaches that "reason does not apprehend *à priori*, self-evident, necessary truth." What Mr. Watson teaches concerning reason we shall see in due time; at present we shall only glance at the term *innate*, leaving the other leading terms to be taken up in order as we shall proceed with our investigations.

Innate. "There is a great deal of difference," says Locke, "between an *innate law* and a law of nature; between something imprinted on our minds in their very original, and something that we, being ignorant of, may attain to the knowledge of by the use and application of our natural faculties. And I think they equally forsake the truth who, running into contrary extremes, either affirm an *innate law*, or deny that there is a law knowable by the *light of nature*, without the help of positive revelation."

The following from Dr. Reid seems to be quite in harmony with the above: "Of the various powers and faculties we possess, there are some which nature seems both to have planted and reared, so as to have left nothing to human industry. Such are the powers which we have in common with the brutes, and which are necessary to the preservation of the individual, or the continuance of the kind. There are other powers, of which nature hath only planted the seeds in our minds, but hath left the rearing of them to human culture." When speaking of natural rights, the doctor uses *innate* as synonymous with natural.

"Among modern philosophers it would be difficult to name any who held the doctrine in the form in which it has been attacked by Locke. In calling some of our ideas *innate* they seem merely to have used this word as synonymous with *natural*, and applied it, as Hutcheson thinks the ancients did, to certain ideas which men, as human or rational beings, *necessarily* and *universally* entertain." (Fleming's "Vocabulary of Philosophy.")

"Though it appears not that we have any *innate* ideas or formed notions or principles laid in by nature, antecedently to the exercise of our senses or understanding; yet it must be granted that we were born with the natural faculty whereby we actually discern the agreement or disagreement of some notions, so soon as we have the notions themselves, as, that we can or do think, that therefore we ourselves are; that one and two make three, that gold is not silver, nor ice formally water; that the whole is greater than its part, &c., and if we should set ourselves to do it, we cannot deliberately and seriously doubt of its being so. This we may call *intuitive knowledge*, or *natural* certainty wrought into our very make and constitution." (Oldfield, "Essay on Reason.")

The above quotations will suffice to show with what propriety Mr. C. uses these terms as though their meaning were fixed and agreed upon by philosophers. Of course the arguments and objections built upon such assumptions are futile and vain. The following are Mr. C.'s views of man's *innate* or *intuitive* powers, as given in the article under review; see pages 183, 184, 197, 205, and 206:

"There are specific *forms* into which human thought must necessarily develop itself, just as a grain of wheat must necessarily develop itself into 'the blade, and the ear, and full corn in the ear,' or an acorn develop into the majestic oak." . . . . . "The human intelligence is configured and correlated to eternal principles of order, and right, and good, as they exist in the Infinite Intelligence. Man is the offspring and image of God. And when a principle or an act is apprehended by the understanding, the mind passes a judgment upon the relation of that principle or act to these laws of order and right and good." . . . . . "Man is so constituted by the great Architect of his mental being—God has imposed upon his intelligence such laws of thought as determine him to form the idea of

God, of right and wrong, of duty, and of accountability." . . . . . "As the vital and rudimental germ of the oak is contained in the acorn—as it is quickened and excited to activity by the external conditions of moisture, light, and heat, and is fully developed under the fixed and determinative laws of vegetative life—so the germ of the idea of God is present in every human mind as the intuitions of pure reason; these intuitions are excited into energy by our experimental and historic knowledge of the facts and laws of the universe; and these facts and intuitions are developed into scientific form by the necessary laws of the intellect." . . . . . "On contemplating the acts of a voluntary agent we immediately apprehend them as having a *moral quality*. The mind intuitively apprehends them as *right* or *wrong*, and spontaneously approves or condemns them. This distinction in the moral quality of actions is felt to be independent of the mind which perceives it, and of any mutable condition of things. Good and evil, right and wrong are immutable. The distinction between them must be the same everywhere, at all times, and to all beings—to God, to angels, and to men. It is as impossible to conceive that there are intelligences to whom falsehood can appear a virtue and justice a vice, as that there are intelligences to whom two and two equal five, or to whom the properties of the triangle can be more or less than they are to us. Accompanying this perception of the immutable distinction between virtue and vice, we have the consciousness of its being our DUTY to avoid the one and perform the other. We feel upon us an OBLIGATION which is imperative. We have also an abiding conviction that moral good is rewardable, and that vice merits punishment. And, finally, we have a conscious apprehension of a future retribution."

Let us try and condense this marvellous accumulation of marvellous assertions, that the whole may be seen at a glance.

The human mind is configured and correlated to eternal principles of order, and right, and good as they exist in the Infinite Mind. God has imposed upon the human mind such laws of thought as determine it to form the idea of God, of right and wrong, of duty and of accountability. The mind intuitively apprehends human actions as right or wrong, and spontaneously approves or condemns them. And all this is independent of the mind which perceives it, and of any mutable condition of things. It is as impossible to conceive that there are intelligences to whom falsehood can appear a virtue and justice a vice, as that there are intelligences to whom two and two equal five. And these intuitions of pure reason are present in every human mind as the vital and rudimental germ of the oak is contained in the acorn. And as the latter is fully developed under the fixed and determinative laws of vegetative life, so these intuitions of pure reason in every human mind are excited into energy by our experimental and historic knowledge of the facts and laws of the universe, and these facts and intuitions are developed into scientific form by the necessary laws of the intellect.

Here is a specimen of the *transcendental*, the *innate*, the *intuitive*, or what you please to call it. And our reviewer "can ill conceal his regrets" that Mr. Watson did not thus believe and teach, instead of "degrading our reason, and casting doubt upon the veracity of our faculties," so that "the foundations of all truth are loosened and unsettled." In short, teaching so erroneous that it "landed, as indeed it must inevitably land, in pure materialism."

We beg to assure our brother that we are very far from being prepared to substitute the above, or anything like it, for the solid Scriptural teachings of Watson's Institutes, and we, too, "can ill conceal our regrets" that such a substitute should be offered. You may talk as loudly as you please about "the intuitions of pure reason," "the facts and laws of the universe," and "the necessary laws of the intellect," *combinedly* and *necessarily* producing the *knowledge* and *faith* you speak of; and that as necessarily as the majestic oak is produced from the acorn, under the fixed and determinative laws of vegetative life; but to all such assertions, however loud and confident, the facts of experience and observation, the facts of history, both ancient and modern, and the teachings of the Bible, give this simple reply: IT IS NOT TRUE! It is also a fact, we claim, that the uniform tendency of fallen man is downward without the intervention of a *supernatural power:* and it too often happens that his course is still onward from bad to worse, notwithstanding that power is exerted with amazing energy. That such statements as those quoted above should be made in the face of these glaring facts, and so completely at variance with them, is truly marvellous. Moreover, if our knowledge and faith are matured into scientific form by fixed and determinative laws, as necessarily as the majestic oak is matured from the acorn by the same or similar laws; if God has imposed upon the human intelligence such laws of thought as determine us to form the idea of God, of right and wrong, of duty and accountability; if the human intelligence is configured and correlated to eternal principles of order, and right, and good as they exist in the Infinite Intelligence, the teachings of Watson and those of his reviewer are alike superfluous and useless; seeing our knowledge and faith are inevitable results of inevitable causes, and, consequently, as destitute of virtue as the majestic oak, being produced by the same or similar laws. In short, if what the reviewer says be true, if the knowledge and faith specified be the inevitable results of inevitable causes, it will follow that the old saying is true after all, "Whatever is, is right!" Or, if there is anything wrong, it is not in man any more than it is in the "majestic oak," seeing the growth of the one, and the knowledge and faith of the other, are alike the inevitable results of inevitable causes, which causes are "fixed and determinative laws."

We regret that the universal and irresistible laws of which the reviewer speaks have not been more powerfully felt in Wyandotte, for it is quite certain that there are many here whose *knowledge* and *faith* are very far from being what is predicated of universal mankind in the above statements of the reviewer. And, what is still more strange, there are those here who teach *that falsehood is a virtue!* And they believe that the Council of Constance, which affirmed this very thing, was infallible. Yea, they believe that "no faith is to be kept with heretics." And they believe that the Emperor Sigismund and the Council of Constance did a truly virtuous act when, acting upon this doctrine, they betrayed and burnt John Huss. And they believe, doubtless, that the act of the Bishop of Landy was a truly virtuous one, when, in the name of the Council, he thus praised the emperor for *falsehood*, *treachery*, and *murder:* "This most holy and goodly labor was reserved only for thee, O most noble prince! Upon thee only doth it lie, to whom the whole rule and ministration of justice is given. Wherefore, thou hast established thy praise and renown; even by the mouths of babes and sucklings thy praise shall be celebrated for evermore." *All this they most steadfastly believe!* Hence, it is clearly possible to believe that falsehood is a virtue, at least when the falsehood is told for the good of "Mother Church." As to whether these are "primitive beliefs," we leave the reviewer to decide. In further proof, however, of "this perception of the immutable distinction between virtue and vice," and which "must be the same everywhere, at all times and to all beings—to God, to angels, and to men;" we will add two more specimens of these "necessary beliefs," these "necessary intuitions," which indicate "the spontaneous energy of the human mind," in forming the idea of God, of right and wrong, of duty and accountability, and of a future retribution."

In 1571 and 1572, Charles IX of France and his great men of state made certain flattering proposals to the Protestants, and confirmed those proposals by the most solemn vows and oaths. By these means they got the Protestants into their power, and slew of them, in Paris alone, some ten thousand, and in all France some thirty thousand. Now, this falsehood, this perjury, to say nothing of the most horrible murder that history records, was considered so *virtuous* that God Almighty, as well as the king of the French, was praised in the most solemn manner, particularly at Paris and Rome, where Te Deum was sung and high mass offered, accompanied by the ringing of bells and other demonstrations of joy. So firmly do they believe the doctrine that "heretics ought to be condemned and executed, notwithstanding the most solemn assurances to the contrary." In other words, so firmly do they "believe that falsehood is a virtue." We will give another specimen of "the intuitions of pure reason;" it may be found in Mr. Wesley's Miscellaneous Works, vol. v, p. 818. Mr. W. says: "Some time since, a Romish priest came to one I knew, and, after talking with her largely, broke out:

'You are no heretic, you have the experience of a real Christian!' And 'would you,' she asked, 'burn me alive?' He said, 'God forbid!—unless it were for the good of the church!'" Such was "the spontaneous energy" of that priest's mind, and so accurate were his "necessary intuitions" in forming "the idea of God, of right and wrong, of duty, and of accountability!" Nor will it mend the matter at all to say that these parties were not sincere, for that would indicate a state still more at variance with the doctrine of "necessary intuitions and beliefs," defended by the reviewer, if any state could be more at variance with it. But the fact is, multitudes of Roman Catholics do believe these teachings of their church, viz., that "no faith is to be kept with a heretic;" in other words, that "falsehood is a virtue;" for they hold that "the end sanctifies the deed." But Roman Catholics are not the only people who believe that "falsehood is a virtue," under certain circumstances; there are many Protestants who believe the doctrine and practise it; in justification of which I have heard the following adduced. Some shipwrecked mariners were cast upon a certain island, among savages; after a long time and much suffering, a ship cast anchor off the island; the savages prepared their canoes to go to the vessel, but would not let the white man go till he promised that he would not disclose the fact that there were other white men on the island, and also that he would return with them; on these conditions he was allowed to accompany the savages to the vessel; he did disclose the fact, and intended to do so when he promised the contrary; neither did he return with them, nor did he intend to return when he promised to do so. Moreover, he obtained the release of his companions in captivity and misery, as well as his own; and all this by telling a *falsehood*, which, consequently, was declared to be a virtue! It follows, then, that even this is not an impossibility: "there are intelligences to whom falsehoods can appear to be a virtue!" nor is it necessary to go to the heathen, either ancient or modern, to find them. And, what we think is much worse, there are, and ever have been, those who justify murder in the same way that they justify falsehood; and this fact is established by the lips of the Most High in the following words: "The time cometh that whosoever killeth you will think that he doeth God service." Such are some of the *beliefs* (call them *intuitive*, *primitive*, or what you please) of "intelligences" which are declared to be "configured and correlated to eternal principles of order, and right, and good as they exist in the Infinite Intelligence."

Before we proceed farther, we will try to fix the point or points in dispute; for on page 196, Mr. C. seems to make a different issue from that which is obviously comprehended in the quotations given above. On the above page he says: "The question is not how the idea of God first became known to man, or how it now becomes known, not whether he has it from the Bible, or from tradition, or independent of any traditional suggestion." All these, we are told, "are irrelevant to the main issue." What! the question is not how the idea first became known, or how it now becomes known, or whether we have it from the Bible. We respectfully beg to differ. These questions certainly are not irrelevant to the main issue, for the question respects man's competency to *originate the idea;* it is admitted that when the idea is once obtained, evidences of its truth are clearly seen in the works of creation and providence. But we will hear what is declared to be the issue.

Can man, from the light of nature, develop a proof of

God's existence which shall be logical, conclusive, and self-sufficient? The main question is as to the competency of human reason, from the facts of the universe and the intuition of the human mind, to demonstrate the existence of God.

Neither have we here a clear exhibit of the doctrine set forth in the quotations which we have given and shall give, for we are not told whether it is *natural* or *regenerate* man that is here spoken of, or whether it is *natural* or *enlightened* and *graciously assisted reason* that is intended. So that arguing from these premises, we are still working in the dark, for certainly it will not be claimed that Watson denies the competency of enlightened reason, already in possession of the idea of a God, to deduce proofs of His being from the facts of the universe. Certainly there can be no controversy with Watson on this point. In vol. i, pp. 271 and 272, his position is thus clearly stated: "Matter of fact does not therefore support the notion that the existence of God is discoverable by the unassisted faculties of man: and there is, I conceive, very slender reason to admit the abstract possibility." "The abundant rational evidence of the existence of God, which may now be so easily collected, and which is so convincing, is therefore no proof that without instruction from heaven the human mind would ever have made the discovery." It is folly, then, to undertake to prove what Watson never denied, and to ignore the real question; to make an issue that he has not made, and leave the real issue untouched; it is worse than folly. Neither is the question in dispute confined to the mere idea of a God; it comprehends man's mental and moral powers: nor is the question what these powers are or may be *graciously*, but what they are *naturally* and *necessarily*. What they are or may be by supernatural communications is a question which certainly has nothing to do with the true issue; no man has more exalted views of the all-sufficiency of such supernatural communications than Richard Watson, nor has any man, we think, more exalted views of the dignity and glory to which man may be raised by this gracious and supernatural aid. The question is not whether the book of nature develops ideas of God's being and attributes, but whether poor, blind, fallen man can read it without gracious assistance; not whether a well instructed Christian can read it. Declaring that to be of nature which is solely of grace, stealing from Jews and Christians the knowledge of God and of the things of God, and then giving the natural, unassisted powers of man credit for the discovery, are the points to which Watson objects, and of which he complains. The question is not, we repeat, what man is or may be *graciously*, but what he is *naturally* and *necessarily*, what he is "constituted by the great Architect of his mental being," unaided by a gracious revelation; and that, too, after and despite the fall; yea, and independent of any act or choice of his own for or against. For it is claimed that "God has *imposed* upon his intelligence such laws of thought as determine him to form the idea of God, of right and wrong, of duty, and of accountability." (P. 184.) "And this distinction of the quality of moral actions is felt to be independent of the mind which perceives it." (P. 205.) This, it will be seen, is very different from what Mr. C., on page 196, represents to be the true issue. When he tells us that reason can draw such and such conclusions from the facts of the universe, he really makes no issue at all, unless he tells us what reason it is he speaks of *graciously assisted* or *unassisted* reason, *enlightened* or *unenlightened* reason; for, I repeat, there is no dispute, at least no room for dispute, with Watson in regard to *enlightened reason.*

To prevent the possibility of mistake as to the true issue, and that it may be seen we are not fighting a man of straw, we will give a few more quotations.

On p. 196, where he defines his position, as stated above, Mr. C. says: "Instead, then, of our knowledge of God resting upon revelation alone, we regard the idea of God as a phenomenon of the universal human intelligence It is in all minds in which reason is in any considerable degree developed, and is there as a *necessary* truth." This knowledge, observe, "*is in all minds as a necessary truth.*" So Mr. Cosh, "The idea of God, the belief in God, may be justly represented as native to man." The propositions on p. 199 may be thus summed up:

"The understanding gives, as the necessary 'concepts,' the 'known' primitive cognitions."

"The reason gives, as the necessary antecedents of the primitive cognitions of the understanding, 'the implied' primitive beliefs."

"The judgment, or logical faculty, gives as the necessary relation between these *understanding* conceptions and these ideas of pure reason, 'the deduced' primitive judgments or *axioms.*"

We think it deserves at least a passing notice, that these mental phenomena are so mathematically exact that "the known primitive cognitions" are just 6, the "implied primitive beliefs," 6, and "the deduced primitive judgments," 6. And all these act so harmoniously and with such combined power that the soul of which they are the phenomena is guided directly and inevitably to "*a moral governor*—A GOD." Hence he adds:

"In each of the above propositions we have an *understanding perception*—'a form' under which the mind necessarily conceives the facts of external and internal perception; we have also an *idea of pure reason*—an implied or implicit belief, arising spontaneously in the human mind in presence of the understanding conception; and lastly, we have *an analytic judgment*—the affirmation of a necessary and universal relation between the two." (P. 200.) "In early infancy this principle of intuitive logic is developed." (P. 201.) "So conclusive is this intuitive logic that no increase of proof can make it clearer, and no argument can make it stronger than when first apprehended." "From the consideration of second and physical causes we are carried forward to the idea of an intelligent cause." On pages 205 and 206 we have specifications of the moral intuitions, by which we have clear and *unavoidable* perceptions "of the immutable distinction between virtue and vice," and "of our duty to avoid the one and perform the other. We have also an abiding conviction that moral good is rewardable, and that vice is punishable. And, finally, we have a conscious apprehension of a future retribution." And "these moral intuitions are confirmed by our experience. The actions which by the conscience are pronounced right, and as such approved, are found to be productive of happiness; and the actions which by the same faculty are pronounced to be wrong and condemned, are found to be productive of misery." So true and accurate are the workings of all the mental and moral powers of all men *naturally*, after and despite the fall! We may just, however, observe in passing, that Paul's conscience, before his conversion at least, was an exception, for there were many actions which his conscience pronounced right, which certainly were not productive of happiness; and we think it is equally certain that the doctrines and practice of the Christians, which the same conscience pronounced wrong, were not productive of misery.

But we will let that pass for the present, till we give two more quotations, from other sources however, but equally illustrative of the same transcendental philosophy, and designed to keep the real issue clearly before us; then we will be prepared to combat the error; and its advocates will not be able to say, "You misrepresent us."

"Schelling and Hegel," says Murdock, "claimed to have discovered the absolute identity of the objective and subjective in human knowledge, or of things and human conceptions of them. And hence, with them transcendentalism claims to have a true knowledge of all things, material and immaterial, human and divine, so far as the mind is capable of knowing; and in this sense the word transcendentalism is now most used."

The following is in harmony with the preceding quotations, and came, doubtless, from the same source, the transcendental school: "We need a revelation of mercy, not of justice; I learn justice in my own breast." This is one of several notes which the writer took while listening to Dr. Dempster preach in the Woodward Avenue Church, Detroit, 29th April, 1860. We assure the doctor we do not wish to have justice administered to us out of the breast of the natural man, unassisted by revelation: from such justice, "good Lord, deliver us!" Nor will we go there to learn justice.

In the quotations here given, we have a clear view of the true issue; in them any one may see at a glance what in this controversy is asserted by the one party and denied by the other as to what man is *mentally* and *morally* in his *natural state;* as to what he is *necessarily* and *universally;* as to what the *natural reason* can and cannot do independent of *supernatural* assistance, independent of *revelation.* Within this compass may be found everything that legitimately belongs to this controversy. With regard to the doctrines necessarily involved, less or more, by the position of either party, they take a wider range, including more particularly the doctrine of the *fall*, the doctrine of the *atonement*, and the doctrine of the *spirit's agency* in the salvation of the soul. For, if the natural man is all that he is declared to be in the above quotations, then we must certainly take a different view of these three leading doctrines of Christianity from that which has been entertained hitherto by those who are denominated the orthodox.

We will now glance at the three leading terms in Mr. C.'s three grand propositions, viz., *understanding*, *judgment*, and *reason*. As with terms already noticed, so with these, Mr. C. takes it for granted that the meaning which he attaches to them is fixed and agreed upon by philosophers and theologians; takes it for granted that each of these mental faculties does the work that he here assigns to it; that the *understanding* gives the primitive cognitions, the *judgment* gives the primitive judgments, and the *reason* the primitive beliefs to the extent claimed: and all this NECESSARILY! Philosophers, however, are very far from being thus agreed as to these mental faculties, as the following quotations will show; and they will show, too, we think, how little reason Mr. C. has for the great confidence which he evidently has in his conclusions, though derived from such premises.

The UNDERSTANDING. "Perhaps," says Coleridge, "the safer use of the term, for general purposes, is to take it as the mind, or rather as the man himself considered as a concipient as well as a percipient being, and reason as a power supervening." And immediately after he says, "it is the whole spontaneity of the representing mind."

"The reason and the understanding," says Whewell,

"have not been steadily distinguished by English writers. The understanding is the faculty of applying principles, however obtained."

"I use the term understanding," says Sir Wm. Hamilton, "not for the *noetic* faculty, intellect proper, but for the *dionoetic*, or discursive faculty, in its widest signification."

"Sir J. Mackintosh," says Haywood, "prefers the term intellect to that of understanding as the source of conceptions." "The word *verstand*" [understanding], says the same writer, "is used occasionally as being synonymous with *vernuft*" [reason].

The JUDGMENT. Our judgments, according to Aristotle, are either *problematical*, *assertive*, or *demonstrable;* or, in other words, the results of *opinion*, of *belief*, or of *science*. Locke says: "*Judgment* implies the comparison of two or more ideas." Dr. Reid says he "applies the word *judgment* to every determination of the mind concerning what is true or false." He adds: "One of the most important distinctions of our judgments is, that some of them are intuitive, others grounded on argument." Thompson says: "Judgments are *analytic*, *synthetic*, and *tautologous*."

The REASON. "There is one faculty," says Aristotle, "by which man comprehends and embodies in his belief first principles, which cannot be proved, which he must receive from some authority; there is another by which, when a new fact is laid before him, he can show that it is in conformity with some principle possessed before. One process resembles the collection of materials for building, the other their orderly arrangement. One is intuition, the other logic. In other words, one is *reason* in its highest sense, the other *understanding*." (See Sewell, "Christ. Mor.," chap. 21.)

"Anselm considers the facts of consciousness under the fourfold arrangement of sensibility, will, reason, and intelligence, and claims that the last two are not identical." (Fleming's "Vocabulary.")

"This word," says Whately, "is used to signify all the intellectual powers collectively; 2, those intellectual powers in which man differs from brutes; 3, the faculty of carrying on the operation of reasoning."

"What some call the intuitive reason and the discursive reason, S. T. Coleridge calls the reason and the understanding, and says the latter is of the nature of the instinct of animals." (Fleming's "Vocabulary.")

"*Reason*," says Cousin, "is a revelation, a necessary and universal revelation which is wanting to no man, and which enlightens every man on his coming into the world. *Reason* is the necessary mediator between God and man, the λογος of Pythagoras and Plato, the Word made flesh, which serves as the interpreter of God, and the teacher of man, divine and human at the same time. It is not, indeed, the absolute God in his majestic individuality, but his manifestation in spirit and in truth; it is not the Being of beings; but it is the revealed God of the human race." The same author is thus quoted by Sir Wm. Hamilton: "*Reason* is a revelation of God in man; the ideas of which we are conscious belong not to us, but to absolute intelligence." It has been well observed that the root and germ of all this is Plato's doctrine, that human *reason* is a ray of the Divine *reason*. It is this notion, doubtless, that led to a denial of the *individuality* of the human soul. "The opinion," says Mr. Watson (vol. i, p. 21), "that the human soul is a part of God, enclosed for a short time in matter, but still a portion of his essence, runs through much of the Greek philosophy. It is still more ancient than that, and, at the present day, the same opinion destroys all idea of accountability among those who in India follow the Braminical system. 'The human soul is God, and the acts of the human soul are, therefore, the acts of God.' This is the popular argument by which their crimes are justified." It is easy to see that the above notions of the ancient heathen and modern Brahmins, and the following from Cousin, are one in *origin*, *nature*, and *tendency:* "Reason or intelligence is not individual, is not ours, is not even human; it is absolute, it is divine." The following notions, too, have a common parentage with the above: "The very ancient notion," says Mr. Watson (vol. i, p. 22), "of an absorption of souls back again into the Divine Essence, was with the ancients what we know it to be now in the metaphysical system of the Hindoos, a denial of *individual* immortality." Thus error leads to error, even as truth leads to truth. "Nor have the demonstrations of reason," continues Mr. Watson, "done anything to convince the other grand division of metaphysical pagans into which modern heathenism is divided, the followers of Budhu, who believe in the total annihilation of men and gods after a series of ages—a point of faith held probably by a majority of the present race of mankind."

Such are a very few of the multitudinous and contradictory definitions which ancient and modern philosophers have given us of these faculties of the mind. Let us sum up the definitions here given, that we may see them all at a glance. *The* UNDERSTANDING *is the man himself; the faculty of applying principles; the discursive faculty. It is synonymous with rèason; it is of the nature of the instinct of animals.* JUDGMENT: *It implies comparison; our judgments are intuitive, analytic, synthetic, tautologous. Our judgments are drawn from opinion, belief, or science.*

2*

REASON: *It is intuition. It is not intelligence. It is all the intellectual powers collectively. It is a revelation from God. It is a mediator. It is a light. It is the Logos. It is the Word made flesh. It is an interpreter. It is a teacher. It is Divine and human. It is the revealed God of the human race. Its ideas belong to absolute intelligence, not to us. It is a ray of the Divine reason.*

Here is a specimen of man's knowledge of himself. Here are some of the conflicting opinions of some of the greatest philosophers with regard to the *nature*, *power*, and *office* of these mental faculties. The *understanding* is reduced to a level with the instinct of brutes. The *reason* is more fortunate, for while it has various fortunes and reverses as it passes through the hands of different philosophers, it is finally elevated to proper divinity and godhead; though at one time, at least, it was so low that it was denied intelligence! Any one may now see how little confidence is to be placed in systems based upon such unfounded and contradictory assumptions. It is worthy of remark that the faculty in which Mr. C. finds so much power, from which so many good works do proceed, and upon which, in short, his whole system depends for its very existence, is that which has had the misfortune of being reduced to a level with the instinct of brutes. Others, however, deal more kindly with it and make it "the discursive faculty," while others declare "it is the man himself."

While reading what philosophers say the *reason*, the *judgment*, and the *understanding* do, and *must* do, we were convinced that while they thus talk they insensibly lose sight of man's *individuality* and *responsibility*. Strictly speaking, it is not proper to say that the *reason*, the *judgment*, or the *understanding* does anything, any more than it is proper, strictly speaking, to say the eye sees, the ear hears, the feet walk, and the hands strike. The fact is, what is thus attributed to the faculties in the one case, and to the bodily members in the other, is done by the *ego*, and is emphatically and essentially the act of the *ego*, which is always a unit, however much we may talk about faculties. If I would speak with strict propriety I must say I see, I hear, I strike, I walk, I understand, I reason, I judge—I, *the ego*, I, *myself*, *do all these things*. This thought is expressed by Sir John Davis in his poem on the immortality of the soul, thus:

> "When she *rates* things, and moves from ground to ground,
> The name of *reason* she acquires from this:
> But when by *reason* she the truth hath found,
> And standeth fixt, she *understanding* is."

While listening to so many transcendental philosophers talk so confidently and so pompously of the faculties of the human mind, we were forcibly reminded of what Archbishop Whately says of certain ecclesiastics as to their manner of talking, and the effects produced. "There is something to many minds awfully and mystically sublime in the idea of the 'decisions of the Catholic Church,' and of 'Catholic Councils, convened in the name of Christ, and whose decrees are authoritative,'" &c., &c., &c., "especially when these matters are treated of in solemn and imposing language of that peculiar kind of dazzling mistiness whose effect is to convey at first sight to ordinary readers a striking impression, with an appearance of being perfectly intelligible at the first glance, but to become more obscure and doubtful at the second glance, and more and more so the more attentively it is studied by a reader of clear understanding, so as to leave him utterly in doubt, at the last, which of several meanings it is meant to convey, or whether any at all. The rule of 'omne ignotum pro mirifico' applies most emphatically to such doctrines treated of in such language." In the foregoing the bishop has given us, we think, an admirable picture of our transcendental philosophers, of the pompous manner in which they speak of "the human intelligence as configured and correlated to eternal principles of order, and right, and good, as they exist in the Infinite Intelligence;" of "the primitive cognitions, intuitions, and beliefs;" "the concepts" and the "ideas of pure reason," which reason "is the Logos of Pythagoras and Plato;" "the Word made flesh;" "the manifestation of God in spirit and in truth." "It is not the Being of beings, but it is the revealed God of the human race." The confidence with which they speak of their own decisions, and the wonderful effect which this sort of talk and its "dazzling mistiness" produce upon certain minds, are equally well described, we think, in the above sketch, and the disappointment experienced after careful investigation is not less accurate and truthful. Oh how sad the disappointment, when the reader turns away from these transcendental descriptions of fallen humanity, and looks upon that humanity as it is! and especially when he follows it in its downward course of ignorance, corruption, and diabolical wickedness, till he can see nothing left but the savage, the cannibal, the fiend incarnate; and then, perhaps, alas! the course is still downward till it terminates in eternal ruin! How sad, I say, is the disappointment when, the "dazzling mistiness" having past away, he is left to look upon the dreadful facts as they are. We are not now speaking, remember, about man when raised by the supernatural remedy; not speaking of what man is *by* that remedy, but of what he is *naturally* and independent of that remedy: for, as we said before, what he is or may be through or by that remedy, has nothing to do with the present controversy. Let it be remembered, too, that whether Watson is right or wrong, we cannot indorse the teaching here objected to; the charges brought against Watson we will answer in due time; at present we are attending to the teachings and assumptions of his opponents as set forth in the quotations which we have given in these pages. To us it seems strange, passing strange, that men will build systems of philosophy and theology upon mere assumptions concerning faculties which the wisest philosophers, whether ancient or modern, have never been able to distinguish from each other and define with any degree of harmony and satisfaction; concerning which, in short, there are, and ever have been, so many conflicting and contradictory opinions; and the wonder is that all this is done with as much confidence as if all were demonstration: while the fact is indisputable that philosophers are and ever have been entirely disagreed as to the very foundation of the systems thus built. And it is still more strange, if possible, that there has been, and still is, such a persistent disposition to be independent of God's word, notwithstanding we are so much indebted to that word for a correct knowledge of the subject under investigation. And if we appeal to that word as decisive and final in its decisions on this subject, immediately it is insinuated, if not broadly asserted, that we are not philosophers, or that we are opposed to philosophy, as though the Bible and philosophy were at variance. Even the author of the article under consideration has only quoted, if we mistake not, Romans i, 19, 20, and Acts xvii, 26–28, and the latter, we think, is irrelevant, and as to the former it shall have our attention in due time. It is not to be wondered at, however, that philosophers of the transcendental school should not seek help from the Bible while they hold such high opinions of man's mental and moral powers. We, however, forming a much lower estimate of those powers, and feeling, consequently, our dependence upon God's word for instruction on such subjects, purpose to make a free use of it, believing, as we do, that "all Scripture is given by inspiration of God, and is profitable for doctrine, for reproof, for correction, for instruction in righteousness; that the man of God may be perfect, thoroughly furnished unto all good works."

"To the law and to the testimony," then: what does God's word say concerning man's mental and moral faculties *naturally?* And let it be distinctly borne in mind that we are not now discussing the *mere question* whether it is possible for man to *derive the idea of a God from the facts of the universe;* for, though we should admit that, still we would object to the teachings of transcendentalism as set forth in the quotations which we have given above; our work at present is to show that those teachings, as to man's *mental* and *moral* faculties *naturally*, are at variance with the teachings of God's word, and with the facts of experience and history.

In his first epistle to the Corinthians, second chapter, fourteenth verse, the Apostle Paul thus speaks: "But the natural man receiveth not the things of the Spirit of God; for they are foolishness unto him; neither can he know them, for they are spiritually discerned." The person thus described is denominated ὁ ψυχικος ἀνθρωπος, the natural man. Any one who will follow the apostle from verse 17 of the preceding chapter will see that he all along speaks of this person as the representative of a certain class, or of the class of which he is the representative. In verse 20 he speaks of ὁ σοφος, and in verse 26 of σοφοι κατα σαρκα, and in verse 22 of the Greeks who seek after σοφιαν, wisdom, and in verse 20 of "the disputer of this world." Now, to this *natural man*, this *wise man*, this *disputer of this world*, these *Greeks*, or, in other words, these philosophers who rejected revelation and boasted of their philosophy, and the discoveries of natural reason, St. Paul opposes ὁ πνευματικος ἀνθρωπος, the spiritual man, in verse 15 of the second chapter. Of these same "wise men after the flesh," the same apostle thus speaks in Romans i, 21, 22: "They became vain in their imaginations, and their foolish heart was darkened; professing themselves to be σοφοι, they became fools." Dr. Adam Clarke, in his comment on this place, says: "This is most strikingly true of all the ancient philosophers, whether Greeks or Romans, as their works, which remain, sufficiently testify." Then, after some further remarks, he adds: "It was from the Christian religion alone that true philosophy and genuine philosophers sprang." Jude gives us a very dark picture of these same ψυχικοι, who, he says, verse 19, "have not the spirit." It is this same "natural man" that is described in the eighth chapter of the epistle to the Romans. His "carnal mind" is declared to be "enmity against God, for it is not subject to the law of God, neither indeed can be." "It is *enmity*," says Mr. Wesley on the place, "to His *existence*, *power*, and *providence*." Now, this man, though a fool, professes to be very wise, and boasts very much of what he calls σοφιαν wisdom, even σοφιαν των σοφων, the wisdom of the wise. But Paul calls it ἀνθρωπινης σοφιας, *man's wisdom*, and the wisdom of this world, and opposes to it σοφιαν Θεου, the wisdom of God, which the natural man hath not, because he "receiveth not the things" or teachings "of the Spirit of God, for they are foolishness unto him; neither can he know them, because they are spiritually discerned." (1 Cor., chap. ii, verses 4, 6, 7, and 14.) This man, we are told, cannot know the things of the Spirit, not because this knowledge is absolutely out of his reach, but because he will not be instructed in God's way, because he rejects the *supernatural* remedy. "That the natural man here," says Whitby on the place, "is the man who rejects revelation, and admits of no higher principle to judge of things by but philosophy and demonstration from the principles of natural reason, is the express assertion of Theodoret, Chrysostom, Photius, Œcumenius, and Theophylact, on the place."

We now see who the natural man is, and what that wisdom is of which he boasted. It is of this wisdom the apostle speaks when he says, chapter i, verse 21, "The world by wisdom knew not God." And this declaration we claim to be decisive of the question; it decides the very question at issue: by this wisdom the world never did know God; this is the positive and unmistakable declaration of the apostle, and this declaration alone must forever set the question at rest in the minds of all who believe the apostle "wrote and spoke as he was moved by the Holy Ghost." Just opposed to this is the equally positive declaration of modern transcendentalists, with whom, consequently, the apostle joins issue as directly as he did with their brethren, the philosophers of his own day. It is this philosophy, so called, that placed itself in opposition to apostolic teaching in apostolic times; and it does so in our times. This is the teaching with which the above-named fathers joined issue, with which the orthodox in all ages joined issue, with which Watson joined issue, and with which we join issue. And with this teaching all must join issue who would not join issue with apostolic teaching.

The importance of this subject will justify us in dwelling upon it yet longer, that we may, if possible, set it in a still clearer light.

We take the ground that when Adam fell there was nothing in him by which he could raise himself again, either less or more; nor could any remedy be found in that order of things which existed before the fall, and which we call the natural order, in contradistinction from that order of things which was introduced after the fall, and which we call the supernatural order. Consequently, so far as Adam and his posterity have been raised from the fall, they have been raised by the *supernatural* remedy thus introduced, and introduced for this very purpose. And to this same *supernatural* remedy we must be indebted for all we shall be raised, as well as for all we have been raised: in the natural man, and the natural order, as thus explained, there was and is no remedy for fallen humanity. This we conceive to be the teaching of the apostle in the eighth chapter of his epistle to the Romans, from which we will now give a somewhat extended quotation, it is so much to the point. "For what the law could not do, in that it was weak through the flesh, God, sending his own Son in the likeness of sinful flesh, and for sin [or by a sacrifice for sin], condemned sin in the flesh: that the righteousness of the law might be fulfilled in us, who walk not after the flesh, but after the Spirit. For they that are after the flesh, do mind the things of the flesh; but they that are after the Spirit, the things of the Spirit. For to be carnally minded is death; but to be spiritually minded is life and peace: because the carnal mind is enmity against God, for it is not subject to the law of God, neither indeed can be. So, then, they that are in the flesh cannot please God. But ye are not in the flesh, but in the Spirit, if so be that the Spirit of God dwell in you. Now, if any man have not the Spirit of Christ, he is none of his." Now, the apostle is speaking of precisely the same persons here that he speaks of in his letter to the Corinthians. The ψυχικος and πνευματικος, or natural and spiritual persons there, are the carnally and spiritually minded persons spoken of here, as any one may see by carefully reading both places, especially if the original be consulted. See the Greek words used by the apostle in 1 Cor. ii, 14, 15, and Romans viii, 5–9. The amount is this: so far as the one has received the *supernatural* remedy, which has been introduced and applied by the Spirit of God, which dwelleth in him, so far he is *spiritual*, he is *wise*, he is *right*, and *no farther;* and all comes through the atonement: so that the *remedy*, the *medium of communication*, and the *mode of applying* the *remedy*, are alike SUPERNATURAL. On the other hand, so far as the other person has rejected this *supernatural* remedy, so far he is *carnal*, and walks after the flesh and not after the Spirit; so far he is *ignorant*, *foolish*, *wrong*, *dead*. In a word, so far he is *natural*, in the sense here explained; that is, so far as he has rejected the *supernatural* remedy, and, consequently, is not renewed, is not spiritual, just so far he is "the natural man who receiveth not the things of the Spirit of God;" and, what is worse, "they are foolishness unto him; neither can he know them;" not as a "natural man," not by "the deductions of natural reason," not by "the pure intuitions of reason;" in a word, not by his natural powers, independent of the *supernatural* remedy provided and offered. "Canst thou by searching find out God?" No, not in this way, for God and the things of God "are spiritually discerned," and the natural man has not that qualification, and cannot have it while he depends upon his natural resources and rejects the *supernatural remedy;* "neither can he know them" while he does so. "This is the condemnation, that light is come into the world, and men loved darkness rather than light." They will even go back to heathenism rather than acknowledge their complete dependence upon this *supernatural remedy* for light and life, nor will they acknowledge their indebtedness to it for the light they have.

Such is the meaning of the terms *natural* and *supernatural*, as used in this connection. Philosophers may attach other meanings to the term *natural*, but theologians must be scriptural in their teaching, let come what will of the technicalities found in the philosopher's vocabulary. With these views we must look upon the teachings of transcendentalism as tantamount to a rejection of the supernatural remedy altogether: for if man is, or may be, by the mere exercise of his natural powers, all that these teachings say he is, or may be, then there certainly is no such necessity for *the atonement* and *the work of the Spirit*, as that which our *Bibles*, our *catechisms*, and our *fathers* have taught us to believe there is.

But, not to insist upon the teachings of our catechisms and of our fathers, at present, we will continue our quotations from the Bible. The case of our first parent immediately after the fall is worthy of notice. Genesis iii. 9, 10, is a record that is very suggestive: "And the Lord God called unto Adam, and said unto him, Where art thou? And he said, I heard thy voice in the garden: and I was afraid, because I was naked; and I hid myself." I HID MYSELF! From whom? From JEHOVAH ELOHIM! Alas! how is the mighty fallen! Poor Adam! And didst thou think thou couldst hide thyself from the Omniscient God? I wonder if the belief of Adam, that he could hide himself from JEHOVAH ELOHIM, was one of the "primitive beliefs" which our transcendental philosophers speak of; or was this happy thought one of those "intuitions of pure reason" which they say are found in every man. If so, we certainly must object; for such beliefs and intuitions are not found even in our children: because the good Book has taught them to say, "Whither shall I go from thy Spirit? or whither shall I flee from thy presence? If I ascend up into heaven, thou art there: if I make my bed in hell, behold thou art there; if I take the wings of the morning, and dwell in the uttermost parts of the sea; even there shall thy hand lead me, and thy right hand shall hold me. If I say, Surely the darkness shall cover me; even the night shall be light about me. Yea, the darkness hideth not from thee; but the night shineth as the day: the darkness and the light are both alike to thee." Thus it is easy to see why our children and our philosophers are wiser than was their first parent immediately after his fall; but it is marvellous that certain philosophers will persist in ascribing to unassisted reason what is due to revelation!

But this poor, fallen, ignorant Adam, we are told "begat a son in his own likeness, after his image;" and soon after we are told that "God saw that the wickedness of man was great in the earth, and that every imagination of the thoughts of his heart was only evil continually." Here is another specimen of the "primitive judgments," and of the "intuitions of pure reason!" "The earth also was corrupt before God; and the earth was filled with violence. And God looked upon the earth, and behold, it was corrupt; for all flesh had corrupted his way upon the earth." Another striking evidence that "the human intelligence is configured and correlated to eternal principles of order, and right, and good as they exist in the Infinite Intelligence." The above quotations are from Gen. vi, 5, 11, 12; the following is from chap. viii, 21, and it shows that the antediluvians, and the postdiluvians, *naturally*, are the same: "for the imagination of man's heart is evil from his youth."

Passing over the abominations of Sodom and Gomorrah, and all other developments of the corruptions and ignorance of "*the natural man*," by which the pages of history are stained and blackened all over, we come to the days of Job, and find the natural man thus described by the wisest and most observant in the land of Uz: "Vain man would be wise, though man be born like a wild ass's colt," Job xi, 12. And again, chap. xv, 16, we are assured that he is "abominable and filthy," and that he "drinketh iniquity like water." It is remarkable that then, as now, there were two parties: one claiming to be *wise*, though *vain;* while the other *degraded the natural reason* quite as much as Watson is said to have done, as is seen in the above declarations of the most thinking men of Uz, who, no doubt, were sensationalists, while the other party were as evidently transcendentalists, though it does not appear that they professed quite as much as do their brethren of the present day. In the days of the psalmist we do not find that "the natural man" is any better; for the Almighty Himself, after careful investigation, "to see if there were any that did understand and seek God," declares, "They are all gone aside, they are all together become filthy: there is none that doeth good, no, not one." In the days of Isaiah and Jeremiah, too, we find "the natural man" just the same; as is evident from the declarations of those prophets, which run thus: "The ox knoweth his owner, and the ass his master's crib: but Israel doth not know, my people do not consider." So it appears that those stupid creatures knew their master and their owner better than "the natural man" knew his God, though in the land of Israel. While Isaiah gives us a mournful picture of the stupidity and ignorance of the natural man, Jeremiah gives us a still more mournful picture of his moral badness, in these few but awfully expressive and comprehensive words: "The heart is deceitful above all things and desperately wicked: who can know it?" Still worse, if possible, is the dark picture which our blessed Lord gives us of the same heart, Matt. xv, 19, and Mark vii, 21, 22. In this picture are fourteen specifications, one of which is blasphemy. Thus while some are "contradicting and blaspheming" the name of God, others are *denying his very being*, as the psalmist tells us in the 14th psalm, in these words: "The fool hath said in his heart there is no God;" and a little after he says, "They are corrupt, they have done abominable works, there is none that doeth good." In the third chapter of his epistle to the Romans the Apostle Paul quotes these words of the psalmist, and, in short, sums up and indorses all that previous inspired writers had said on this subject. And dark as is the dreadful painting, he declares it is a true picture of the natural man, whether a Jew or a Gentile. "What then," says he, "are we," Jews, "better than they," Gentiles? "No, in no wise; for we have before proved both Jews and Gentiles, that they are all under sin." And to know what he means by being "under sin," the specifications which follow must be carefully read.

Now, what does our blessed Lord, and all the inspired writers of the Old and New Testaments, mean in those declarations which we have quoted, and others which might be quoted? What is the specific meaning of these their statements? Do they mean to convey the idea that every human being upon the earth at every period of its history, was, is, and shall be all that is specified in the above and similar declarations? Do they by such utterances mean to teach us that every child of man was, is, and shall be as ignorant of God and as corrupt as is asserted in the words here quoted? To this question there is but one answer: they did not, and could not, mean this; for there have been wise and good people on the earth at every period of its history. What, then, did they mean? I answer: they meant just what they said, viz., that this is the character of the ψυχικος ἀνθρωπος, *the natural man*, whenever and wherever found; and the natural man is the man that is not renewed by the supernatural remedy; and the πνευματικος is the man that is thus renewed: hence, while the former receiveth not the things of the Spirit of God, and regards them as the veriest foolishness, because, as a natural man, he cannot know them; the latter *discerneth all things*, all those things which the other *cannot know*, "*because they are spiritually discerned*," which spiritual discernment he has not, and, *as a natural man*, cannot have.

We now see *who* the natural man is, and *what* he is. And we see, too, that the teachings of the Bible and those of transcendentalism, with regard to the *mental* and *moral* character of the *natural man*, are completely at variance; it is not possible to reconcile them; so completely are they at variance that it is not possible to hold the one, intelligently, and not reject the other. And that this same teaching is at variance with the facts of experience also, will be shown in due time.

Our reviewer professes to have shown "that human reason can demonstrate from the facts of the universe and the intuitions of the mind that God exists, and consequently that 'our knowledge of the existence of God is not derived from revelation alone.'" Then follows what he calls "an analysis of the belief in God as developed in the human intelligence."

This analysis we have already examined, and have shown

that what he claims cannot be granted, that his whole system rests upon mere assumptions as to the office and work of certain mental faculties concerning which philosophers are not and never have been agreed. We have shown, too, that what he asserts concerning these faculties in the natural man, is utterly opposed to the teachings of God's word; and will show that it is equally opposed to the facts of experience. And as to the πνευματικος, the spiritual man, the man that is already in possession of the idea of a God, and is enlightened and renewed by the *supernatural remedy*, his ability to prove the being of a God is not questioned. So far as we know, certainly Watson does not question it; on the contrary, he asserts it. Therefore, to prove that this man can do this thing is to prove what is not denied, and to prove that the ψυχικος ἀνθρωπος, the natural man, car do this, is to prove what the word of God declares to be impossible. Neither does it follow that, because the spiritual man can demonstrate the being of a God from the facts of the universe, therefore he is not indebted to revelation for this "knowledge of the existence of God," seeing his ability thus to demonstrate this great truth in this way, may result entirely from his knowledge of God thus received; therefore, till this is disproved, we must reject the inference as altogether illegitimate. We must say, then, and we do it with all deference, that the reviewer has been entirely unsuccessful in his undertaking; he has utterly failed to prove what he undertook to prove, unless he undertook to prove what is not denied, viz., that the spiritual man can do this, and even then his inference is illegitimate.

We confess that we question the *possibility* of man's *originating* the idea of a God, even in his primeval state, supposing that his Creator had left him without that idea for a given time, which we do not believe. When we speak of the idea of a God, we mean, of course, the God of the Bible, for there is no other. That man, even in his fallen state, has the idea of a superior being whom he worships as God, is not questioned; nor will he be satisfied with one, for he will have gods many and lords many. But the question is: could man, even in his primeval state, *originate the idea of the true God, the God of the Bible?*

In reply to this question perhaps we cannot do better than give a quotation from our published review of a sermon by Rev. Henry Ward Beecher. In reply to his assertion that "the natural world and the human soul are the only two sources from which men derived their ideas concerning the Divine nature," we said then, and now say again, "Is it possible for our weakness to suggest the idea of omnipotence? Our utter ignorance of the future to suggest the idea of absolute prescience? Our very limited knowledge, our ignorance and blindness, I had almost said, to suggest the idea of omniscience? Is it possible for a being who, by his very nature, is necessarily confined to a given point of space at every given moment of time, to derive from this same nature the idea of omnipresence? Will he not rather argue, 'If I, who am a spirit, am, by my very nature, necessarily confined to a given point of space, at every given point of time, every spirit is subject to the same limitation; but God is a spirit, ergo, God is confined to a given point of space at every given point of time.' Thus arguing from his own nature, and from that of all other creatures, however exalted, he legitimately reaches the conclusion that God is not omnipresent, is not *omniscient, is not omnipotent; in a word, is a located and* limited being. Nor is it possible for any creature, however exalted, to derive from itself, or from any other creature, or from any number of creatures, the idea of the God of the Bible: for it is not possible to derive from anything what it does not possess. Creation, however extensive, is limited, and would be, if it were ten thousand times more extensive than it is. And being limited, it cannot give the idea of the unlimited; being *finite*, it cannot impart the idea of the INFINITE: because, we repeat, it cannot possibly impart what it does not possess. It follows, then, that so sure as we have the true idea of the true God, so sure we have it from himself *originally*, and *directly*. We say directly; by which we mean, it was not inferred by any intelligent creature from its own nature, nor yet from the nature and extent of creation at large; for there was not, and could not be, anything in either, or in both, that could suggest the idea of omnipresence, omniscience, or omnipotence. In a word, nothing that could suggest the idea of the *unlimited*, the *Infinite;* for whatever be the nature and extent of creation, still it must be *limited*, still it must be *finite;* and consequently, we repeat it yet again, could not possibly suggest the idea of the *unlimited*, of the INFINITE; and what cannot suggest the idea of the *unlimited*, the INFINITE, cannot suggest the idea of the God of the Bible; for the suggestion, the idea, that stops short of this, stops infinitely short of the true God!

If Mr. C. had confined himself to what he considered objectionable in Watson's Metaphysics, or Institutes, our course, like his in that case, would have been straightforward. But this he has not done. The fact is, his article contains a mere exhibit, and an attempted defence of the teachings, the most extravagant teachings, of transcendental philosophy, accompanied by a marvellous representation, or rather, misrepresentation, of the philosophical and theological teachings of Richard Watson. Hitherto we have confined our attention principally to the former, now we will give our attention principally to the latter.

In listening to the charges brought against the author of the Institutes, we purpose to place him upon his trial alone, and of the people there shall be none with him; not even the empirical or sensational philosophers, amongst whom Mr. C. has forced him to dwell like the psalmist "in the tents of Kedar."

Instead of listening to general and sweeping charges brought against Watson on the assumption that he belonged to a certain school of philosophers, we will now hear such specific charges as may be brought against Watson himself.

On p. 185, Mr. C. continues to bring his sweeping charges against Watson thus: "That Watson was, in philosophy, a sensationalist, must, we think, be evident to every discriminating mind furnished with even a very slender acquaintance with the history of modern philosophy. A careful perusal of the chapters 'On the Presumptive Evidences,' in Part I, the chapter 'On the Existence of God,' in Part II, and the first chapter of Part III, 'On the Moral Law,' will be decisive of this question in every intelligent mind. He affirms, with earnestness and emphasis, that we have no idea of God, of right and wrong, and of immortality, except as derived from *without* by *instruction* and *verbal revelation;* that, indeed, we have *no faculty of knowing* on any of these subjects except faith." In proof of the truthfulness of these charges, general charges as usual, he refers us to the Institutes, vol. i, pages 10, 11, 272, and 274, and gives us the following as specifications: "We are all conscious that we gain our knowledge of God by *instruction*. . . . We owe our knowledge of the existence of God and of his attributes to *revelation* ALONE."

He also gives us the following as the words of Ellis, and as being approved by Watson: "God is the only way to himself; he cannot be *in the least* come at, defined, or demonstrated by human reason." He then charges Watson with asserting, at page 10, vol. i, "that *nothing* appears in the constitution of nature, or in the proceedings of the Divine administration, to indicate it to be the will of God that the appetites should be restrained within the rules of sobriety, except that, by a connection which has been established by him, the excessive indulgence of those appetites usually impairs health." . . . The design of the whole of this chapter ii," continues the reviewer, "is to prove 'that the rule which determines the quality of moral action must be presumed to be matter of [oral] revelation from God.'" Finally, as a quotation from page 11, vol. i, we have the following: "*All observation lies directly against the doctrine of the immortality of man.* He dies! and the probabilities of a future life, which have been established upon the unequal distribution of rewards and punishments in this life, and the capacities of the human soul, are a presumptive evidence which has been adduced only by those to whom the doctrine had been transmitted by *tradition*, and were, therefore, in possession of the idea." Our reviewer now reaches this sweeping and marvellous conclusion: "It is, therefore, but natural that he should enter his solemn protest against the attempt to construct a science of NATURAL THEOLOGY, or of MORAL PHILOSOPHY, as a design which is not only 'visionary and impossible, but of mischievous tendency,' and they who are engaged in it are accessary to the infidel crusade against the word of God."

Now although we profess to have a "slender acquaintance with the history of modern philosophy," and with that of ancient philosophy too; and though we profess to have a little *intelligence* and *discrimination*, yet, after "a careful perusal of the chapters" referred to by the reviewer, and of all other parts of the Institutes, we confess we have utterly failed to find the errors which the reviewer professes to have found there. On the contrary, we are more and more convinced of the soundness and of the importance of both the theological and philosophical teachings of the Institutes. Nor do we hesitate to express our deep conviction that the chapters referred to are *specially* important; because truth *specially* important, and error *specially* dangerous, are there set forth—the former defended, and the latter exposed—by a pen evidently wielded by a master's hand; not by the hand of an empiric! We have also to object to what are given above as quotations from the chapters referred to, because, though they profess to be accurate quotations, they are not; but are very inaccurate, so much so, that we are convinced no one by reading them would obtain, to say the very least, a correct knowledge of the teachings of Richard Watson.

The design of chap. ii, vol. i, of the Institutes is thus given by Mr. C. in the quotation given above: "The design of the whole of this chapter ii is to prove 'that the rule which determines the quality of moral action must be presumed to be matter of [oral] revelation from God.'" The design of the same chapter is thus given by its author in the closing paragraph:

"The whole of this argument is designed to prove that, had we been left, for the regulation of our conduct, to infer the will and purposes of the Supreme Being from his natural works and his administration of the affairs of the world, our knowledge of both would have been essentially deficient; and it establishes a strong presumption in favor of a direct revelation from God to his creatures, that neither his will concerning us, nor the hope of forgiveness, might be left to dark and uncertain *inference,* but be the subjects of an express declaration."

Now we think that Mr. Watson knew the design of his own argument quite as well as Mr. Cocker, and if the latter considered that design pernicious, he should have given it to his readers in the author's own words, and then point out its pernicious character, and not set up a man of straw of his own making and fight that as though he were fighting Mr. Watson. Why Mr. C. has done the latter and not the former we will not take upon us to say, but we must say that by doing so he has misrepresented Mr. Watson and led his readers, who were not acquainted with Mr. Watson's writings, astray. And we say, too, that to object to the teaching of Mr. Watson, in this chapter, as set forth in his own words, is virtually to take the position of infidels and deists, who hold that the book of nature is sufficient, and that the book of revelation consequently is, to say the least, superfluous and uncalled for. We have this moment looked over the chapter again, and find that the argument is directed to these very characters. Hence, the following quotation from Bolingbroke, in a note at the foot of page 9: "By employing our reason to collect the will of God from the fund of our nature, physical and moral, we may acquire not only a particular knowledge of those laws which are deducible from them, but a general knowledge of the manner in which God is pleased to exercise his supreme powers in this system." Thus, in opposition to Bolingbroke and all others who assert that "our reason can collect the will of God from the fund of our nature," and, consequently, that a written revelation is not necessary, Mr. Watson asserts the necessity of a direct revelation, and by a masterly and most conclusive argument he establishes his position, as we will now show.

The question to be discussed is thus stated by Mr. Watson on page 10, vol. i: "Are there, in the natural works of God, or in his manner of governing the world, such indications of the will of God concerning us, as can afford *sufficient* direction in forming a *perfectly virtuous character*, and *sufficient* information as to the means by which it is to be affected?" Now the reviewer of Watson takes the negative or the positive of this question; if the *negative*, he is one with Watson, and there is no dispute: if the *positive*, then he occupies the position of Bolingbroke and all others who reject a direct revelation, as being unnecessary, to say the least, and hold natural reason and the book of nature to be sufficient for these purposes; the latter, of course, is the reviewer's position. The reader now sees, beyond the possibility of mistake, the true position of Watson, and that of his reviewer, and can take which side he pleases. To assist him, however, in his choice, we will give an outline of the argument. We do this the more readily, because the reviewer professes to find so much deadly error in this chapter, as is seen in the quotations which we have given above.

"The Theist will himself acknowledge that *temperance*, *justice*, and *benevolence* are essential to moral virtue."

Mr. Watson now proceeds to show that the indications of the constitution of nature, and of God's natural government, in favor of temperance, are not *sufficient* for the purpose, and concludes by saying: "The rule is therefore IMPERFECT." The capitals are mine: my object is to fix the attention of the reader upon the point that Watson claims to have established. The rule is IMPERFECT: that is all; it requires a direct revelation from God to afford *fallen man* a PERFECT rule of temperance. The next element in "a perfectly virtuous character" is *justice.* Mr. W. goes on to say that neither "are the obligations of justice in this way indicated with ADEQUATE CLEARNESS;" and closes his argument on this point thus: "Rules of justice, therefore, thus indicated would, like those of temperance, be very IMPERFECT." He now takes up the third element, and with his characteristic clearness conducts his argument to this conclusion: "The rule would therefore be UNCERTAIN and DARK, and ENTIRELY SILENT as to the extent to which beneficence is to be carried, and whether there may not be exceptions to its exercise as to individuals, such as *enemies, vicious persons*, and *strangers.*" Concerning all the indications of God's will, in the ways above specified, he concludes thus: "It follows then that they form a rule too vague in itself, and too liable to different interpretations to place the conduct of men under adequate regulation, even in respect of *temperance, justice,* and *benevolence.*" Mr. Watson now goes on to show that the information derived from the aforementioned sources is still more defective as to other and still more vital points.

"For instance," he says, "there is no indication in either nature or providence that it is the will of God that his creatures should worship him. . . . . There is no indication that God will be approached in prayer. . . . . Nor is there a sufficient indication of a future state of rewards and punishment, because there is no indubitable declaration of man's immortality, nor any facts and principles so obvious as to enable us confidently to infer it. Hence some of the wisest heathens, who were not wholly unaided in their speculations on these subjects by the reflected light of revelation, confessed themselves unable to come to any satisfactory conclusion. The doubts of Socrates, who expressed himself the most hopeful of any on the subject of a future life, are well known; and Cicero, who occasionally expatiates with so much eloquence on this topic, shows by the skeptical expressions which he throws in that his belief was by no means confirmed." Here follow some of Cicero's own words with regard to the human soul after the present life:

"Show me first, if you can, and if it be not too troublesome, that souls remain after death; or, if you cannot prove that (for it is difficult), declare how there is no evil in death."

"If, therefore," continues Mr. Watson, "without any help from direct or traditional instruction, we could go as far as they, it is plain that our religious system would be deficient in all those motives to virtue which arise from the doctrine of man's accountability and a future life, and in that moral control which such doctrines exert, the necessity of which for the moral government of the world is sufficiently proved by the wickedness which prevails even where these doctrines are fully taught."

"Still further," continues our author, "there is nothing in those manifestations of God and of his will which the most attentive contemplatist can be supposed to collect from his natural works and from his sovereign rule, to afford the hope of pardon to any one who is conscious of having offended him, or any assurance of felicity in a future state, should one exist."

Our author now goes on to show, in a very forcible and pathetic manner, how impossible it is for the sinner to obtain from such sources even a hope that his offences will be forgiven. "All observation and experience," he says, "lie against this; and the case is the more alarming to a considerate mind, that so little of the sad inference that the human race is under a rigorous administration, depends upon reasoning and opinion: it is a fact of common and daily observation. The minds of men in general are a prey to discontent and care, and are agitated by various evil passions. The race itself is doomed to wasting labors of the body or the mind, in order to obtain subsistence. Their employments are for the most part low and grovelling, in comparison of the capacity of the soul for intellectual pleasures and attainments. The mental powers, though distributed with great equality among the various classes of men, are only in the case of a few individuals ever awakened. The pleasures most strenuously sought are, therefore, sensual, degrading, and transient. Life itself, too, is precarious; infants suffer and die, youth is blighted, and thus by far the greater part of mankind is swept away before the prime of life is attained. Casualties, plagues, famines, floods, and war carry on the work of destruction." Our author goes on thus to eumerate painful facts similar to the above, and adds, "The very religions of the world have completed human wretchedness by obdurating the heart, by giving birth to sanguinary superstitions, and by introducing a corruption of morals destructive of the very elements of well ordered society. Part of these evils are *permitted* by the Supreme Governor, and part *inflicted*. . . . But whether permitted or inflicted, they are *punitive* acts of his administration, and present him before us, notwithstanding innumerable instances of his benevolence, as a Being of terrible majesty."

So close is the argument in this chapter, and so much to the point is all that is said, and so important withal, that we would like to give the whole of it; but as that cannot be, we find it difficult to decide what should be left out.

Our author goes on to show how unsuccessful have been the efforts of great men "to remove in part the awful mystery which overhangs such an administration," without the light of a direct revelation from God; and, admitting that we were even certain of existing in a future state, he closes this part of the argument by saying, "The idea of a future life does not, therefore, relieve the case. If it be just that man should be punished here, it may be required by the same just regard to the principles of a strictly moral government that he should be punished hereafter." Thus darkness still rests upon the future, and, at best, fallen man has too much reason to fear the worst. Hence "The Theist," continues our author, "in order to support this hope [of a future life], dwells upon the proofs of the goodness of God with which this world abounds, but shuts his eyes upon the demonstrations of his severity; yet these surround him as well as the other, and the argument from the severity of God is as forcible against pardon as the argument from his goodness is in its favor. At the best it is left entirely uncertain; a ground is laid for heart-rending doubts and fearful anticipations; and, for anything he can show to the contrary, the goodness which God has displayed in nature and providence may only render the offence of man more aggravated, and serve to strengthen the presumption against the forgiveness of a *wilful* offender, rather than afford him any reason for hope." Here follows the concluding paragraph, in which the author specifies *the design of the whole argument.* This paragraph we have given above.

Such is the chapter in which the reviewer professes to have found so much error. Such is the design of the chapter, and such is the argument which our author employs to support his position, all of which we pronounce worthy of the author of the THEOLOGICAL INSTITUTES, and supported by Scripture and experience.

CHAPTER II.

In proof of the charges already cited, we are referred "to the chapter 'On the Existence of God,' in Part II." This chapter contains 203 pages, yet the reviewer gives us only two quotations. One from page 274, so broken from its connection as to give no correct idea of Mr. Watson's argument, and the other from Ellis, on page 272, in these words: "God is the only way to himself; he cannot be *in the least* come at, defined, or demonstrated by human reason."

I do not see that these words of Ellis teach anything different from the following scriptures: "No one knoweth the Son but the Father; neither knoweth any one the Father save the Son, and he to whom the Son will reveal Him." .... "Flesh and blood hath not revealed it [this knowledge] unto thee, but my Father, which is in heaven." .... "No man hath seen God at any time; the only begotten Son which is in the bosom of the Father, He hath declared Him." (Matt. xi, 27; xvi, 17; John i, 18.)

The question is not as to whether there is something eternal, for that will not admit of dispute. The question is, as Dr. Samuel Clarke observes, as to the CHARACTER *of that eternal.* The reasoning of Ellis, from which the above words are quoted, involves the simple question, whether it is in the power of the human reason to originate the conception of the Eternal God, the God of the Bible, clothed, as he is, with infinite perfections, natural and moral; whether the unassisted reason could derive the knowledge of such a being from the phenomena of creation. Mr. Ellis takes the negative of this question, and reasons thus: "Where would the inquirer fix his beginning? He is to search for something, he knows not what; a nature without known properties, a being without a name. It is impossible for such a person to declare or imagine what it is he would discourse of, or inquire into; a nature he has not the least apprehension of; a subject he has not the least glimpse of, in whole or in part, which he must separate from all doubt, inconsistencies, and errors; he must demonstrate without one known sure principle to ground it upon, and draw certain necessary conclusions whereon to rest his judgment, without the least knowledge of one term or proposition to fix his procedure upon, and, therefore, can never know whether his conclusions be consequent or not consequent, truth or falsehood, which is just the same in science as in architecture, to raise a building without a foundation."

Now it is much easier to quote two lines from this noble production, and then pronounce its author and its admirers sensationalists, than it is to answer the manly reasoning contained therein; but while the former is much the easiest, the latter would certainly be much the noblest way of disposing of it, and we think the safest too. In the mean time we are free to confess that we admire Ellis as well as Watson, at least so far as the above goes, for therein we think he appears to good advantage.

But seeing the reviewer asserts that "a careful perusal" of this, and the other chapters specified, "will be decisive of this question in every intelligent mind," we will now examine it, and see whether it contains the error which we have failed to find in the chapters "On the Presumptive Evidences." This important chapter commences thus:

"The *Divine authority* of those writings which are received by Christians as a revelation of infallible truth, having been established, our next step is seriously, and with simplicity of mind, to examine their contents, and to collect from them that ample information on religious and moral subjects which they profess to contain, and in which it had become necessary that the world be supernaturally instructed." Mark, SUPERNATURALLY instructed.

Such is the work which our author proposes to accomplish in this chapter; let this work, as here specified, be carefully noticed and kept in view. What is proposed in this chapter is simply this: the "Divine authority" of the sacred writings being established, we are "to collect from them that ample information on religious and moral subjects which they profess to contain."

"The doctrine which the first sentence in this Divine revelation unfolds," namely, "*that there is a God, the* CREATOR *of heaven and earth*," is the first doctrine taken up. "In three distinct ways," he continues, "do the sacred writers furnish us with information on this great and essential subject, the existence and the character of God." Mark the knowledge for which, it is claimed, we are indebted to a direct revelation from God: *the knowledge of a* GOD POSSESSING THE CHARACTER HERE DESCRIBED. The three ways in which the sacred writers furnish this knowledge are thus specified: "From the *names* by which he is designated; from the *actions* ascribed to him; and from the *attributes* with which he is invested in their invocations and praises, and in those lofty descriptions of his nature which, under the inspiration of the Holy Spirit, they have recorded for the instruction of the world. . . . . . The names of God recorded in Scripture convey at once ideas of overwhelming greatness and glory, mingled with that awful mysteriousness with which, to all finite minds, and especially to the minds of mortals, the Divine essence and mode of existence must ever be invested." Here follow some of the principal names of the Almighty, such as ELOHIM, JEHOVAH, EL, EHIEH, SHADDAI, ADON. Then follow the names of this Almighty Being as given in the thirty-fourth chapter of Exodus, with their import as given by Dr. Adam Clarke. Here our author specifies some of those sublime ideas of God which the sacred writers derive from his *actions*. "More at large," he continues, "do we learn what God is, from the *declarations* of the inspired writings." Here he furnishes us with numerous quotations from the Old and New Testaments, containing declarations which convey the most lofty conceptions of the Divine attributes, both natural and moral; adding: "Under these deeply awful, but consolatory views, do the Scriptures present to us the supreme object of our worship and trust, dwelling upon each of the above particulars with inimitable sublimity and beauty of language, and with an inexhaustible variety of illustration; nor can we compare these views of the Divine nature with the conceptions of the most enlightened of pagans, without feeling how much reason we have for everlasting gratitude that a revelation so *explicit* and so *comprehensive* should have been made to us on a subject which only a revelation from God himself could have made known." Mark the sum of all that is claimed in the above: "only a revelation from God himself" could give us those sublime conceptions of the nature and attributes of the God of the Bible, as here specified. Hence he adds: "It is thus that Christian philosophers, even when they do not use the language of the Scriptures, are able to speak on this great and mysterious doctrine in language so clear and with conceptions so noble; in a manner too so *equable*, so different to the sages of antiquity, who, if at any time they approach the truth, when speaking of the Divine nature, never fail to mingle with it some essentially erroneous or grovelling conception." Confirmatory of these remarks, some fine specimens from the writings of Dr. Barrow, Bishop Pearson, Lawson, and Sir Isaac Newton, are now furnished.

Our author now notices the fact "that neither Moses, the first of the inspired penmen, nor any of the authors of the succeeding canonical books, enters into any *proof* of this first principle of religion, *there is a God*." "There is indeed," he adds, "in the sacred volume no allusion to the existence of atheistical sentiments till some ages after Moses, and then it is not quite clear whether speculative or practical Atheism be spoken of. From this circumstance we learn that, previous to the time of Moses, the idea of one supreme and infinitely perfect God was familiar to men, that it had descended to them from the earliest ages; and also that it was a truth of original revelation, and not one which sages of preceding times had wrought out by rational investigation and deduction." "No man," he observes, "claims to have made any such discovery; had any one man done so, some grateful mention of so great a sage, of so celebrated a moral teacher, would have been made." "If those views of God which are found in the Pentateuch had been discovered by the successful investigations of wise men among the ancients, the progress of this wonderful discovery would have been marked by Moses." The way in which a clear knowledge of the God of the Bible was communicated to man, is thus stated: "The first man, we are informed, knew God, not only from his works, but by sensible manifestation and converse; the same Divine appearances were made to Noah, to Abraham, to Isaac, to Jacob; and when Moses wrote, persons were still living who had conversed with those who conversed with God or were descended from the same families to whom God, '*at sundry times*,' had appeared in visible glory, or in angelic forms. These Divine manifestations were also matters of public notoriety among the primitive families of mankind." The idea being once communicated to mankind, it "was confirmed," he adds, "by every natural object which they saw around them."

"That the idea of the Supreme First Cause was at first obtained by the exercise of reason, is thus contradicted by the facts, that the first man received the knowledge of God by sensible converse with him, and that this doctrine was transmitted, with the confirmation of successive visible manifestations, to the early ancestors of all nations. Whether the discovery, therefore, of the simple truth of the existence of a first cause be within the compass of human powers, is a point which cannot be determined by matter of fact; because it may be proved that those nations by whom that doctrine has been acknowledged, had their origin from a common stock, resident in that part of the world in which the primitive revelations were given. They were therefore never in circumstances in which such an experiment upon the power or weakness of the human mind could be made." It is declared probable that there are some in whose minds "the idea of a Supreme Being is entirely obliterated; although some notion of spiritual existences superior in power to man still remains;" but our author declares it to be a fact, that no man, having lost the knowledge of the true God, has ever been able, of himself, to recover it again. He then finally closes thus: "Matter of fact does not therefore support the notion, that the existence of God is discoverable by the unassisted faculties of man; and there is, I conceive, very slender reason to admit the abstract probability." (Pp. 263 to 271.) Such is the modest conclusion reached by Mr. Watson, after presenting such arguments and facts as the above. Yet in the face of all this, the author of the review, page 188, represents him as saying on page 270, vol. i, that "the simple truth of the existence of a first cause is not within the compass of human powers." There is no such statement there! The words of Watson on page 270, and his final conclusion on page 271, we have given above: the reader can compare. And as to the errors which the reviewer professes to have found in this chapter, we will only say here, as yet we have found none of them. With Watson we claim it to be a simple fact that the knowledge of God was originally communicated to man in the way here specified, that Moses found man in possession of the idea, that there is no intimation of any man claiming the honor of having originated it, that where the knowledge of God was once lost, unassisted reason has never recovered it again. When opposite facts are adduced we will conclude Mr. Watson is wrong; as yet we hold that his *arguments*, his *facts*, and his *conclusions* are unrefuted, and, in fact, untouched!

On page 271, Mr. Watson goes on to reason thus: "If therefore we suppose a first cause to be discoverable by human investigation, we must seek for the instances among a people whose civilization and intellectual culture have roused the mind from its torpor, and given it an interest in abstract and philosophic truth; for to a people so circumstanced as never to have heard of God, the question of the existence of a first cause must be one of mere philosophy."

But where the idea of a God is not, he argues, men could never rise to such a state of mental culture and civilization. For "a mere barbarian," "without" any "degree of education," would be incapable "of such a course of inquiry as might lead him to a knowledge of God." A person so ignorant and degraded "would be wholly occupied with the gratification of his appetites or his sloth. Should we however suppose it possible, that those who had no previous knowledge of God, or of superior invisible powers, might be brought to the habits of civil life, and be engaged in the pursuit of various knowledge (which itself however is very incredible), it would still remain a question whether, provided no idea from tradition or instruction had been suggested of the existence of spiritual superior beings, or of a Supreme Creator or Ruler, such a truth would be within the reach of men, even in an imperfect form. We have already seen, that a truth may appear exceedingly simple, important, and evident, when once known, and on this account its demonstration may be considered easy, which nevertheless has been the result of much previous research on the part of the discoverer. The abundant rational evidence of the existence of a God, which may now be easily collected, and which is so convincing, is therefore no proof that without instruction from heaven the human mind would ever have made the discovery." Here follows the quotation from Ellis, which we have already given. Also quotations from Hare, Van Mildert, and Gleig's "Stackhouse Intro.," each the production of a master mind, and all designed to establish the same proposition; yet our author, with great modesty, simply says of the whole: "These observations have great weight, and though we allow that the argument which proves that the effects with which we are surrounded must have been *caused*, and thus leads us up through a chain of subordinate causes to one First Cause, has in it a simplicity, an obviousness, and a force, which when we are previously furnished with the idea of God, makes it at first sight difficult to conceive, that men, under any degree of cultivation, should be inadequate to it; yet, if the human mind ever commenced such an inquiry at all, it is highly probable that it would rest in the notion of an *eternal succession* of causes and effects, rather than acquire the ideas of creation in the proper sense, and of a Supreme Creator."

The amount is this: to be able to investigate so as to originate a knowledge of God implies a state of mind that we have no reason to believe could exist where, as yet, the idea of a God did not exist. But should we even suppose this possible, it would still remain a question whether such a discovery were possible; for if such a mind should ever commence "such an inquiry at all, it is highly probable that it would rest in the notion of an *eternal succession* of causes and effects, rather than acquire the ideas of creation in the proper sense, and of a Supreme Creator." In proof of this he says: "Scarcely any of the philosophers of the most inquisitive ages of Greece, or those of their followers at Rome, though with the advantage of traditions conveying the knowledge of God, seem to have been capable of conceiving of creation out of nothing, and they consequently admitted the eternity of matter. This was equally the case with the theistical, the atheistical, and the polytheistical philosophers. It was not among them a subject of dispute; but taken for a point settled and not to be contradicted, that matter was eternal, and could not therefore be created." In support of this the following quotation from Leland's "Necessity of Revelation" is given by Mr. Watson: "Few, if any, of the ancient pagan philosophers acknowledged God to be, in the most proper sense, the Creator of the world. By calling him Δημιουργος, 'the maker of the world,' they did not mean that he brought it out of non-existence into being, but only that he built it out of pre-existent materials, and disposed it into a regular form and order." "This was the opinion of Plato," says Mr. W., vol. i, p. 21, "who has been called the Moses of philosophers. Through the whole *Timæus*, Plato supposes two eternal and independent causes of all things: one, that by which all things are made, which is God; the other, that *from* which all things are made, which is *matter*. Dr. Cudworth has in vain attempted to clear Plato of this charge. The learned Dr. Thomas Burnet, who was well acquainted with the opinions of the ancients, says that 'the Ionic, Pythagoric, Platonic, and Stoic, all agreed in asserting the eternity of matter; and that the doctrine, that matter was created out of nothing, seems to have been unknown to the philosophers, and is one of which they had no notion. Aristotle asserted the eternity of the world, both in matter and *form* too, which was but an easy deduction from the former principle, and is sufficiently in proof of its atheistical tendency." The fact is, this idea, and a proper idea of the true God, cannot possibly exist in the same mind at the same time; either one must necessarily exclude the other. Hence all who believed thus must have been ignorant of the true God.

"Since the revelation of truth to man," continues our author, "philosophy has been able to adduce a very satisfactory argument" against the above notion; "but, though it is not a very recondite one, it was never discovered by philosophy while unaided by the Scriptures. In like manner philosophy can *now* furnish cogent arguments against an infinite succession of causes and effects; but it does not appear probable that they could have been apprehended by those to whom the very notion of a First Cause had not been intimated. If, however, it were conceded that some glimmering of this great truth might, by induction, have been discovered by contemplative minds thus circumstanced, by what means could they have *demonstrated* to themselves that that great collection of bodies which we call the world had but one Creator; that he is an incorporeal spirit; that he is eternal, self-existent, immortal, and independent? Certain it is, that the argument *à posteriori* does not of itself fully confirm all these conclusions; and the argument *à priori*, when directed to these mysterious points, is not, with all the advantages which we enjoy, so satisfactory as to leave no rational ground of doubt as to its conclusiveness. No sober man, we apprehend, would be content with *that* as the only foundation of his faith and hope."

Now, after producing all these fine arguments on the topics here specified, and after corroborating them with so many facts as to what the wisest of the heathen philosophers did and did not believe, and as to what they utterly failed to discover; our author, with his characteristic modesty and caution, only questions the possibility of fallen man being able to originate the idea of a *creation* and of a *creator*, in the proper sense. This much however he does assert, finally, viz., that "the argument *à posteriori* does not *of itself* fully confirm all these conclusions [specified page 274, vol. i]; and the argument *à priori*, when directed to these mysterious points, is not, with all the advantages which we enjoy, so satisfactory as to leave no rational ground of doubt as to its conclusiveness." Let those who please take the affirmative of these questions, for our part we heartily join with Watson in the negative: and we as heartily unite with him in saying, "No sober man, we apprehend, would be content with *that* as the only foundation of his faith and hope." The truth is, if Mr. Watson's position in every instance were fairly stated and opposed, we would be willing to leave the whole with the intelligent reader, without any fear as to the result. But while Mr. Watson simply questions the possibility of fallen man's rising "to a state of civil and scientific cultivation," without even the idea of a God, and then, assuming this to be possible, simply says "it would still remain a question" whether by his investigations he would reach the idea of *creation* and *creator* in the proper sense, or whether he "would rest in the notion of an eternal succession of causes and effects;" I say while Mr. Watson simply does this, producing, as some of his reasons for taking this ground, the unsuccessful efforts of the wisest philosophers of antiquity, Mr. Cocker represents him as asserting what he never did assert, as we have already shown, and will show more fully immediately. That man had the idea *originally* and *directly* from God himself, and, consequently, that he had not the chance to originate it even if he originally had the ability, and that he never has, by his unassisted reason, recovered the idea when once it was lost, Mr. Watson asserts to be facts! And, in harmony herewith, he denies (page 274) that the idea of God is *innate*. "If indeed the idea of God were *innate*," he says, "as some have contended, the question would be set at rest. But then every human being would be in possession of it. Of this there is not only no proof at all, but the evidence of fact is against it; and the doctrine of innate ideas may with confidence be pronounced a mere theory, assumed to support favorite notions, but contradicted by all experience." Mark, he still deals in facts; that every human being is in possession of the idea of God, which would be the fact if the idea were innate, is not only destitute of all proof, but the evidence of fact is against it." The following are some of the facts adduced. "Peter the wild boy, who in the beginning of the last century was found in a wood in Germany, far from having an innate sense of God or religion, seemed to be incapable of instruction; and the aboriginal inhabitants of New Holland are found, at this day, in a state of knowledge but little superior, and certainly have no idea of the existence of one Supreme Creator." And this, observe, is the point in dispute. In favor of this, argues our author there is "no proof at all," there is not one fact to support it: while against it there is much evidence, there are positive facts; and some of the facts are here given. And to these may be added all the atheists that ever lived, all those fools who have said in their hearts, "There is no God;" for if the idea of God is *innate*, is *intuitive*, as Mr. Watson denies, and as his opponents assert, there could be no atheists, and to assert this is to assert what is contrary to matter of fact and the word of God. Yet notwithstanding this, some have doubted, or at least professed to doubt, whether there ever was an atheist, and they have done so, probably, rather than give up the notion here opposed; for if this notion, that the idea of God is innate, be true, there could be no atheist. But surely Vanini was an atheist, and so obstinate was he that rather than admit the being of a God he suffered himself to be burnt at Paris, February 19th, 1619. And what better was Rabshakeh, or his master the king of Assyria, who said they had whipped "the gods of the nations," and the God of Israel should fare no better? Their knowledge, whether intuitive or not, served them to little purpose when they could see no difference between the God of Israel and the gods of Hamath, Arphad, Sepharvaim, Gozan, Haran, and Rezeph: these gods, said the king of Assyria, could not deliver their people out of my hand, or out of the hand of my fathers; neither can the God of Israel! And this, observe, is a fair specimen of the *intuitions* of the heathen generally. I have been at the trouble of searching out the substance of all that is known of the religion and worship of the ancient heathen, and could fill a volume with their gross and absurd ideas of the objects of their worship, and in the whole volume one correct idea of the true God would not be found. Occasionally I find some correct ideas, evidently communicated through Israel from Israel's God; but, as Mr. Watson says, they soon corrupted it, for in every nation they had "gods many, and lords many," and the mind that embraced the idea of a plurality of gods, could not, of course, at the same time, embrace the idea of the God of the Bible. "To show that there are *real literal* atheists in the world," Mr. Wesley mentions two whom he knew, and who had confidently denied the being of a God for many years: they both lived in London. Such too were all those "hell-fire clubs," as they were called, in England, Ireland, and Scotland, in the last century. Such too were Altamont, D'Alembert, and Diderot, notwithstanding their various abilities, natural and acquired: the first mentioned especially had great abilities, yet he was an obstinate atheist. And, in short, such were multitudes at that time in Great Britain and France, but whom we are in the habit of denominating infidels; they were, however, evidently downright atheists. Hence Hume, as Mr. Watson observes, denies the axiomatic truth that "Nothing exists or comes to pass without a cause." And I really do not think we would be far astray, if we were to class infidels generally with atheists. I mean such as those whom I have heard say, "Nature is God and God is nature."

The late Robert Owen gives us the meaning of such phraseology in the lips of infidels, in his "Book of the New Moral World," pages 65 and 66, where he denies that there is a "personal deity," and says, "truth is nature, and nature God; God is truth, and truth is God." With these and similar facts, meeting us among every people in every country and age, and scattered over almost every page of the history of our fallen race, we are forced to say with Watson that "the doctrine of innate ideas may with confidence be pronounced a mere theory, assumed to support favorite notions, but contradicted by all experience."

That man is utterly incapable of originating those sublime ideas of God which are developed in the book of revelation, is asserted by Watson with the utmost confidence; nor did we suppose that any would join issue with him here, unless such as Lord Herbert and his followers, who lay it down as a first principle of their religious system that "everything necessary to be believed is discoverable by the natural faculties." From this principle the conclusion is legitimately reached that a revelation is unnecessary. "This specious kind of infidelity," says Mr. Watson (page 236, vol. i), "known by the name of '*Deism*,' made its appearance in Italy and France about the middle of the sixteenth century, and in England early in the seventeenth. Under this appellation, and that of 'The Religion of Nature,' each adopted to deceive the unwary, the attack upon Christianity was at first cautious, and accompanied with many professions of regard for its manifold excellencies." Concerning the above principle of Lord Herbert and his followers, which, indeed, is the very basis of all infidelity, Mr. Watson further says, on page 237: "The history of infidelity from this time is a striking comment upon the words of St. Paul, "*But evil men and seducers shall wax worse and worse, deceiving and being deceived.'*" In proof of this, he mentions, among other things, the fact that "all Lord Herbert's five articles of natural religion have been questioned or given up by those who followed him in his fundamental principle, i. e., 'that nothing can be admitted which is not discoverable by our natural faculties.'" His five articles were: *There is a Supreme God—He is chiefly to be worshipped—Piety and virtue are the principal part of his worship—Repentance expiates offence—There is a state of future rewards and punishments.* But even these principles were not retained by those who adopted his first principle; hence Mr. Watson says, "between this grand principle of error and absolute atheism there are but a few steps." It is in opposition to this principle of error, which is the very basis of infidelity, that Mr. Watson asserts our indebtedness to revelation for a correct knowledge of God, particularly for those sublime ideas of his infinite perfections, developed in the word of God, and which we could not possibly originate or derive from the works of God. For this "knowledge of the existence of God and of his attributes we owe to revelation alone." (Page 274.) Accordingly, he says on this same page, "We are all conscious that we gain the knowledge of God by *instruction*, and we observe that, in proportion to the want of instruction, men are ignorant, as of other things, so of God." This knowledge of God and of his attributes, for which we are indebted to revelation, and which we received by instruction, Mr. Watson specifies in a preceding part of this chapter, pages 266 and 267, and gives us quotations from Barrow, Pearson, Lawson, and Newton, to show that, for the correct and sublime conceptions of God therein contained, they are indebted to revelation; seeing, as he shows, that many of the heathen philosophers who, in every other respect, were fully their equal, were, nevertheless, painfully destitute of this knowledge, so much so as to assert the eternity of matter, and a plurality of gods, and doubt, if not deny, everything essential to a correct religious system. Such is Mr. Watson's position, as set forth, and we think established, in this chapter, by *facts*, by *experience*, by *observation*, and by *the word of God.* If his opponents can prove that these four witnesses are in favor of their position and against his, we will embrace the doctrine of *innate ideas*, which we now oppose; but, as we believe this never can be done, and are sure it never has been done, we purpose to defend Watson and his position to the last.

Just here we pause to make two remarks which result from these investigations. The grand principle of Lord Herbert, from which infidelity has legitimately flowed, and between which and atheism Mr. Watson says there are but a few steps; I say this great principle of Lord Herbert, and the transcendentalism which we here oppose, and which Mr. Cocker sets forth and attempts to defend in the article under consideration, *are essentially one!* To be convinced of this, it is only necessary to compare that principle, as quoted above, with those quotations which we have already given from the article under review, and also with those which we will now give. Any one who will be at the trouble of comparing will see, I am convinced, that Mr. Cocker claims as much in favor of our natural faculties as Lord Herbert does. Take the following quotations in proof:

"The idea of God is a necessary deduction from the facts of the universe and the primary intuitions of the mind. . . . . It is present in every human mind as the germ of the oak is in the acorn. . . . . And it is developed into scientific form by the necessary laws of intellect, as the germ of the oak in the acorn is fully developed under the fixed and determinative laws of vegetative life." (Review, page 197.) "There are specific forms into which human thought must necessarily develop itself, just as a grain of wheat must necessarily develop itself into the blade, and the ear, and the full corn in the ear; or as an acorn must develop itself into the majestic oak. There are fundamental laws of the human intelligence which constrain man, in view of the facts of the universe, to form certain necessary judgments and beliefs. . . . . The human intelligence is configured and correlated to eternal principles of order, and right, and good, as they exist in the Infinite Intelligence." (P. 183.) So much so that "the mind intuitively apprehends them [our acts] as *right* or *wrong*, and spontaneously approves or condemns them. This distinction in the moral quality of actions is felt to be independent of the mind which perceives it and of any mutable condition of things." See much more of the same kind on page 205, and which we quoted in another connection. Much more follows, but we only add the following: "Accompanying this perception of the immutable distinction between virtue and vice, we have the consciousness of its being our DUTY to avoid the one and perform the other. We feel upon us an OBLIGATION which is imperative. We have also an abiding conviction that moral good is *rewardable*, and that vice merits *punishment*. And, finally, we have a conscious apprehension of a future *retribution*."

Of course we could easily contradict these high-sounding assertions, as we have done before, by facts; but this is not what we aim at just now; we only request the reader to compare these, and the quotations of a similar character formerly given, with Lord Herbert's grand principle quoted above, and we have no doubt that he will be convinced, as we are, that the *transcendentalism* which we here oppose is none other than the Herbertism which Watson opposed. It comes now, as it did then, with many fair professions and imposing titles, BUT IT IS THE SAME DEADLY ERROR. We will simply add the single remark, that there is one point in which our reviewer claims more for the natural faculties than Lord H. does. The latter only declares man to be *capable* of these attainments by the exercise of his "natural faculties," while the former declares all the attainments, which he specifies, to be the *necessary* results of *necessary* and *fixed* laws! The one says he *may*, the other says he *must* be all this, independent of revelation.

Our second remark is this: If Lord Herbert's doctrine and the transcendentalism here opposed are essentially one, and if the former led to infidelity, and is only a few steps from atheism, as Mr. Watson asserts, and history shows, the conclusion is inevitable; this same transcendentalism leads to infidelity, notwithstanding its fair pretensions and high sounding-titles. That the principle adopted and advocated by Lord Herbert led to infidelity in England, and to atheism, too, is a fact that will not be disputed by any one acquainted with the history of those times. These teachings first and principally corrupted the higher ranks of society, amongst whom were many real scholars, possessed of varied and splendid abilities. This "Religion of Nature," this *Deism*, this *philosophy*, as it was variously called, was admirably adapted to flatter their vanity, which increased more and more till the old Book, called the Bible, was utterly rejected as only suitable for the vulgar and the superstitious; while the Book of Nature, which always lay open before them, was so worthy the study of the philosopher, and fully competent to teach them all they desired to know of God and religion. In this book, they contended, *everything necessary to be believed is discoverable by our natural faculties.* Amongst those who embraced, and were almost or utterly ruined by these teachings, were the Hon. Francis Newport, the Earl of Chesterfield, Sir John Pringle, Lord Littleton, the Earl of Rochester, William Emmerson, David Hume, Soame Jenyngs, Captain John Lee, and many others, amongst whom was an accomplished youth, an account of whom is given us under the fictitious name of Antitheus. Some of these were reclaimed, some became obstinate atheists, and some ended their miserable life in the most terrible agonies of utter despair. And all this resulted from teachings which, in their beginning, were comparatively plausible, and with which the teachings of modern transcendentalism are, as we have shown, essentially one; and, consequently, have the same tendency; because they lead from the Bible, and ascribe to the *natural man*, and to the *Book of Nature*, what they do not possess; because they lead man to seek in the *natural*, what can only be found in the *supernatural.* In short, they lead away from God while they profess to lead to him; they cad away from "God in Christ," who is "the way, the truth, and the life;" they lead away from the Holy Spirit by teaching that the *unassisted natural faculties can do what they cannot possibly do without the assistance of that Spirit.* They lead away from the faith of the Christian to that of the Deist, by teaching that *faith cometh by seeing the works of God; while Paul teaches that faith cometh by hearing the word of God.* Thus we turn the tables by showing that transcendentalism—not Watson's philosophy—tends to infidelity, if not to "pure materialism." And in proof of this we have given some terrible instances in connection with the history of this error in England, and could give still more numerous and terrible instances connected with its history in France.

Having denied that the knowledge of the being and attributes of God is *innate*, and having asserted our indebtedness to revelation for that knowledge, and having given his reasons for so doing, Mr. Watson concludes thus: "But being now discovered, the rational evidence is both copious and irresistible; so much so that Atheism has never been able to make much progress among mankind where this revelation has been preserved." In proof of this position Mr. Watson gives the following quotation from Ellis, and we think it is a very forcible expression of the same sentiment: "Tell men there is a God, and their mind embraces it as a necessary truth; unfold his attributes, and they will see the explanation of them in his works. When the foundation is laid sure and firm that there is a God, and his will the cause of all things, and nothing made but by his special appointment and command, then the order of beings will fill their minds with a due sense of the Divine Majesty." The amount is this: the Book of Nature is read in the light of the torch of revelation; in that light "the heavens declare the glory of God, and the firmament showeth his handiwork."

Mr. Watson now takes up the arguments *à priori* and *à posteriori*, on page 281. The former, he says, "is an argument from something *antecedent* to something *consequent;* from *principle* to *corollary;* from *cause* to *effect.*" Concerning this argument he says, on page 330: "It may be ranked among the overzealous attempts of the advocates of truth. It is well intended, but unsatisfactory, and so far as on one hand it has led to a neglect of the more convincing and powerful course of argument drawn from '*the things which do appear*,' and on the other, has encouraged a dependence upon a mode of investigation, to which the human mind is inadequate, which in many instances is an utter mental delusion, and which scarcely two minds will conduct in the same manner; it has probably been mischievous in its effects by inducing a scepticism not arising out of the nature of the case, but from the imperfect and unsatisfactory investigations of the human understanding, pushed beyond the limit of its power. In most instances it is a sword which cuts two ways; and the mere imaginary assumptions of those who think they have found out a new way to demonstrate truth, have in many instances either done disservice to it by absurdity, or yielded principles which unbelievers have connected with the most injurious conclusions. We need only instance the doctrine of the *necessary* existence of the Deity when reasoned *à priori*." From this doctrine, "*when reasoned à priori*," he says, "some acute infidels have drawn the conclusion that the Supreme Being cannot be a free agent, and have thus set the first principles of religion at variance with the Scriptures."

With Mr. Watson's definition and views of the *à priori* argument, as here given, Mr. Cocker has no patience. His want of *honesty*, it would seem, and his want of *intelligence*, are alike annoying to Mr. C. Hence on page 190, he expresses himself thus: "It would appear from Mr. Watson's treatment of this argument that he did not fully apprehend it. He characterizes it as an argument from cause to effect, whereas it is an argument from *à priori* truths." In addition to the above objections to the *à priori* argument, Mr. Watson says, on page 331: "But if there is in reality nothing *prior* to the being of God, considered as the first cause and causality, nothing in *nature*, nothing in *reason*, then the attempt to argue from it is fruitless; and we improperly pretend to search into the grounds or reasons of the first cause, of whom antecedently we neither do nor can know anything." To all this Mr. C. replies thus: "What a misapprehension of the argument! Surely Mr. Watson must have known that the question is not, Is there anything prior to God? but, Are there any *à priori* truths of reason? To instance one such truth: 'every event must have a cause;' here is an *à priori* truth, a necessary belief of the human intelligence." Yes, sir, Mr. Watson did know very well that the question is not, "Is there anything before God?" Hence he assumes that as a truth acknowledged on all hands, and from that acknowledged truth he both *honestly* and *intelligently* deduces one of his objections to the *à priori* argument; therefore the only question here, is, whether the deduction is legitimate and conclusive, and that we leave the reader to decide, at least for the present. Mr. Watson also knew that the question which he was discussing was not, "Are there any *à priori* truths of reason?" He was discussing, as the above quotations show, the merits of the *à priori* argument; nor do we see any reason to conclude with Mr. C., from anything Mr. W. has said in reference to the *à priori* argument, "that he did not fully apprehend it;" on the contrary, we are forced to turn the tables again, and say it is Mr. C., and not Mr. W., that fails to apprehend the argument. We adopt Mr. W.'s definition of the *à priori* argument, though Mr. C. assumes, as usual, that the definition which he gives us is agreed upon, and adopted by all. We believe with Sir W. Hamilton, and Watson knew, and Mr. C. should have known, that, "Previously to Kant the terms *à priori* and *à posteriori* were, in a sense which descended from Aristotle, properly and usually employed—the former to denote a reasoning from cause to effect—the latter a reasoning from effect to cause. The term *à priori* came, however, in modern times, to be extended to any abstract reasoning from a given notion to the conditions which such a notion involved; hence, for example, the title *à priori* bestowed on the ontological and cosmological arguments for the existence of the Deity. The latter of these, in fact, starts from experience—from the observed contingency of the world, in order to construct the supposed notion on which it founds. Clarke's cosmological demonstration called *à priori*, is, therefore, so far, properly an argument *à posteriori*."

What Mr. Watson says on page 331, is precisely the same in substance as the above from Sir W. Hamilton. Regarding Dr. S. Clarke's *à priori* argument, he says the doctor was "one of the earliest and ablest advocates of this mode of demonstrating the existence of God." But, he adds, "He first proceeds *à posteriori* to prove, from the actual existence of dependent beings, the existence from eternity of 'one unchangeable and independent Being!'" And just so it is that Mr. Cocker reasons, after all that he says about the conclusiveness and importance of the *à priori* argument, which he says is deduced from "*à priori* truths;" of which he gives the following as a specimen: "Every event must have a cause." Now in this *à priori* truth, as he calls it, there is clearly nothing from which to deduce an argument, but the *event* or *effect* therein specified; and in attempting to prove the being of a God from that *event* or *effect*, he is clearly arguing from effect to cause; his argument, therefore, is clearly an *à posteriori* argument! The fact is, in proving the being of a God there cannot be such a thing as an *à priori* argument, properly so called; for wherever you start you must start with the creature or the Creator; if with the latter, you assume what is to be proved, and then attempt to prove your *assumption* from your *assumption!* If with the former, you are evidently arguing from effect to cause, and your argument, consequently, is an *à posteriori* argument. The reader can now judge who it is that has failed to apprehend the *à priori* argument, Watson or his reviewer! And as to his "*à priori* truth," we simply remind him, as Watson has already done, that although it is an obvious truth, *axiomatic* if you please, it is not so to infidels, at least not so to all infidels, for Hume denies that it can be proved to be a truth; so that although *we* admit it to be an evident truth, still it failed to afford to Hume an argument demonstrative of the being of a God. It follows, that the failure to apprehend the *à priori* argument is wholly on the part of Mr. C., for if we should even grant that his mode of constructing the *à priori* argument is the right mode, still it fails to answer the end for which he employs it, and this is the fact previously asserted by Mr. Watson.

Mr. Watson now takes up the *à posteriori* argument. On page 275 he says: "Nature, as one justly observes, proceeds from causes to effects; but the most certain and successful investigations of man, proceed from effects to causes, and this is the character of what logicians have called the argument *à posteriori*." From page 281 we have this argument as conducted by Locke, Howe, and Paley. The last two named are quoted at great length, and concerning the whole he thus speaks: "The above arguments, as they irresistibly confirm the Scripture doctrine of the existence of an intelligent first cause, expose the extreme folly and absurdity of Atheism." Of this argument, as conducted by these masters, he not only speaks in the highest terms, but says of the *à posteriori* argument itself, when properly conducted, that it is "both copious and irresistible," page 274. And again, on page 335, he says: "The proof of the *being* of a God reposes wholly then upon arguments *à posteriori*, and it needs no other; though we shall see as we proceed that even these arguments, strong and irrefutable as they are when rightly applied, have been used to prove more as to some of the attributes of God, than can satisfactorily be drawn from them. Even with this safe and convincing process of reasoning at our command, we shall find at every step of inquiry into the Divine nature, our entire dependence upon Divine revelation, for our primary light. That must both originate our investigations, and conduct them to a satisfactory result." On page 281, vol. i, Mr. Watson says: "The existence of God, once communicated to us by his own revelation, direct or traditional, is capable of ample proof, and receives an irresistible corroborative evidence *à posteriori*." Again, on page 274, he says: "It is therefore to be concluded, that we owe the knowledge of the existence of God, and of his attributes, to revelation alone, but, being now discovered, the rational evidence of both is copious and irresistible." Now, not only in defiance, but in direct contradiction of all this, Watson's reviewer says, on page 188: "Some of Mr. Watson's admirers have concluded his doctrine to be, that when once the idea of God has been suggested by revelation the human reason can elaborate the demonstration of his existence. . . . . . A more exact and critical attention to the entire scope and structure of his argument must, however, result in the conviction that this is a misapprehension." Again, on page 198, he says: "It is solely because Watson degrades the *reason*—the faculty which apprehends eternal, necessary, universal truth—and undervalues and disregards its *à priori* intuitions, that he is unable to apprehend and feel the logical conclusiveness of the *à posteriori* demonstration of a God." Poor Watson! He "degrades the reason, and undervalues and disregards its *à priori* intuitions," and "he is unable to apprehend and feel the logical conclusiveness of the *à posteriori* demonstration of a God." This is about as conclusive as it is modest; and the following on page.185 is in keeping: "He affirms, with earnestness and emphasis, that we have no idea of God, of right and wrong, and of immortality, except as derived from *without* by *instruction* and *verbal revelation;* that, indeed, we have no *faculty of knowing* on any of these subjects, except by faith." The reviewer does not tell us where Mr. Watson affirms this, only he assures us that, "A careful perusal of the chapters 'On the Presumptive Evidences in Part I, the chapter On the Existence of God in Part II, and the first chapter of Part III, On the Moral Law,' will be decisive of this question in every intelligent mind!" If the reviewer considers this decisive he is welcome to do so; we apprehend, however, that most people will wonder, as we do, why Mr. Watson is thus misrepresented, which we have shown to be the fact in our review of the chapters referred to. As to the *à posteriori argument*, as given by Locke, Howe, and Paley, so far from disparaging it, Watson speaks of it in the highest terms, as we have shown, and we do not hesitate to say that the argument, as thus quoted and endorsed by Watson, is the fullest and clearest exhibit of it that has yet been given, as far as our knowledge goes, and for anything Mr. C. has shown to the contrary. And we do verily believe that Mr. W. has given it credit for all the merit it possesses; nor do we hesitate to say that Watson's reviewer has left it unimproved.

As Mr. Cocker mentions *space*, on page 203, as a source

from which we may derive a knowledge of God, we will give Mr. Watson's views of arguments derived from this source also; and thus close our examination of the chapter "On the Existence of God," to which we were referred by the reviewer. His remarks on this topic are found at the close of the chapter, on page 335, and run thus: "Equally unsatisfactorily, and therefore quite as little calculated to serve the cause of truth, is the argument from *space;* which is represented by Newton, Clarke, and others, as an *infinite mode* of an *infinite substance*, and that *substance* God. . . . . . Berkeley, Law, and others have however shown the fallacy of considering space either as a *substance*, or a *mode*, and have brought these speculations under the dominion of common sense, and rescued them from metaphysical delusion. They have rightly observed, that space is a mere *negation*, and that to suppose it to have existence, because it has some properties, for instance, of penetrability, or the capacity of receiving body, is the same thing as to affirm that *darkness* must be something because it has the capacity of receiving light, and *silence* something because it has the capacity of receiving *sound*, and *absence* something because it has the property of being supplied by *presence*." After exposing these and similar metaphysical sophisms, at some length, and showing that *nothing* may, in this way, be exalted into *something*, he closes with these remarks: "The whole of this controversy has left us only to lament the waste of labor which has been employed in erecting around the impregnable ramparts of the great arguments on which the cause rests with so much safety, the useless incumbrances of mud and straw." The fact is, any one who is acquainted with what philosophers, ancient and modern, have said of space, knows, that, to undertake to prove from it the being of a God, is to undertake to prove the *unknown* from the *unknown!* Or, if it is assumed that God is already known, then such arguments profess to increase our knowledge of the *known* from the unknown! To show how little we know about space we will here give a few of the singular definitions of it, which great men have left on record: *Space is vacuum; it is the mere form of the sensibility; Space and time are in themselves non-existing; Space is nothing but the order of things co-existing; Space is not pure nothing, for it has the capacity of receiving; Space is infinite and eternal; Space and time are really something; Space is but a relative to body, and to body only; Space is an affection or property of the Deity; Space is an infinite quality of an infinite substance!*

Now, in view of the above definitions, we really cannot represent Watson as degrading the human reason because he will not admit the utility of arguments drawn from such a source to prove the being of a God. On the contrary, we really think with him that they are at best "useless incumbrances of mud and straw!" Thus have we carefully examined and passed through the chapter in which Watson's reviewer professes to have found so much error, and have utterly failed to find the error specified. On the contrary, we admire and love its weighty and truly scriptural teachings more and more.

But we are assured that we shall find the error "in the first chapter of Part III, 'On the Moral Law.'" To a "discriminating mind," it is affirmed that "a careful perusal" of this chapter "will be decisive of this question." That it will be "decisive of the question" is quite certain, for that is the last chapter appealed to; hence, if we do not find the error there, as we are sure we will not, we have nowhere else to go to find it, and must, therefore, conclude that it is not to be found in "Watson's Institutes."

We are glad that we have been referred to this chapter, for several reasons; one is, it so happens that the part more especially objected to is that which we more especially admire, because it contains, we believe, one of the happiest and most successful efforts to expose one of the most pernicious and subtle errors. For this reason, and also that we may do both Watson and his reviewer justice, we must be allowed to quote that part of the chapter to which the reviewer so strongly objects, and in reference to which we differ so very widely. We sincerely regret, however, that we have still to complain of misrepresentation, and such misrepresentation as we cannot even attempt to account for.

CHAPTER III.

On page 186 of the review, Mr. C. brings the following sweeping charge against our author:

"It is, therefore, but natural that he [Mr. Watson] should enter his solemn protest against the attempt to construct a science of NATURAL THEOLOGY or of MORAL PHILOSOPHY, as a design which is not only 'visionary' and 'impossible,' but of 'mischievous tendency,' and they who are engaged in it are accessory to the infidel crusade against the word of God."

Here Mr. Watson is represented as "entering his solemn protest against the attempt to construct a science of Natural Theology or of Moral Philosophy." Nay more, he is represented as asserting that the thing is "visionary, impossible, and of mischievous tendency." And in his introduction, on the first page, the reviewer conveys the idea that Mr. Watson and other theologians condemn philosophy altogether. "Many theologians," he says, "have condemned philosophy, shutting it, as they supposed, out of the region of theology, and cautioning their hearers to 'beware that no man beguile them through philosophy.'" Doubtless it was, on reading these statements in the Quarterly, that the good doctor of the Repository was moved to fly with so much haste and zeal to the rescue of philosophy out of the hands of these mistaken theologians who were about to shut it out of the region of theology, and abandon it forever. In the June number of the Repository, in connection with his notice of the article under consideration, the doctor thus speaks: "The true way to escape being spoiled through philosophy is not to let all philosophy alone, but to ground ourselves upon the true. Never yet have men succeeded in erecting a wall high enough to secure a total separation between the domains of philosophy and theology." This deep concern for the safety of philosophy brings to our mind what Bishop Morris tells about a certain city official who, in his great zeal for the peace of his city, on a certain occasion demanded the cause of the tumult, when an honest Dutchman replied, "It is only one bird that did get out of him cage." But in the present instance there is not even that much cause for alarm; for all this talk about Mr. Watson's deadly opposition to philosophy is simply untrue! If the editor of the Repository had examined the Institutes as well as the Quarterly, he would have seen that the attempt "to secure a total separation between the domains of philosophy and theology" is one of those evils to which Mr. Watson objects, and which he exposes in that very chapter to which Mr. Cocker refers us for proof of the above charges. To prevent such mistakes in the future, and to show how Mr. Watson has been misrepresented, we will now hear him speak for himself.

After speaking of the "perfection and glory" of the moral law, as given in the Old, and more fully developed in the New Testament, he says, on page 472:

"It has, however, fared with morals as with doctrines, that they have been often and by a strange perversity studied without any reference to the authority of the

Scriptures. As we have had systems of NATURAL RELIGION drawn out of the materials furnished by the Scriptures, and then placed to the sole account of human reason, so we have also various systems of morals drawn, as far as the authors thought fit, from the same source, and put forth under the title of MORAL PHILOSOPHY, implying too often, or at least sanctioning, the inference that the unassisted powers of man are equally adequate to the discovery of doctrine and duty [this, as we have seen, is the teaching of the article under review]; or, at least, that Christianity but perfects what uninspired men are able not only to commence, but to carry onward to a considerable approach to perfection. This observation may be made as to both, that whatever is found correct in doctrine and pure in morals in ancient writers or systems, may be traced to indirect revelation, and that, so far as mere reason has applied itself to discovery in either, it has generally gone astray. The modern systems of natural religion and ethics are superior to the ancient, not because the reason of their framers is superior, but because they have had the advantage of a light from Christianity, which they have not been candid enough generally to acknowledge. For those who have written on such subjects with a view to lower the value of the Holy Scriptures, the remarks in the first part of this work must suffice; but of that class of moral philosophers who hold the authority of the sacred books, and yet sedulously omit all reference to them, it may be inquired what they propose by disjoining morals from Christianity, and considering them as a separate science? Authority they cannot gain, for no obligation to duty can be so high as the command of God; nor can that authority be applied in so direct a manner as by a revelation of his will; and, as for the perfection of their system, since they discover no duties not already enjoined in the Scriptures, or grounded upon some general principles they contain, they can find no apology, from the additions they make to our moral knowledge, to put Christianity, on all such subjects, wholly out of sight."

The reader is requested to notice the *connection* of the words "mischievous tendency" in what follows, and compare with the quotation which we have given above from page 186 of the Review; and also with the quotation which we have given from Dr. Clarke of the Repository, and then tell us what ground there is for the charges of the one, and the fears of the other; in other words, say whether Watson is the enemy of philosophy that he is represented to be, or whether he is its true and intelligent defender; say whether he is for separating philosophy and theology, as has been assumed, or whether, with Dr. Clarke, he is opposed to the separation, and a defender of the union of philosophy and theology. That the latter is the fact, "must, we think, be evident to every discriminating mind," after reading the quotations here given. Thus we turn the tables again, by not only clearing Watson of the charge of separating philosophy and theology, but by showing that it is his opponents who do this very thing. And, as Mr. Watson complains, "they have not been candid enough generally to acknowledge" the source from which they obtained the moral teachings which they thus separate from theology; for although they are entirely indebted to "the sacred books" for all that is valuable in their moral teachings, they "sedulously omit all reference to them." We will now hear our author continue his defence.

"All attempts to teach morals, independent of Christianity, even by those who receive it as a Divine revelation, must, notwithstanding the great names which have sanctioned the practice, be considered as of mischievous tendency, although the design may have been laudable, and the labor, in some subordinate respects, not without utility."

His reasons for objecting to "all attempts to teach morals" *in the* WAYS *here specified*, now follow. These reasons are so weighty, and so well expressed, we must be permitted to give them in the author's own words; for, let it be distinctly noticed—Watson's opponents *must fairly meet and invalidate these reasons, or adopt the position in support of which they are advanced.* And this they will find to be very different work from making and fighting a man of straw; which is really all they have yet done. He objects to such attempts, then:

"1. Because they silently convey the impression that human reason, without assistance, is sufficient to discover the full duty of man toward God and toward his fellow creatures. [That the teaching of the article under review conveys this impression, we have already seen. See Review, pages 183, 184, 205, and 206.]

"2. Because they imply a deficiency in the moral code of our religion, which does not exist; the fact being that, although these systems borrow much from Christianity, they do not take in the whole of its moral principles, and, therefore, so far as they are accepted as substitutes, displace what is perfect for what is imperfect.

"3. Because they turn the attention from what is fact, the revealed LAW of God, with its appropriate sanctions, and place the obligation to obedience either on fitness, beauty, general interest, or the natural authority of truth, which are all matters of opinion; or, if they ultimately refer to the will of God, yet they *infer* that will through various reasonings and speculations, which in themselves are still matters of opinion, and as to which men will feel themselves to be in some degree free.

"4. The duties they enjoin are either merely outward in the act, and so they disconnect them from internal principles and habits, without which they are not acceptable to God, and but the shadows of real virtue, however beneficial they may be to men; or else they assume that human nature is able to engraft those principles and habits upon itself, and to practise them without abatement and interruption; a notion which is contradicted by those very Scriptures they hold to be of Divine authority.

"5. Their separation of the *doctrines* of religion from its morals, leads to an entirely different process of promoting morality among men to that which the infinite wisdom and goodness of God have established in the Gospel. They lay down the rule of conduct, and recommend it from its excellence *per se*, or its influence upon individuals and upon society, or perhaps because it is manifested to be the will of the Supreme Being indicated from the constitution of human nature and the relations of men. But Christianity rigidly connects its doctrines with its morals. Its doctrine of man's moral weakness is made use of to lead him to distrust his own sufficiency. Its doctrine of regeneration by the influence of the Holy Spirit, implies the entire destruction of the love of evil, and the direction of the whole affection of the soul to universal virtue. Its doctrine of prayer opens to man a fellowship with God, invigorating to every virtue. The example of Christ, the imitation of which is made obligatory upon us, is in itself a moral system in action, and in principle; and the revelation of a future judgment brings the whole weight of the control of future rewards and punishments to bear upon the motives and actions of men, and is the source of the fear of offending God, which is the constant guard of virtue, when human motives would in a multitude of cases avail nothing.

"It may indeed be asked whether the teaching of morals must then in all cases be kept in connection with religion? and whether the philosophy of virtues and vices, with the lower motives by which they are urged upon men, may not be usefully investigated? We answer, that if the end proposed by this is not altogether speculative, but something practical; if the case of an immoral world is taken up by moralists with reference to its cure, or even to its emendation in any effectual degree, the whole is then resolved into this simple question—whether a weaker instrument shall be preferred to that which is powerful and effective? Certain it is that the great end of Christianity, so far as its influence upon society goes, is to moralize mankind; but its infinitely wise Author has established and authorized but ONE process for the correction of the practical evils of the world, and that is the teaching and enforcement of THE WHOLE TRUTH as it stands in his own revelations; and to this only has he promised his special blessing. A distinct class of ethical teachers imitating heathen philosophers in the principles and modes of moral tuition, is, in a Christian country, a violent anomaly; and implies an absurd return to the twilight of knowledge after the sun itself has arisen upon the world.

"Within proper guards, and in strict connection with the *whole* Christian system [so far is Mr. W. from building a high wall between theology and philosophy], what is called moral philosophy is not, however, to be undervalued; and from many of the writers above alluded to much useful instruction may be collected, which, though of but little efficacy in itself, may be invigorated by uniting it with the vital and energetic doctrines of religion, and may thus become directive to the conduct of the serious Christian. Understanding then by moral philosophy, not that pride of science which borrows the discoveries of the Scriptures, and then exhibits itself as their rival, or affects to supply their deficiencies; but as a modest scrutiny into the reasons on which the moral precepts of revelation may be grounded, and a wise and honest application of its moral principles to particular cases, it is a branch of science which may be usefully cultivated in connection with Christianity."

The above is all that this chapter contains that is strictly relevant to the points at issue, unless it be the closing paragraph, in which our author sums up thus:

"To the revealed will of God we may now turn for information on the interesting subject of morals, and we shall find that the ethics of Christianity have a glory and a perfection which philosophy has never heightened, and which its only true office is to display, and keep before the attention of mankind."

We have now before us a verbatim exhibit of all that this chapter contains strictly relevant to the subject in hand. And any one who will be at the trouble of reading these quotations will see that Watson speaks highly of "what is called moral philosophy," and which he defines to be "a modest scrutiny into the reasons on which the moral precepts of revelation may be grounded." "This," he says, "is a branch of science which may be usefully cultivated in connection with Christianity, and may thus become directive to the conduct of the serious Christian." "From many of the writers above alluded to much useful information may be collected." Therefore, "what is called moral philosophy is not to be undervalued." To this end, however, it must be kept "in strict connection with the whole Christian system;" therefore, to "all attempts to teach morals independent of Christianity," he decidedly objects, and his reasons are given above. As we only aim at a defence of Watson and the truth, we leave it to others to divine why it is, in face of the above, that Watson is represented as being the unqualified enemy of philosophy, and as attempting to separate and build a wall between philosophy and theology! That precisely the reverse is true, in each particular, is as evident as the strength of the English language can make it! Why his true position, and his weighty and masterly arguments in support thereof, should be left utterly unnoticed, we also leave to others to divine. We must say, however, that to us this is truly marvellous, and its marvellousness is increased by the fact that this is done by ministers of high standing in the M. E. Church; not because we expect them to be wiser or better than other ministers; but because we expect them to be better acquainted with the Theological Institutes of Richard Watson, and should unite with him in saying "that the ethics of Christianity have a glory and perfection which philosophy has never heightened, and which its only true office is to display, and to keep before the attention of mankind."

Mr. Watson raises no objection to philosophers or philosophy properly so called; but to "that pride of science which borrows the discoveries of the Scriptures, and then exhibits itself as their rival, or affects to supply their deficiencies." Mr. Watson takes the ground, as every sound theologian must do, that the *doctrines* and *morals* of Christianity are both *perfect* and *inseparable*; and, accordingly, objects, as God himself does, to all attempts to add to, take from, or separate them. He objects to the dishonest and pernicious practice of stealing Scripture truth, and giving *reason* credit for the discovery thereof. With such philosophers and philosophy Mr. Watson has no sympathy, because he is a sound philosopher, and a lover of sound philosophy, as his writings do most clearly show. And we are fully convinced that we would have better theologians and better philosophers if Watson's writings were more carefully and more generally studied; and, as a consequence, we would have less of "that pride of science" above specified, and which sound theologians and philosophers hate as the very *bane* of both philosophy and theology, and which abounds in the present age as much as in any previous age—perhaps I should say more, for it always grows out of, and accompanies the *superficial.*

We have long been convinced that the error of *separating the morals of Christianity from their doctrines, and divesting them of their proper authority and motives, is very common,* and very pernicious, and that it demands from theologians far more attention than it receives. It originated with those who were very far from being the friends of either the Church or the word of God; but, assuming the garb and name of philosophy, it obtained countenance and support from many who were the friends of both; and to the latter it is indebted for most of the success which it has had in the Christian world. We believe the sacred cause of Temperance has suffered more from this error than from any other thing—perhaps we might say, more than from all other things put together. This branch of Christian morals has of late been separated more or less from the Christian doctrines whence it naturally springs; it has been divested of the motives and authority with which Christianity invested it; and it has been taken out of the hands of the Church, or people of God, and put into the hands of those who, in many instances, made no pretensions to the Christian character, and were very far from being friendly to the Church and cause of God. In such hands, and divested of all that which gave it force and vitality, the cause of Temperance has languished and died, or been made a mere tool to promote other and even pernicious ends!

We have now examined all those parts of the Institutes to which we have been referred, and have discovered that the charges brought against Mr. Watson are without foundation. Instead of error, we have found the sublime doctrines of Christianity developed and enforced with the abilities of a master; and much of the teachings said to be erroneous, we have not only shown to be entirely Scriptural, but such as is specially needed at the present time: we have also shown that Mr. Watson is strangely misquoted and misrepresented. In a word, we "have found no fault in this man, touching those things whereof ye accuse him."

But Mr. Watson's logic is quite as objectionable, it would seem, as his metaphysics. On pages 191, 192, 193, and 194, the reviewer records some of his objections to Mr. Watson's reasoning, and gives us some specimens of his own, which shall now have a brief notice.

"The question whether the Scriptures are a revelation from God is referred solely to the arbitration of a faculty which is pronounced to be 'weak, uncertain, and erring,' 'which may be the reverse of the Divine reason,' and in whose demonstrations of the existence of God I am not permitted to repose any confidence. Now if *reason* is totally unreliable in *this* case, it must be in *that;* if it mislead me in the one instance, I cannot trust it in the other; if it is wholly incompetent to produce certitude when the existence of God is under consideration, it must also when the truth of the Bible is under consideration." (Pages 191 and 192.) This is a small specimen of much more that possesses as little, and even less merit, but with which we will not trouble the reader, as this contains the point at issue, and will, consequently, answer our purpose.

That reason, *human reason, without the supernatural assistance* of which we have already spoken at some length, is "a weak, uncertain, and erring faculty," especially in reference to those subjects specified by Mr. Watson, is certainly asserted by the latter, and we join with him in the assertion; for to join issue with him here, is to take the ground *that unassisted reason is strong, unerring, and certain, in its investigations and decisions on the aforesaid subjects;* a ground which we did not suppose any man in his senses would take, and which we know is utterly untenable, being at variance with the facts of universal experience.

We join issue with the reviewer, however, when he asserts, "if it [reason] is wholly incompetent to produce certitude when the existence of God is under consideration, it must also when the truth of the Bible is under consideration." By "the truth of the Bible" we suppose the reviewer means its being what it professes to be, the word of God. That reason is competent to produce certitude as to this, but entirely incompetent to originate the idea of the God of the Bible, is Watson's position; that it is incompetent to the former, if it be incompetent to the latter, is the reviewer's assertion: but as he simply asserts, we simply deny till he attempts the proof; in the mean time we will give Watson's position in his own words.

The chapter in which this subject is discussed commences on page 95, vol. i, and is entitled, "The use and limitation of reason." After several remarks, which it is not necessary to quote, our author proceeds thus, on page 95:

"We are not, in the first instance, to examine the doctrine, in order to determine from our own opinion of its excellence, whether it be of God (for to this, if we need a revelation, we are incompetent), but we are to inquire into the credentials of the messengers, in quest of sufficient proof that God hath spoken to mankind by them. Should a slight consideration of the doctrine, either by its apparent excellence, or the contrary, attract us strongly to this examination, it is well; but whatever prejudices, for or against the doctrine, a report, or a hasty opinion of its nature and tendency may inspire, our final judgment can only safely rest upon the proof which may be afforded of its Divine authority. If that be satisfactory the case is determined, whether the doctrine be pleasing or displeasing to us. If sufficient evidence be not afforded, we are at liberty to receive or reject the whole, or any part of it, as it may appear to us to be worthy of our regard; for it then stands on the same ground as any other merely human opinion."

On pages 102, 103, our author speaks of the use and limitation of reason thus: "The USE of reason, therefore, in matters of revelation, is to investigate the evidences on which it is founded, and fairly and impartially to interpret it according to the ordinary rules of interpretation in other cases. Its LIMIT is the authority of God. When he has explicitly laid down a doctrine, that doctrine is to be humbly received, whatever degree of rational evidence may be afforded of its truth, or withheld; and no torturing or perverting criticisms can be *innocently* resorted to, to bring a doctrine into a better accordance with our favorite views and systems, any more than to make a precept bend to the love and practice of our vicious indulgences. A larger scope than this cannot certainly be assigned to human reason in matters of revelation when it is elevated to the office of *judge*—a judge of the evidences on which a professed revelation rests, and a judge of its meaning after the application of the established rules of interpretation in other cases. But if reason be considered as a *learner*, it may have a much wider range in those fields of intelligence which a genuine revelation from God will open to our view. . . . . Thus it is that reason, instead of being fettered, as some pretend, by being regulated, is enlightened by revelation, and enabled from the first principles and by the grand landmarks which it furnishes, to pursue its inquiries into many subjects to an extent which enriches and ennobles the human intellect, and administers continual food to the strength of religious principle. This, however, is not the case with all subjects. Many, as we have already seen, are from their very nature wholly incapable of investigation. At the first step we launch into darkness, and find in religion as well as in natural philosophy, beyond certain limits, insurmountable barriers, which bid defiance to human penetration."

Thus it is that Mr. Watson specifies the USE and LIMITATION of reason; specifies what it *can*, and what it can *not* do; what is its legitimate work, and what is not; wherein it is weak, erring, and uncertain, and wherein it is a sure guide; wherein it is reliable, and wherein it is not. "Its LIMIT is the authority of God;" its USE "in matters of revelation," is not to decide *what a revelation should be*, "for to this, if we need a revelation, we are incompetent;" but "to investigate the evidences on which it is founded, and fairly and impartially to interpret it according to the ordinary rules of interpretation in other cases." But the reviewer says, "if reason is wholly incompetent to produce certitude when the existence of God is under consideration," it is equally incompetent to do this; if it cannot decide what a revelation from God *should* be, it cannot examine the seals thereof. In a word, if it cannot do the greater it cannot do the less! We now leave the reader to decide whether Watson's logic or that of his reviewer is most at fault! We also leave it to the impartial reader to say whether Watson has degraded the human reason by specifying its LIMIT and USE as above. Thus we again turn the tables, by showing that it is the reviewer's logic that is at fault, not Mr. Watson's! The appropriate work of reason, in this connection, is thus stated by Leslie in his "Short and Easy Method with a Deist:" "I suppose, then, that the truth of the Christian doctrines will be sufficiently evinced if the matters of fact recorded of Christ in the gospels are proved to be true; for his miracles, if true, established the truth of what he delivered. The same may be said with regard to Moses. If he led the children of Israel through the Red Sea, and did such other wonderful things as are recorded of him in the book of Exodus, it must necessarily follow that he was sent by God; these being the strongest evidences we can require, and which every Deist will confess he would admit if he himself had witnessed their performance. So that the stress of this cause will depend upon the proof of these matters of fact." The work here assigned to reason is simply to ascertain whether the things here specified are matters of fact, and this being done, "the truth of the Christian doctrines," says Mr. Leslie, "will be sufficiently evinced." It is difficult, perhaps impossible, to conceive of any two works more different than the above, and that of originating the idea of an Infinite Intelligence; yet Mr. Cocker says, if reason cannot do the latter it cannot do the former! Mr. Leslie, however, like Mr. Watson, shows that reason is quite competent to the one task, though utterly incompetent to the other; and he also shows that to establish the above *facts*, with which God seals his own truth, is to establish "the truth of the Christian doctrines," and the first of these is the being of an Infinite Intelligence!

On page 193 the reviewer further objects to Mr. Watson's logic, thus: "In order, therefore, to prove the truth of the Holy Scriptures, *he has first to assume what he cannot prove*, namely, the existence of God, and then having, as he supposes, proved the truth of revelation, he proves *from* revelation the existence of God. In other words, he says: Grant me that God exists, and I will prove the Bible to be true, and then from the Bible I will prove the being of a God. If this be not an example of the *petitio principii*—a mere begging of the question—then we do not understand his argument. He is all the while arguing in a vicious circle."

That the reviewer does not understand Mr. Watson's argument is sufficiently obvious, and to admit this is the very best apology we can make for him, for he has never once given Watson's argument to his readers, though he has often professed to do so. In the quotations given above he says Watson "has first to assume what he cannot prove, namely, the existence of God." And he represents him as saying, "Grant me that God exists, and I will prove the Bible to be true." No, sir; Watson says no such thing, nor anything like it; neither does he assume what cannot be proved. He says: "It is, therefore, to be concluded that we owe the knowledge of the existence of God, and of his attributes, to revelation alone; but, being now discovered, the rational evidence of both is copious and irresistible; so much so that Atheism has never been able to make much progress among mankind where this revelation has been preserved." And, as corroborative of this sentiment, he quotes the following words of Ellis: "Tell men there is a God, and their mind embraces it as a necessary truth; unfold his attributes, and they will see the explanation of them in his works." The amount is this: the knowledge of an Infinite Intelligence cannot be derived from what is created, however extensive, for that would be to DERIVE THE INFINITE FROM THE FINITE; but God himself having communicated to man a knowledge of his own being and attributes, that knowledge is corroborated and illustrated by all the works of God. In a word, *Revelation* ORIGINATES *and Creation* ILLUSTRATES *the great* IDEA. Instead, then, of assuming "what cannot be proved," Watson simply assumes *a naked fact*, namely, that the *idea* of an Infinite Intelligence *is already in man's possession;* and he asserts that "Moses and all the inspired writers" assume the same fact, and assume it because it was *a fact admitted, believed, and known.* That some "did not like to retain God in their knowledge," and, consequently, "had not the knowledge of God," is not only not denied, but asserted, both by Watson and the inspired writers; but this does not affect the fact here claimed; it only goes to establish that other point claimed by Watson, viz., that the knowledge of God is not *intuitive, universal,* and *inevitable.* But while Watson, like the inspired writers, assumes the fact here specified, he does not assume, but attempts to prove, that the idea of an Infinite Intelligence was not originated by man, but communicated to him directly from God himself; and we believe he is quite successful in his attempt. Here, then, is no "begging of the question," no "arguing in a vicious circle." Watson, we repeat, simply recognizes the undisputed fact, viz., that in his time, as well as in the time of Moses and Adam, the idea of an Infinite Intelligence was in man's possession, whether he believed it or not; and by a masterly and, we think, conclusive argument, he professes to have shown that man had this knowledge originally and directly from God himself. The difference between Watson and his opponents on this last point is simply this: Watson takes the ground, with Paul, that "faith cometh by hearing the word of God;" while his opponents take the ground that *faith cometh by seeing the works of God.* We have already seen that man could not in this way originate a knowledge of the being and attributes of the God of the Bible; and we now say that this is equally true of all the essential doctrines of Christianity. It is quite evident, for instance, that we cannot by contemplating the works of creation originate a knowledge of the doctrine of the trinity, nor that of the atonement; there is nothing in the earth, the sun, the moon, or the stars, by seeing which we can learn how "God can be just and the justifier of the ungodly." The same is true of the doctrine of the Spirit's agency in man's salvation, of the resurrection of the human body, of a general judgment, and of prayer offered to God in the name of another. No part of this faith, we affirm, *cometh by seeing the works of God;* it all comes by HEARING THE WORD OF GOD, either communicated directly by God himself, or by a messenger who shall give satisfactory evidence that God hath sent him; and to investigate this evidence is the legitimate work of reason. It is thus that Mr. Watson has proved the truth of revelation; and, in connection with his own, he gives the famous argument of Mr. Leslie, already referred to. To examine the seals of revelation, and thus prove it to be from God, man is quite competent if he will avail himself of the help within his reach; but to originate a knowledge of the doctrines specified above, he is entirely incompetent; for this knowledge he is indebted to a direct revelation from God.

But the reviewer takes the ground that the Bible is simply of no use, that it admits of no proof, and has no authority, unless you can *first,* and *independent of it,* prove the being and attributes of God. I say the being and attributes of God, for the question is not whether there be something eternal (that is not disputed), but whether there be an Eternal Intelligence, clothed with infinite attributes; if this cannot be proved, independent of the Bible, then the Bible itself is insusceptible of proof, and is, consequently, of no more authority than the Koran or the Zendavesta.

As this is a point upon which the reviewer lays much stress, and upon which he grounds, if I mistake not, his weightiest objections to Watson's views, we will quote his own words to an extent that will prevent the possibility of mistake. "'How am I to certify myself of the being of a God?' That he does exist must be determined before I can consider the evidence of a revelation professing to be from him." (P. 187.) "Finding that the *à priori* and *à posteriori* argument are both alike insufficient to furnish a complete and independent demonstration of the being of a God, and that human reason is unable, without a revelation from God in human language, to certify itself that God exists, he 'concludes that we owe the knowledge of the existence of God to revelation alone.'" . . . . "If we owe our knowledge of the existence of God to revelation *alone, then it is impossible to prove, logically, the existence of God.*" Mark the words, "a complete and independent demonstration of the being of a God." That reason can do this is what Mr. C. affirms, and that if this cannot be done *independent of revelation*, "then it is impossible to prove, logically, the existence of a God." As the words "in human language," in the above quotation, are calculated to lead astray, and as Mr. C. seems to assume that the word revelation, as used by Mr. Watson, means something written in a book, we will just here give Mr. Watson's own definition of a revelation, which he adopts from Dr. Doddridge.

"A Divine revelation has been well defined to be 'a discovery of some proposition to the mind, which came not in by the usual exercise of its faculties, but by some miraculous Divine interposition and attestation, either mediate or immediate.'" It will be seen that this is very different from what Mr. Cocker gives as Mr. Watson's idea of a revelation. It will be necessary to keep in view this definition of a revelation, as it shows the sense in which Mr. W. uses the word.

We will now proceed with our quotations from the review for the purpose of showing Mr. Cocker's position. "If we owe the knowledge of the existence of God to revelation alone, then we cannot, by human reason, prove that the Bible is a revelation from God." . . . . . "We must either *postulate* or *prove* the existence of God before we can attempt the first argument to prove the truth of the Bible." (P. 192.) We might give much more of the same kind, but the quotations here given are quite sufficient. *Till you demonstrate the being of a God independent of a Divine revelation, your best attempt to prove that* "the Bible is a revelation from God," is "a mere begging of the question," it is "arguing in a vicious circle."

Dr. Dempster takes the same ground, as may be seen in his series of articles which are now being published in the "North-Western Christian Advocate." The following quotation from article No. 3, in the issue of the 24th December, 1862, will suffice to show the doctor's position; indeed, the whole series is evidently designed to perfect what is lacking in Mr. Cocker's effort to place the argument beyond the possibility of successful contradiction. His first article, in particular, is, to a considerable extent, a mere rehearsal of Mr. Cocker's words, so that we need not give more than a single quotation in this connection. "The conclusion is, then, logically forced upon us, if there be no prior proof of God's existence *out of the Bible*, there can be no proof that the Bible is of God." * So that we must do the work independent of the Bible, and then, after the work is done, the Bible may come along and offer its superfluous and uncalled-for service!

Now with all deference to all doctors, and all others, we take the ground that the Bible is complete, not only in its teaching, but also in EVIDENCE. So that the issue is fairly joined in this particular also! And notwithstanding the evident confidence with which Watson's opponents rest in the supposed security of their position, as stated above, we cannot resist the conviction that we can expose its utter weakness in five minutes! Now, why may I not prove that the inspired writers lived, as is recorded of them, and that they said and did certain things; without first proving the being of a God from the facts of creation, and the intuitions of pure reason? I say, why may I not do the

* The following quotations from Fowler the phrenologist are, we think, quite in harmony with the above:

"Modern Christianity makes too much of her Bible, by ascribing to it more than it claims, or was ever designed to accomplish. Christianity, or the doctrines of the Bible, are only the *supplement* of religion, while *natural* theology, or the existence of God, or the fundamental principles of religion to be presented in the essay, are the foundation. The human mind requires somewhat more of *proof* than it finds in the Bible. The Bible gives us its *ipse dixit* simply; but the human mind requires *evidence* —requires to understand the *why* and the *wherefore*, and the *philosophy* of that which it receives. That philosophy the Bible does not give—does not even *pretend* to give. It requires belief on the ground of a 'thus saith the Lord,' and there leaves it."

According to Fowler, the Bible contains mere *ipse dixit;* according to Dempster, "words uttered by we know not who." We, however, take the ground that the Bible is complete in itself, both in *teaching* and *evidence*.

former, without first doing the latter? Why, sirs, you may as well tell me that I cannot prove that Aristotle, Socrates, Plato, and Cicero lived, as is recorded of them, and that they said and did certain things, without first proving the being of a God from the facts of creation! I say you might as well tell me the latter, as tell me the former. Nay, you might as well tell me that I cannot prove a case of murder, without first proving the being of a God, as tell me that I cannot prove that Elijah and Jesus Christ restored life, till I first prove the being of a God! Why may I not prove that life was restored, just as well as that it was taken away? And all this without first proving the being of a God. I maintain that *the simple facts*, that the sacred writers lived, as is recorded of them, and that they wrought certain miracles, and delivered certain prophecies, are as susceptible of proof as any other *facts;* and that there is no conceivable necessity for my first proving the being of a God, before proving *such facts.* And I take the ground, that when these facts are proved, i. e., that the sacred writers lived and acted as is recorded of them, the claims of the Bible are established beyond the possibility of successful contradiction: for the miracles and prophecies *thus proved to be facts*, are God's seals affixed to what they "wrote and spoke," *and affixed for the declared purpose of proving that they* "wrote and spoke as they were moved by the Holy Ghost." We cannot so much as conceive of any possible way of evading this conclusion, save that adopted by the Sadducees, for on all hands the miracles were admitted to be above the power of man, and, therefore, must be ascribed to God or the devil; and as the Sadducees would not do the former, they were forced to do the latter, and Jesus Christ pronounced their malignant utterances blasphemy, and declared it to be unpardonable!

Although the points here claimed are exceeding plain, yet believing, as we do, that it will give increased vividness and force to our argument, we will give a quotation or two from the good old Book which we claim to be complete in itself, not only as to teaching, but also as to EVIDENCE.

The following passages are, we think, to the point: "And Moses answered, and said, But, behold, they will not believe me, nor hearken unto my voice: for they will say, The LORD hath not appeared unto thee. And the LORD said unto him, What is that in thine hand? And he said, A rod. And he said, Cast it on the ground. And he cast it on the ground, and it became a serpent; and Moses fled from before it. And the LORD said unto Moses, Put forth thine hand, and take it by the tail. And he put forth his hand and caught it, and it became a rod in his hand: that they may believe that the LORD GOD of their fathers, the GOD of Abraham, the GOD of Isaac, and the GOD of Jacob, hath appeared unto thee. And the LORD said furthermore unto him, Put now thine hand into thy bosom. And he put his hand into his bosom: and when he took it out, behold, his hand was leprous as snow. And he said, Put thine hand into thy bosom again. And he put his hand into his bosom again, and plucked it out of his bosom; and, behold, it was turned again as his other flesh. And it shall come to pass, if they will not believe thee, neither hearken to the voice of the first sign, that they will believe the voice of the latter sign. And it shall come to pass, if they will not believe also these two signs, neither hearken unto thy voice, that thou shalt take of the water of the river, and pour it upon the dry land: and the water which thou takest out of the river shall become blood upon the dry land. And Moses said unto the Lord, O my Lord, I am not eloquent, neither heretofore, nor since thou hast spoken unto thy servant: but I am slow of speech, and of a slow tongue. And the Lord said unto him, Who hath made man's mouth? or who maketh the dumb, or deaf, or the seeing, or the blind? have not I, the Lord? Now therefore go, and I will be with thy mouth, and teach thee what thou shalt say." "And thou shalt take this rod in thine hand, wherewith thou shalt do signs." "Thus shalt thou say unto the children of Israel, I AM hath sent me unto thee. "And Moses and Aaron went, and gathered together all the elders of the children of Israel. And Aaron spake all the words which the LORD had spoken unto Moses, and did the signs in the sight of the people. And the people believed: and when they heard that the LORD had visited the children of Israel, and that he had looked upon their affliction, then they bowed their heads and worshipped." These quotations are taken from the third and fourth chapters of the book of Exodus. We will simply call attention to the following particulars: First, Moses saw, "And, behold, the bush burned with fire, and the bush was not consumed." He also witnessed the other phenomena, some of which we have given in the above quotations. Moreover, he heard the voice of the LORD God, and he felt his power in his body, and in his soul, and all to this end, that he might know that the message which he carried, and the authority under which he acted, were from the LORD God of his fathers, Abraham, Isaac, and Jacob. And the God who did all these things, for the ends here specified, also said to Moses, "Certainly I will be with thee; and this shall be a token unto thee, that I have sent thee; when thou hast brought forth the people out of Egypt, ye shall serve God upon this mountain." And, finally, the LORD God said unto him, "Thou shalt take this rod in thine hand, wherewith thou shalt do signs."

Such are the means which God employed, and such the end for which he employed them. And the end was answered, for Moses never doubted for one moment that it was the Lord God of his fathers that sent him; and being invested with power to work miracles, to convince others that I AM had sent him, he went forth.

Meantime, "The Lord said to Aaron, Go into the wilderness to meet Moses. And he went, and met him in the mount of God, and kissed him. And Moses told Aaron all the words of the Lord who had sent him, and all the signs which he had commanded him." Thus Aaron had all the evidence necessary to satisfy his mind on the same points. And being thus satisfied, and qualified, they, "Moses and Aaron, went and gathered together all the elders of the children of Israel. And Aaron spake all the words which the LORD had spoken unto Moses, and did the signs in the sight of the people. And the people believed: and when they heard that the LORD had visited the children of Israel, and that he had looked upon their affliction, then they bowed their heads and worshipped." Here, again, the means employed are quite successful; the people are as satisfied as are Moses and Aaron, that the message and the authority are from the Lord God of their fathers. And no marvel, for the facts were as indisputable as their very existence, and the facts established the claims. Thus, as might be expected, Infinite Wisdom employs the best means to the best end, and, of course, where such means fail, nothing can possibly succeed. "If they believe not Moses and the prophets, neither will they be persuaded though one rose from the dead." It will be seen, of course, that the parties more immediately interested in the miracles here specified, were such as already had the *idea*, and to some extent, the knowledge, of the true God, and the miracles were designed to convince them that it was this God, the God of their fathers, that spake to and by Moses. The knowledge that the God of Abraham was an Infinite Spirit, clothed with omnipotence, omniscience, and omnipresence, was not communicated by the miracles; miracles could not do this, any more than the heavenly bodies; but miracles could, and did, convince them that Moses had his commission from this true God, the God of their fathers, a knowledge of whose being and attributes they were already in possession of. Hence the Egyptians, though they saw the miracles, had no such lofty conceptions of the God that wrought them: on the contrary, while they had no doubt that it was by the power of Israel's God that the miracles were wrought, they still supposed that their own gods were equal, if not superior, to the God of Israel; it was to have this matter fairly tested that Pharaoh called for the magicians, that they might work by the power of the gods of Egypt, while Moses wrought by the power of the God of Israel. But let us suppose that the Egyptians are as fully instructed, by revelation, as the Israelites are, as to the character of the true God, and let miracles be wrought to convince them that Moses comes to them with instructions from that God, then the miracles will be calculated to produce the same effect upon their minds that they did upon the minds of the Israelites. I say by *revelation;* for it was by *revelation* that Moses and the Israelites had the knowledge of God here specified. Moses never pretended that his sublime conceptions of God were inferred from the miracles which he had witnessed, any more than that they were inferred from the heavenly bodies; nor does the sacred text intimate for a moment that this is the end for which they were wrought, as we have already seen. Moses derived his sublime conceptions of God, partly from his pious and divinely instructed ancestors, and partly by *direct revelation* from God himself.

Of course we are not now speaking of a written revelation, for although man was *never without a revelation from God*, as yet he had no *written revelation;* nor does it appear that the knowledge of letters was even known till God with his own "finger" wrote the ten commandments upon two tables of stone. "God wrote now," says Dr. Adam Clarke, "on tables of *stone* what he had originally written on the *heart* of man, and in mercy he placed that before his eyes which by sin had been obliterated from his soul; and by this he shows us what, by the Spirit of Christ, must be rewritten in the mind." By the way, Dr. Dempster, in his article of the 17th December, speaks of "the heathen which were without revelation." I suppose he means without a *written* revelation; though if he does, his consequences will not follow; and if he means absolutely without any revelation save that which is given in the works of creation, we object to the premise from which he draws his conclusions; for we do not believe that man was ever left absolutely without a *revelation*, understanding the *term* as Watson and Doddridge define it; for not only did God speak to Adam and others, and "to the fathers by the prophets," but we are assured that Jesus Christ is "the true Light, which lighteth every man that cometh into the world."

We now turn to the *written* revelation, and will endeavor to show that the Bible imparts to us both the *idea* and the *knowledge* of God, and that it contains *in itself* satisfactory *evidence* of the truthfulness of that *idea* and that *knowledge* of God which it imparts.

I make a distinction between these three particulars, namely, the *idea* of the *being* of a God, the *knowledge* of his character, and the *evidence*, or *proof*, of both.

The *idea*, the *knowledge*, and the *evidence* are thus obtained. I take up the Bible, and the first sentence in that book strikes my eye, and reads thus: "God in the beginning created the heavens and the earth." Here I have two *ideas*. The first is, that there is a being whose name is Elohim, or God; and the second is, that this God created the heavens and the earth. Now as soon as I read this sentence, I have these two ideas; I say I have them, whether I believe them or not; or whether I like them, or dislike them; the fact is the same, I have them; and it is absolutely out of my power to make it otherwise. Now let it be supposed that I was, up to this time, like one of those philosophers whom Watson mentions, and whom we shall notice in due time, who never had the idea of *creation*, or of a *creating God;* and lived and died without the idea, because they had not the Bible, or a revelation of these two ideas contained in this first sentence of the Bible: I say suppose this, and it will follow, not only that I have these two ideas as soon as I read this sentence, but that I am indebted to the Bible for them. Or if my opponents should deny that there ever was such a man, still it must be admitted that if there was, it would be possible for him to obtain these *two ideas in this way;* and this is all that my argument requires, namely, that I have, or may have these ideas from the Bible alone, independent of any previous help from any other source, as to *these two ideas.*

Well, now I have these ideas; and they are of such an extraordinary character that my mind acts as it never did before. I look up to the heavenly bodies, and I say, "Certainly, this is an extraordinary conception, that there was a time when these were *created*, before which they had no being, not even as to their substance! And what a Being that must be who *create*d them all, yea 'the heavens and the earth!'" I am now induced to read on, and am surprised beyond measure as I read the sublime utterances, which are only exceeded by the still more sublime conceptions contained in the short history of the creation and formation of the heavens and the earth. "Let there be light, and there was light!" "Certainly," I exclaim again, "these are conceptions utterly unknown, even in the schools of our philosophers; and whether they are true or not, they are at least interesting, and are worthy of the most careful consideration." I proceed with increased interest, and mark with pleasing wonder the sublimity and simplicity which alike characterize this brief but altogether wonderful history. My wonder, together with the most pleasing emotions, are still increased as I read, "And God said, Let the earth bring forth grass, the herb yielding seed, and the fruit tree yielding fruit after his kind, whose seed is in itself, upon the earth: and it was so." Again, I pause, with still increased wonder and delight, as I read, "And God made two great lights; the greater light to rule the day, and the lesser light to rule the night: he made the stars also. And God set them in the firmament of the heaven to give light upon the earth." I proceed with this wonderful narrative till, lo! my wonder and delight are increased beyond utterance as I read, "And God said, Let us make man in our image, after our likeness: and let them have dominion over the fish of the sea, and over the fowl of the air, and over the cattle, and over all the earth, and over every creeping thing that creepeth upon the earth. So God created man in his own image, in the image of God created he him; male and female created he them. And God blessed them, and God said unto them, Be fruitful, and multiply, and replenish the earth, and subdue it; and have dominion over the fish of the sea, and over the fowl of the air, and over every living thing that moveth upon the earth." Finally, the narrative closes in these words, as my wonder and delight reach their climax: "And God saw every thing that he made: and, behold, it was very good." "Thus the heavens and the earth were finished, and all the host of them." And all in six days! And, what is also wonderful, the whole history would only cover about one page of a pamphlet! Could any man who never saw the Bible, write such a history as this? Have any of the schools of learning, whether ancient or modern, produced anything like this? Could any man by his natural powers originate these conceptions, and write this history? Our answer, our unhesitating answer, to these questions is, No.

But, having these *ideas*, I become increasingly anxious to know more about this God who "created the heavens and the earth and all the host of them," and who upholds and moves all and every part thereof; and, what is still more interesting, is the Father of my Spirit. I say I am increasingly anxious to know more about this God; yea, I already begin to feel that "this is life eternal, to know thee the only true God." Hence, to this end, I continue to read the wonderful book to which I am indebted for the wonderful conceptions by which I am thus moved and charmed. And as I read, the character of this great First Cause is developed more and more. He is ETERNAL; he is *being itself.* "I AM THAT I AM." "*From everlasting to everlasting.*" "I AM GOD." *He is Spirit, not body; mind, not matter.* He is "*the Father of spirits.*" "*The God of the spirits of all flesh.*" We are not allowed to conceive of him as having any form. *He is a pure Spirit unconnected with body.* Hence he is declared to be "*the invisible God, whom no man hath seen nor can see.*" "*The King eternal, immortal, invisible.*" "*Remember ye saw no similitude.*" "*God is a Spirit.*" The idea of a plurality of gods has no place in this book. "Hear, O Israel, the LORD thy God is one LORD." "The LORD he is GOD; there is none else beside him." "There is none other God but one." Yet this ONE GOD is manifested, or held forth to us in this book, as *Father*, *Son*, and *Holy Spirit*; each possessing the same attributes, and claiming and receiving the same worship. Hence we have a TRINITY in UNITY; THREE PERSONS, ONE GOD. I am taught, too, that God is everywhere present. "Do not I fill heaven and earth? saith the Lord." "Behold, heaven and the heaven of heavens cannot contain thee." "In him we live, and move, and have our being." His power, like his presence, knows no bounds. "Is there any thing too hard for God?" "He spake and it was done, he commanded and it stood fast." "He upholdeth all things by the word of his power." As this book teaches me that God is omnipresent, it also teaches me that he is omniscient, and perfect in knowledge. He sees and knows all persons and things. "Known unto him are all his works." "Hell and destruction are without a covering before him, how much more the hearts of the children of men!" "Lord, thou hast searched me and known me; thou knowest my down-sitting and my up-rising." "The darkness hideth not from thee, but the night shineth as the day." "Great is the Lord, his understanding is infinite." This wonderful book teaches me that this wonderful Being is immutable. This is indicated by the sublime title I AM. It is also asserted in the most striking language: "I am the Lord, I change not." He is "the Father of lights, with whom is no variableness, neither shadow of turning." "The same yesterday, to-day, and forever." His wisdom, like his other perfections, is declared to be perfect. As to his works, it is said: "In wisdom hast thou made them all." And he is emphatically declared to be "the only wise God." "He is mighty in strength and wisdom." "To the intent that now unto the principalities and powers in heavenly *places* might be known by the church, the manifold wisdom of God." On the subject of God's *goodness*, the writers of this book employ language the most elevated, glowing, and rapturous. His goodness they represent as *goodness of nature*, as being one of his essential perfections. "Thou art good and doest good." "The LORD is good to all, and his tender mercies are over all his works." We are assured that "He delights in mercy," that his is "loving kindness and tender mercy." His very names import the goodness of his nature, and convey the most overwhelming ideas of that goodness; such as "The gracious one," "The all-sufficient and all-bountiful pourer forth of all good." So critics interpret some of the wonderful names of this wonderful Being, who is as good as he is great. Nor are the writers of this book satisfied with asserting the essential goodness of the Divine nature, but, becoming rapturous in view thereof, they exclaim: "O that men would praise the LORD for his goodness and for his wonderful works to the children of men!" And becoming still more rapturous, they exclaim in a burst of holy joy: "Let every thing that hath breath praise the LORD."

Everywhere in this book I meet with the most sublime and elevated conceptions of the *holiness* of this God, and of his law. He is the "HOLY, HOLY, HOLY, LORD God Almighty." And his "Law is holy, and the commandment holy, and just, and good." He is "*The* HOLY ONE *of Israel.*" Here, too, the sacred writers become rapturous and exclaim: "Who is like unto thee, O LORD, among the mighty ones? Who is like thee, glorious in holiness, fearful in praises, doing wonders ?" And again, "Who shall not fear thee, O LORD, and glorify thy name, for thou only art HOLY." The book that teaches these sublime lessons as to the *holiness* of the Divine nature also teaches, as a matter of course, that the justice and truth which flow from this *holiness* are, like their source, *infinite.* "A God of truth, and without iniquity, just and right art thou." "A just God and a Saviour, there is none beside me." "The judgments of the Lord are true and righteous altogether." "Thy word is truth." "Thy word is true from the beginning." "These things saith he that is holy, he that is true." "Just and true are thy ways, thou King of saints." Being thus just and true, we are assured he "will render to every man according to his works." "The LORD our God is the God of gods, and Lord of lords, a great God, a mighty and terrible, which regardeth not persons, neither taketh rewards. He accepteth not the person of princes, nor regardeth the rich more than the poor, for they are all the work of his hands." "God is no respecter of persons." "Shall not the Judge of all the earth do right?" Seeing this God is represented in this book as making promises to and entering into covenant with man, his *faithfulness* is frequently asserted with an absoluteness similar to that which certifies to us his goodness, justice, and truth." "He is not a man that he should lie, nor the son of man that he should repent." "God is faithful." "Faithful is he that calleth you, who also will do it." "But the Lord is faithful, who shall stablish you and keep you from evil." "Thy faithfulness reacheth unto the clouds." "Thy faithfulness shalt thou establish in the heavens." "Thy faithfulness is unto all generations." "Great is thy faithfulness."

Such are some of the wonderful conceptions which this

book gives us of that God whose book it is. But it gives us to understand that even these are but feeble conceptions of his infinite glory and majesty. While Paul gazes with adoring wonder and rapturous delight upon this Almighty Being as manifested in his own word, he can only exclaim: "O the depth of the riches, both of the wisdom and knowledge of God! how unsearchable are his judgments, and his ways past finding out!" "For of him, and through him, and to him are all things: to whom be glory for ever. Amen." Mr. Watson, too, after contemplating the teachings of this wonderful book with reference to the being and attributes of God, gives expression to his sentiments and feelings in the following very appropriate and beautiful language: "God is *unsearchable.* All we see or hear of him is faint and shadowy manifestation. Beyond the highest glory, there is yet unpierced and unapproached light, a track of intellectual and moral splendor untravelled by the thoughts of the contemplating and adoring spirits who are nearest to his throne. The manifestation of this nature of God, never fully to be revealed, because infinite, is represented as constituting the reward and felicity of heaven. This is 'to see God.' This is 'to be forever with the Lord.' This is to behold his glory as in a glass, with unveiled face, and to be changed into his image, from glory to glory, in boundless progression and infinite approximation. Yet, after all, it will be as true, after countless ages spent in heaven itself, as in the present state, that none by 'searching can find out God,' that is, 'to perfection.' He will even then be 'a God that hideth himself;' and widely as the illumination may extend, clouds and darkness will still be round about him." With these thoughts in the mind, and still lingering as in the presence of this "God of glory," I must be permitted to give still further expression to my present sentiments and feelings in the following words from the 29th chapter of First Chronicles: "Blessed be thou, Lord God of Israel our Father, for ever and ever. Thine, O Lord, is the greatness, and the power, and the glory, and the victory, and the majesty: for all that is in the heaven and in the earth is thine; thine is the kingdom, O Lord, and thou art exalted as head above all. Both riches and honor come of thee, and thou reignest over all; and in thine hand is power and might; and in thine hand it is to make great, and to give strength unto all." Equally appropriate are the following words from the seventy-second psalm: "Blessed be the LORD God, the God of Israel, who only doeth wondrous things. And blessed be his glorious name for ever: and let the whole earth be filled with his glory. Amen, and Amen."

Thus it is that this book imparts to us the idea of God and of creation, and thus it is that it gives perfect instruction with regard to God's character, the perfection of his government, and the boundlessness of his reign. So perfect that, as Watson observes, not a single additional conception, worthy of God, has ever been originated by man. And its teachings as to man are equally ample and satisfactory. It gives perfect information as to my *origin*, *nature*, and *destiny*. As to my *origin*, it tells me that this *spirit*, this *ego*, I myself, came directly from God, and that he formed my body "out of the dust of the earth." It gives ample information as to the derangement and weakness of man's spiritual faculties, the badness of his moral nature, the troubles and sorrows with which he is loaded, the evils, both natural and moral, with which he is surrounded, and also as to the infirmities and death of the body. *Sin*, *rebellion against God*, is the cause of all. It points me to a glorious and complete remedy for all this evil in the infinite goodness, wisdom, and power of God, working through the atonement and intercession of Jesus Christ his Son and my Saviour, and not mine only, but also "the Saviour of all men, especially of those that believe." It tells me that the Holy Spirit, in consideration of this atonement, will come in answer to my believing prayer, and not only teach, enlighten, and regenerate my soul, but will also "bear witness with my spirit" to the fact of my sonship by regeneration and adoption; that he will apply the blood of Jesus so as to cleanse me from all sin; that he will guide me into all truth, help my infirmities, and even be my comforter. As to my destiny, it tells me *that* is eternal union with God himself in ineffable glory upon his own eternal throne. Nor is my dead and consumed body forgotten: this book tells me that God will raise it from the grave and make it like unto Christ's glorious body. And all this, I am told, is secured by believing in Jesus Christ, and being faithful unto death. In other words, by following the plain teachings of this book, the sum of which is, *hear*, *repent*, *believe*, *obey*. This book tells me, finally, that there will be a general resurrection, and a general judgment, at which all intelligences will have their final destinies fixed, eternally fixed, in the bliss of heaven or the misery of hell. And all this, I am told, will be done by the unerring decision of that God whose book this is, and in which I have all the information specified above.

Now, all this information man has or may have from the Bible alone, without previously proving the being of a God from the material world. *This is a fact.* And it will be remembered that Watson admits man's ability to collect evidence of the being of a God when once he has the *idea;* but here is not only the *idea*, but complete instruction, so complete that nothing can be added to it, and all this from the Bible alone, without any help from any other quarter. As to the proof that there is just such a God as is here described, and that the other teachings specified are true, that is the next point that we proposed to take up. We take the ground that the Bible contains *evidence* or *proof* of the truth of its own teachings. The objectors to Watson take the negative of this question. That the point or points in dispute may be before the reader, we will give the words of our opponents just here.

"If we owe our knowledge of the existence of God to revelation *alone, then it is impossible to prove, logically, the existence of God.*" (Review, p. 191.) Mark what it is that is declared to be impossible. "If we owe the knowledge of the existence of God to *revelation* ALONE, then we cannot by human reason prove that the Bible is a revelation from God." (Review, p. 192.) Mark again what it is that cannot be done.

"The conclusion is, then, logically forced upon us, if there be no prior proof of God's existence *out of the Bible*, there can be no proof that the Bible is of God." (Dr. Dempster, "N. W. C. Advocate" of 24th December, 1862.) Mark again what it is that cannot be proved.

Now, whether there is proof "out of the Bible" or not, we hope to show that there is sufficient proof *in* the Bible. And, if we do, it will follow, as a matter of course, that the above conclusions are not true, and the systems built upon them must of necessity fall to the ground.

We take the ground that miracles are God's seals upon his own truth, and that they afford the evidence or proof claimed. That is, every revelation or truth that has this seal affixed to it, is thereby proved to be from that God whose seal it is. Before proceeding with our argument from the Bible, we will give the following quotations, which we think will be quite in place just here.

"Every real miracle is a work of God." (Richard Watson.)

"And thus we see that the only question concerning the truth of Christianity is, whether it be a real revelation." (Butler.)

Speaking of Paul's heavenly visions, Grotius says: "If we believe his miracles, what reason is there why we should not believe him in his heavenly visions, and in his receiving his instructions from Christ?" And again, "God cannot more effectually recommend the authority of any doctrine delivered by man than by working miracles. But some say that these wonders were done by the help of devils; but this calumny has been already confuted from hence, that as soon as the doctrine of Christ was made known, all the power of the devils was broken." He quotes the Fathers in proof of this, and we might quote modern missionaries in proof of the same thing. The following quotation from Ambrose, as given by Grotius, is also worthy a place here: "Whom should I rather believe concerning God than God himself." When God gives a revelation of *himself*, and seals that revelation with a miracle, that is God speaking concerning himself; and yet there are three witnesses, viz., the *messenger*, the *word*, and the *miracle;* the messenger, as we have already shown, has evidence that he has his message from God; the word declares the character and will of God; and the miracle, which none but God can work, seals the message and avouches the whole to be *from* God.

CHAPTER IV.

Being now in possession of perfect instruction as to the *being*, *attributes*, *government*, and claims of God, and, in short, as to every other particular, all we want now is the *proof*, and for this we return to Moses and his "wonders in the land of Ham." Here he is before us, with "the rod of God in his hand." Himself, Aaron, and the people of Israel in general, particularly the elders, have been convinced already that he has his commission and authority from the true God, the God of their fathers; and now the Egyptians, before whom this same God is set forth clothed with infinite attributes, are to have satisfactory evidence of the same truths by the same or still more wonderful miracles. And remember, so far as the facts are certified to us, the miracles afford us the same evidence that they afforded the Israelites and the Egyptians.

The history of the ten plagues may be read in the seventh and five following chapters of the book of Exodus, and a very striking epitome of this history may be found in the 105th psalm, so that we need only make a few remarks for the purpose of fixing attention upon the more striking features of these wonderful occurrences.

Notice then, first, that Moses and Aaron act simply as they are commanded by that God from whom they have their commission and authority; second, that to that God they ascribe all the miracles; third, they give previous notice of the wonderful event, stating the very time of its occurrence; fourth, at the time specified they *publicly* put forth an act, and the result *immediately* follows; fifth, the miracles are such as are felt and seen throughout the land of Egypt, except, sixth, that part occupied by the children of Israel; that part was exempted from all the plagues. "In the land of Goshen, where the children of Israel were, was there no hail." "And Moses stretched forth his hand toward heaven, and there was thick darkness over all the land of Egypt three days; they saw not one another, neither rose any from his place for three days, but all the children of Israel had light in their dwellings." Seventh, these plagues were of long continuance, so that all had time not only to feel, but to test their terrible reality. For instance, all the waters of Egypt being turned into blood, continued so for seven days, and the "thick darkness" continued three days. Eighth, these plagues not only came at the word of Moses and Aaron, which they uttered in the name of the LORD, "in the sight of Pharaoh, and in the sight of his servants," but they went away also at their word, and that instantaneously. Ninth, these miracles were such that none but the God of Israel could work them, and there was no power that could resist them, for, if God permitted the magicians to practise deception for a time, or work lying wonders by satanic influence, it was only to expose them, and manifest his power still more. Tenth, the end for which these miracles were wrought is thus *distinctly* and *often* stated: "Thus saith the LORD, In this shalt thou know that I am the LORD." "That thou mayest know that there is none like unto the LORD our God." "And I will sever in that day the land of Goshen, in which my people dwell, that no swarms of flies shall be there, to the end thou mayest know that I am the LORD in the midst of the earth." "Thus saith the LORD God of the Hebrews, Let my people go, that they may serve me. For I will at this time send all my plagues upon thine heart, and upon thy servants, and upon thy people, that thou mayest know that there is none like me in all the earth." "And in very deed for this cause have I raised thee up [margin: made thee stand], for to show in thee my power, and that my name may be declared throughout all the earth."

So frequently, emphatically, and unmistakably, is the great end of all these miracles stated; even to demonstrate the *being*, and *will*, of that God whose *eternity*, *character*, and *government* are so forcibly asserted, and developed by Moses and the other inspired writers. Nor was this for the conviction of the Egyptians only, but that, saith the LORD, "My name may be declared throughout all the earth." I say the end was not only to demonstrate the being of a God, but to demonstrate the being of *that* God, whom Moses declared to be eternal, and clothed with infinite perfections; yea, and *to demonstrate that there is no other god;* and also to establish the fact that all the teachings of Moses are the teachings of this very God. Now seeing an infinitely wise God employs these means for the accomplishment of the end or ends here specified, it follows that they are the very best means that can be employed under the circumstances. It follows, too, that when Watson's opponents assert, as above, that the being of a God must first be proved "from the facts of creation and the intuitions of pure reason," and that till this be done "we cannot prove that the Bible is a revelation from God," they not only join issue with Watson, but with God himself, who has adopted this very method, and has adopted it as the very best, if not the only method, and that, too, without any attempt, before or after, to prove the being of a God from the works of creation. If any one should attempt to evade this conclusion by saying that the Egyptians already knew God, as all men do, by *intuition*, it is only necessary to say that this assumption is contradicted by facts, and by the history before us. It also represents God as undertaking to teach the Egyptians what they already knew, and as working miracles to produce a faith which they already possessed. But if, notwithstanding all facts and consequences, any one should still persist in saying that the Egyptians had already a knowledge of God by *intuition*, it is only necessary to refer them to Pharaoh, who himself rejects their assumption, and corrects their mistake, by saying: "Who is the LORD, that I should obey his voice to let Israel go? *I know not the* LORD, neither will I let Israel go." Now it was to convince Pharaoh and other atheists of the being of Israel's God, and of the truth of revelation, that God wrought *miracles*, without first attempting a proof from the works of creation; nor was it altogether in vain that he did so, as the following quotations do most clearly show: "He that feared the LORD among the servants of Pharaoh made his servants and his cattle flee into the houses. And he that regarded not the word of the LORD left his servants and his cattle in the field." Thus while the masses of the people "regarded not the word of the LORD," there were some who "feared the word of the LORD." They "feared the word of the LORD" by Moses, in view of the six preceding plagues, or miracles; so completely have these miracles proved the being of a God and the truth of revelation. Nay, conviction is riveted even on the mind of Pharaoh by these miracles; so that the following utterances are wrung from him: "And Pharaoh sent and called for Moses and Aaron, and said unto them, I have sinned this time: the LORD is righteous, and I and my people are wicked. Entreat the LORD (for it is enough) that there be no *more* thunderings and hail; and I will let you go, and ye shall stay no longer." And again: "Then Pharaoh called for Moses and Aaron in haste; and said, I have sinned against the Lord your God, and against you. Now therefore forgive, I pray thee, my sin only this once, and entreat the Lord your God that he may take away from me this death only." But if, notwithstanding all this, it should still be asserted that revelation, though sealed by miracles, is of no use till the being of a God is first proved "from the facts of creation and the intuitions of pure reason," and that before this is done it is even "impossible to prove, logically, the existence of a God," the authors of such assertions must not blame us for drawing from their own premises conclusions that are inevitable. And one of these conclusions is this: those who take this ground resist evidence which not only convinced Pharaoh and the Egyptians mentioned above, but even constrained the magicians themselves to exclaim: "This is the finger of God!" This faith and this confession of faith were produced by the third plague, and that too without any "prior proof of God's existence." So that those who, in the face of all this, still persist in maintaining the position here opposed, prove that they are more unbelieving even than Jannes and Jambres, who candidly acknowledged the evidence to be irresistible and declared their faith in Israel's God, and in his revelation by Moses, by giving up the contest and exclaiming: "This is the finger of God." They evidently believed with Watson that "every real miracle is a work of God." And with Grotius they seemed to say: "If we believe his miracles, what reason is there why we should not believe him in his heavenly visions, and in his receiving his instructions" from the God whom he declares to be eternal in his being, and infinite in his attributes? They evidently conclude with Butler, too, "that the only question concerning the truth of Christianity is, whether it be a revelation." And that the truth delivered by Moses was a revelation from God, was just what it professed to be, was, according to their own showing, demonstrated by the stupendous miracles which they had witnessed, and which had been wrought, avowedly, to prove this very thing. We formerly showed that man could not possibly originate a knowledge of the God of the Bible, that he could not derive such knowledge from the works of creation; and it is equally evident that the works of creation could not prove that the teachings of Moses were a revelation from the God of the Hebrews; but miracles proved this, even to the conviction of Pharaoh and his magicians. And what is true of the teachings of Moses, is true of the teachings of all the inspired writers. The teachings that are declared to be from the God of the Bible, and in proof thereof are sealed by the miracles that are recorded in the Bible, must be from that God, and cannot possibly be from any other. This conclusion seems to us inevitable. The miracles and the teachings of the Bible evidently come from the same source; for none but the God of the Bible could work these miracles, and he certainly would not, he could not, work them to prove that these teachings were his, if they were not his. It follows that to establish the miracles of the Bible, is to establish the teachings of the Bible; and he who knows the end from the beginning wrought these miracles for this very end, as we have shown above; and they answer this end, as might be expected, for God never makes a mistake. Thus it is that the Bible contains in itself, and imparts to man, the *idea* of God, *perfect teaching*, and *demonstrative proof*. And the process is so simple and easy, that you have only to prove the *single fact* that *the miracles were wrought*, and you thereby prove that the *teachings of which they are the seals, are from the God of the Bible;* and the teachings thus proved to be from the God of the Bible, are, like their Almighty Source, PERFECT: so perfect that we are commanded on pain of eternal death neither to add to nor take from them. The following lines contain a sublime and glorious truth:

> "What glory gilds the sacred page!
> Majestic like the sun,
> It gives a light to every age;
> It gives, BUT BORROWS NONE."

The reader is now prepared to judge between these conclusions, and those with which we join issue; the sum of which is contained in Dr. Dempster's grand proposition, which it may be well to repeat just here:

"If there be no prior proof of God's existence *out of the Bible*, there can be no proof that the Bible is of God."

Now, in opposition to this, we hold that the Bible is complete in itself, both as to *teaching* and *evidence*. We say with Grotius, if we believe its miracles, we must believe its teachings. And we say with Butler, "The only question concerning the truth of Christianity [or the Bible], is whether it be a revelation?" And we not only say that miracles prove this, but that they prove it as nothing else will. In proof of this, let us turn to Moses again. God sends him to teach his will, say to the Israelites; now, how is he to convince the Israelites that he has this teaching from

God Almighty? Is he to appeal to the facts of creation? It would be perfect nonsense; there is no connection whatever. Even if the being and attributes of the God of the Bible could be proved from the visible world, that would not prove that Moses had his teaching from that God, any more than it would prove that Jannes and Jambres had their teaching from him. Would you have him appeal to the harmony of his teachings, the agreement of all the parts thereof? That would be little better, for multitudes declare that the Pentateuch is full of contradiction. Would you have him appeal to the moral purity of his teachings? That, too, would be to little purpose, for multitudes declare that although much of his teaching is excellent, there is also much that is wicked in his teaching; hence they say they will just take and reject as they see fit; so that they are left to their own opinion after all. Even prophecy will not substitute for miracle, for it affords no evidence save in its fulfilment, and that, being yet in the future, will not answer for the present. But when stupendous miracles are wrought, miracles that are seen and felt throughout the land of Egypt, then the most stupid Egyptian will both understand and fear; while Pharaoh himself acknowledges his guilt, and the magicians exclaim, "This is the finger of God." How is it possible, I say, to doubt that Moses speaks the *word*, and acts by the *authority*, of God Almighty, when, to prove these very points, *that* God works the stupendous miracles specified above, and then leads some three millions of people through a sea some twelve miles across? I say, how is it possible to doubt in view of such evidence? There is a road cut through the sea where the waters are some twenty-eight yards deep! And these waters form a wall on either hand, perhaps some forty yards high, and immovable as a wall of brass; while some three millions of people, pursued by mighty armies of their enemies, urge on, in their escape from bondage and death, between these wonderful walls, and through depths hitherto unexplored, save by leviathan or other creatures whose home is in the mighty waters. There they go! I say, in the depths of the sea, yet on "dry land!" Methinks I hear the solid tread of some six millions of feet, as they momently fall upon the highway which God has prepared for them away down in the depths of the Red Sea. There they go! during the silent watches of the night, when all, save Israel, is wrapped in darkness: but the God that gave Israel light in Goshen, while the Egyptians were wrapped in thick darkness, now gives Israel light during midnight darkness, even in the depths of the sea; whilst the same Egyptians are still in darkness, though only separated from Israel by a pillar of cloud. This cloud, however, gives light to Israel, while it only increases the midnight gloom with which Israel's enemies are shrouded. Let it be distinctly noticed, that these miracles in the Red Sea, like those in Egypt, occur instantaneously when Moses simply lifts up his hand, which he does by the command of the LORD. Here is the record: "And the LORD said unto Moses * * * * lift up thy rod, and stretch out thine hand over the sea, and divide it: and the children of Israel shall go on dry ground through the midst of the sea." He did so, and the sea divided, and Israel passed through. "And the LORD said unto Moses, Stretch out thine hand over the sea, that the waters may come again upon the Egyptians, upon their chariots, and upon their horsemen. And Moses stretched forth his hand over the sea, and the sea returned to his strength when the morning appeared; and the Egyptians fled against it; and the LORD overthrew [margin: shook off] the Egyptians in the midst of the sea.

And the waters returned and covered the chariots, and the horsemen, and all the host of Pharaoh that came into the sea after them: there remained not so much as one of them. But the children of Israel walked upon dry *land* in the midst of the sea; and the waters *were* a wall unto them on their right hand, and on their left. Thus the Lord saved Israel that day out of the hands of the Egyptians: and Israel saw the Egyptians dead upon the sea shore. And Israel saw that great work which the LORD did upon the Egyptians: and the people feared the LORD, and believed the LORD, and his servant Moses." Mark the results of these miracles: "The people feared the LORD, and believed the LORD, and his servant Moses." They not only believed in the being of an Intelligent First Cause, but they believed in that very God whose eternity and infinite perfections are proclaimed by Moses in language so forcible and elevated, and in strains so sublime and rapturous. And the people, too, caught those sublime conceptions of God, and gave expression to them in the rapturous and glorious song which immediately follows the words quoted above. And they not only believed in this God, but they "believed in his servant Moses." That is, they received his teaching, and submitted to his authority, as coming from this God. And they did so because God affixed his seal to these teachings by working the miracles here recorded.

But all such conclusions from such premises, according to Watson's reviewer, are "a mere begging of the question." Such persons are "all the while arguing in a vicious circle." "As yet the truth of revelation is under discussion, and is itself in abeyance;" and must continue so till the being and attributes of God are first proved from "the facts of the universe and the intuitions of the human mind." It is even so, says Dr. Dempster: "The conclusion is logically forced upon us, if there be no prior proof of God's existence *out of the Bible*, there can be no proof that the Bible is of God." Regardless of the above miracles, and of all the miracles and prophecies recorded in the Old and New Testaments, and by which God seals every word of revelation, I say, regardless of all this, Mr. Watson's reviewer exclaims, "How am I to certify myself that such a revelation has been given? True, we have a book which professes to be a revelation from God—a book which says, 'There is a God!' and which records numerous appearances of God to men in bygone days. But that assertion is not proof that such a Being does exist, any more than the assertion of the Koran or the Zendavesta, until I have rationally demonstrated that the Bible is an authentic revelation, and that here I have the veritable words of God." Thus, while all Israel are fully satisfied that Moses proclaims "the veritable words of God," being convinced of this by the wonderful miracles recorded in Exodus, and are singing their triumphant song in consequence; Watson's reviewer has no song to sing! While the millions of Israel, whom the Lord brought up out of Egypt with a high hand and an outstretched arm, and through the sea, as on dry land; I say, while these millions are singing their rapturous song in all the triumphs of faith in God, and in his revelation; Watson's reviewer stands disconsolate and sad, exclaiming, "How am I to certify myself that such a revelation has been given?" And no marvel, for, strange to say, he sees nothing in it but mere *assertion;* and "that assertion," he says, "is not proof that such a Being does exist, any more than the assertion of the Koran or the Zendavesta." Now we readily admit that mere assertion will prove nothing; but pray, does the Bible contain no more than mere assertion? That any one who ever read the Bible should assume so, is little less marvellous than the miracles and prophecies which such an assumption ignores. Now suppose Watson's reviewer should be sent to Mr. Jefferson Davis, of the Southern Confederacy, as Moses was sent to Pharaoh; suppose the call, the authority, the evidence, and every other particular were the same. And suppose he should go to the President of the Southern Confederacy, with the rod of God in his hand, and in the name of the LORD God, demand the release of all the slaves; and on his refusing to grant that request, which he certainly would, suppose Mr. C. should distinctly warn Mr. Davis of the consequences, as Moses did Pharaoh; and let it be supposed that he should then speak and act, as is recorded of Moses and Aaron in the seventeenth and four following verses of the seventh chapter of Exodus; and let us suppose that the Mississippi and all the waters in the Confederate States are turned into blood, and continue so for seven days; and all this, it is supposed, takes place according to previous and public notice, given by Mr. C., and that too, immediately on his lifting up his hand in the open day, "in the sight of" Mr. Davis "and in the sight of his servants." Now let it be supposed, further, that after similar notice in each case, nine more plagues are poured out upon the Confederate States, just such as were poured out upon Egypt, and each plague follows the lifting up of Mr. C.'s hand, or on some similar signal being given by him, and on his raising his hand, or offering up a prayer, these plagues go as quickly as they came. We will now suppose that after the first-born of man and beast, throughout the Confederate States, are slain, Mr. C. is permitted to depart with, say, three millions of slaves, men, women, and children, "and a mixed multitude with them; and flocks, and herds, even very much cattle." There Mr. C. goes at the head of this vast multitude, as mixed as it is vast, but "not a dog" is permitted to "move his tongue against man or beast." "And the Lord went before them by day in a pillar of cloud, to lead them the way; and by night in a pillar of fire, to give them light: to go by day and night. He took not away the pillar of the cloud by day, nor the pillar of fire by night, from before the people." We will now suppose that Mr. C. and his three millions of slaves have arrived at the Chesapeake Bay, and that the President and all the armies of the Confederate States overtake them there, being determined to bring them back or destroy them; but, we will suppose Mr. C. lifts his rod again, and points it across the bay, upon which the waters divide and stand as a wall some thirty to forty yards high on either hand, leaving a road sufficiently wide for the millions that are to travel upon it. In the evening they commence their journey and in the morning they are in Maryland; in the mean time the pillar of cloud has passed from the front to the rear, dividing the escaped slaves from the Southern armies who are still pursuing; but as soon as Mr. C. and his people reach the other side and are safe in Maryland, he again points his rod over the bay, "and the sea returned to his strength when the morning appeared," and the Confederate armies "fled against it; and the Lord overthrew the" Confederate armies "in the midst of the sea . . . there remained not so much as one of them." We will now suppose that Mr. C. composes such a hymn as is found in the 15th chapter of Exodus, and he and all the people sing it, and after suitable devotions, wherein they give all the praise to the Lord God of their fathers, they pursue their journey till they come to the Blue Mountains, and there, from the highest of these mountains, as from Sinai, God speaks to the people, while the thunders peal, the lightnings flash, the mountains tremble, and " burn with fire unto the midst of heaven, with darkness, clouds, and thick darkness." "And when the voice of the trumpet sounded long, and waxed louder and louder," Mr. C. spake, "and God answered him by a voice," in the hearing of all the people. He also gave him, we will suppose, a law for the people "written upon two tables of stone with the finger of God." You may suppose too, that Mr. C. journeyed with this people forty years; they were all fed with manna from heaven, their shoes and clothing did not wax old, neither did their feet swell, during these forty years. Finally, in short, we will suppose that Mr. C. wrought all the miracles recorded in the Pentateuch, and at the age of an hundred and twenty years he took leave of the Africans as Moses did of the Israelites: "His eye was not dim nor his natural force abated." And God took his spirit to heaven, and buried his body we know not where. Now let us suppose that the people whom God thus delivered by the hand of Mr. C. became a great nation, and a record of all these miracles is laid up in the archives of the nation; and annual celebrations of these great events are kept by the whole nation to the present day. Let us, I say, suppose all this, and we must suppose a thousand times more to make out a parallel case, but let us suppose this much, and then let us suppose that Mr. C. has written a book in which all these wonders are recorded, and which contains teachings so perfect, and so original, that ever after nothing of importance could be found in systems of philosophy, jurisprudence, theology, and religion, that was not in Mr. C.'s book, at least in its principle. Finally we will suppose that Dr. Dempster has written an able work in defence and in explanation of Mr. C.'s book, similar to that which Mr. Watson has written in defence and in explanation of the Bible. Now suppose I should publish a review of the doctor's work, and declare it to be "a mere begging of the question," and that he was "all the while arguing in a vicious circle," and further, that "if there be no prior proof of God's existence out of" Mr. C.'s book, "there can be no proof of its truth." Suppose, too, that I should assume that Mr. C.'s book contained nothing but mere assertion, and insist, withal, that till the being and attributes of a God are proved "from the material universe and from the intuitions of the human mind," his book affords no evidence of the being of a God, or that it contains a revelation from God. "True," I continue, "we have a book which professes to be a revelation from God—a book which says 'there is a God!' and which records numerous 'appearances of God to men in bygone days.' But that assertion is no proof that such a being does exist, any more than the assertion of the Koran or the Zendavesta, until I have rationally demonstrated that" this book "is an authentic revelation, and that here I have the veritable words of God." Now suppose Dr. Dempster to have written largely to prove the genuineness and authenticity of Mr. C.'s book, and suppose him to have written some two hundred pages to prove that the miracles and prophecies recorded in Mr. C.'s book were established facts, and that these miracles and prophecies proved those teachings, of which they are the seals, to be from that God in whose name Mr. C. wrought the miracles, and by whose inspiration he delivered the prophecies; I say, suppose I should ignore all this, and speak of Mr. C.'s book and of the doctor's defence of it as they have of the Bible and of Watson's Institutes, what would those gentlemen think of me? What would they say of me? Would they consider it highly creditable to my intelligence and candor to ignore all the miracles and prophecies recorded in Mr. C.'s book, and proceed to argue against it on the assumption that it contained no more than mere assertion, and that, consequently, till evidence is brought from a source independent of Mr. C.'s book, it is of no more authority than the Koran or Zendavesta? Would they not claim that the fact of the passage through the Chesapeake Bay, and the facts of the other miracles, deserved at least a passing notice? Nay, would they not claim that these facts remained facts, whether they did or did not, whether they could or could not, prove the being of a God from the material universe? Would they not insist that there is no connection whatever between such facts and the question whether the being of a God can be proved from the visible world? Would they not be likely to ask, "Even if we should 'prove the existence of a God from the facts of the material universe,' how would that prove Mr. C.'s book to be the word of God? And even though we could not prove, from the material universe, the being of a God clothed with infinite attributes, would not the miracles and prophecies prove the being of the God in whose name Mr. C. wrought the miracles, and by whose inspiration he prophesied?" Other questions might be asked, but these will suffice, and the application is sufficiently obvious. Here it is: "Whatsoever you would that men should do unto you, do ye even so unto them, for this is the law and the prophets." Following this rule, the Bible and Watson's Institutes would never be represented as they are in the quotations which we have given above. From miracles and prophecy, Mr. Watson claims to have proved the Scriptures to be "a revelation from God." As the above quotations from Watson's reviewer indicate that Watson has taken all this for granted without even attempting a proof, we will give a quotation from vol. i, p. 237. "The great principle of the English proto-infidel, 'the sufficiency of our natural faculties to form a religion for ourselves, and to decide upon the merits of revealed truth,' is, however, the principle of all [all the infidels whose views he had just stated]; and this being once conceded, the instances just given are sufficiently in proof that the cable is slipped, and that every one is left to take his course wherever the currents may impel his *unpiloted*, *uncharted*, and *uncompassed* bark The *grand principle* of error ['the sufficiency of our natural faculties to form a religion for ourselves, and to decide upon the merits of revealed truth'], between which and absolute atheism there are but a few steps, has been largely refuted in the foregoing pages, and the claims of the Holy Scriptures to be considered as a revelation from God, established by arguments, the force of which in *all other cases* is felt, and acknowledged, and acted upon even by unbelievers themselves. If this has been done satisfactorily, the objections which remain are of little weight, were they even less capable of being repelled."

We will simply call attention to four particulars in the above quotation. First, the great principle of infidelity, and the terrible consequence of embracing it. This principle, he says, "has been largely refuted in the foregoing pages." And in refuting this principle, he has refuted the great principle of transcendentalism, as we showed formerly. Second, the Scriptures claim to be a revelation from God. Third, this claim, he says, he has "established by arguments, the force of which in *all other cases* is felt, and acknowledged, and acted upon even by unbelievers themselves." Fourth, this being done, "the objections which remain are of little weight, were they even less capable of being repelled." This conclusion is exactly in harmony with that of Butler, i. e., "The only question concerning the truth of Christianity is, whether it be a revelation." The arguments by which he claims to have "established" this grand truth cover about one hundred and sixty pages, and are based upon miracles and prophecy, for upon the *internal* and *collateral* evidences he does not lay much stress, at least not upon the former. Of these miracles, however, Watson's reviewer takes no notice, and, without attempting to refute the arguments based upon them, he tells his readers that Watson "has first to assume what he cannot prove," viz., the being of a God, and he asserts this simply because Watson, after giving numerous reasons, cannot see reason to conclude that man originated a knowledge of the God of the Bible, and concludes by saying: "Matter of fact does not, therefore, support the notion that the existence of God is discoverable by the unassisted faculties of man; and there is, I conceive, very slender reason to admit the abstract possibility." For this he is represented as "doing business on a fictious capital—passing what we know is not good coin." We claim, however, that he has established by irrefragable argument what Butler declares to be "the only question concerning the truth of Christianity." Indeed, this seems to us so obvious we know not how any one can fail to see it; for, to prove the Bible to be a revelation from that Being whose natural and moral attributes are declared to be infinite, is to prove it to be *true*, unless you suppose such a Being to be capable of making a mistake, or of saying what is not true; but such a supposition is, of course, impossible. The conclusion, therefore, is inevitable: to prove the Bible to be a revelation from God, is to prove it to be "true and righteous altogether." And as its miracles and prophecies afford such a *proof*, it follows that THE BIBLE IS COMPLETE IN ITSELF, complete both as to its teaching as to the evidence which it affords that its teachings are of God. Indeed, it seems to us unreasonable in the very extreme to suppose that God would give us a book upon the truth of which we are to rest our eternal all, and which we are to believe upon pain of eternal damnation, though it does not contain evidence that it is a revelation from God, and is, therefore, utterly destitute of authority, and utterly unreliable. It is, therefore, good for just nothing at all, unless so far as it may happen to take our fancy. Such an idea is utterly inadmissible; it cannot be entertained for a moment. If I believed that the Bible contained no evidence that it is a revelation from God, how could I go forth and enforce its teachings upon my fellow men by the sanction of eternal life and eternal death? How could any man do so? Nor will it help the matter in the least to say that the being of a God can be proved from "the facts of the universe," for, as I said before, that would not prove that the Bible is a revelation from God; if it does not *contain in itself* evidence that it is a revelation from God, "the facts of the universe" cannot impart that evidence to it. And if it does contain evidence that it is a revelation from God, then its teachings are as *true* as they are *complete*, and as complete as they are true. It will follow, of course, that Watson is right, transcendentalism wrong, and the controversy is forever decided, by proving that the Bible contains *in itself* evidence that it is a revelation from that God beside whom there is not another; in other words, by proving that it contains *in itself* evidence that it is what it professes to be. On the other hand, if it does not contain such evidence, then, as Watson says, "the cable is slipped, and every one is left to take his course wherever the winds and the currents may impel his *unpiloted*, *uncharted*, and *uncompassed* bark." So true it is "that the only question concerning the truth of Christianity is, whether it be a revelation." Thus we turn the tables again, by showing that the teachings of Watson's opponents, not those of Watson, tend to infidelity!

The following sketch on the inspiration of the Scriptures, though not originally designed for this work, seems to comprehend all we wish to say here, and perhaps all that need be said on this subject:

As to the nature and extent of the inspiration of the Scriptures, I conceive it consists in such a communication of assistance, by the Holy Spirit, as enabled the sacred writers to write and speak *with infallible truthfulness.*

As to the extent of that assistance or inspiration, that would vary with what they wrote and spoke.

For instance, when, as historians, they recorded facts or events, they were so assisted as to do so *with infallible truthfulness.* When the facts or events recorded consisted simply of what they had seen or heard perhaps years before, then it was principally their memory that was assisted; according to that promise, "He [the Holy Spirit] shall bring all things to your remembrance whatever I have said unto you." When they were called upon to speak impromptu, as they frequently were, before their enemies, and various authorities, then perhaps we might say it was their judgment principally that was assisted, according to that promise, "The Holy Ghost shall teach you in that same hour what ye ought to say." When they wrote and spoke as prophets, all we can say is, they were so assisted as to announce certain events which should take place long after the announcement, and which did take place according to their announcement; as, for instance, the birth and acts of Cyrus, and those of Jesus Christ. Sometimes the sacred writers recorded events which had taken place before they themselves were born; for instance, the history of the creation, by Moses. In this instance, it is clear the assistance was not communicated to the memory, nor does it seem proper to say that it was communicated either to the judgment or to the perceptive faculty; all that can be said is that which the inspired writers themselves have said: they "wrote and spoke as they were moved by the Holy Ghost."

With regard to the moral teachings of holy writ, we may observe that the sum thereof was written by the finger of God upon two tables of stone, and delivered to Moses in the presence of millions of people, accompanied by the supernatural phenomena of which we have already spoken. And in writing those moral precepts which are included, though not specified, in the ten commandments, and applying them to all the purposes of life, as they have done, the sacred writers had the infallible guidance of the Holy Spirit. It should be observed, too, that Jesus Christ himself, who is the source of all light and truth, teaches us the nature and use of the ten commandments when he tells us that the sum is love to God and man.

All the doctrines also the inspired penmen had from God by direct revelation. For instance, God made known his own being and attributes to Moses, to whom he showed his glory, and with whom he talked as a man with his friend. The doctrine of the resurrection, and that of the general judgment, St. Paul tells us, he had "by the word of the Lord." And many of the doctrines they had from the lips of Jesus Christ while he was present with them on earth. And in recording his words, as already stated, they were so guided by the Holy Spirit as to make the record with infallible truthfulness. At other times they announced doctrines and prophecies under the plenary inspiration of the Holy Ghost. So that the entire teaching of holy writ comes to us by direct revelation from God.

As to the evidence by which these teachings are proved to be from God, it is necessary to observe that there are three distinct parties occupying three distinct positions, and each party has evidence adapted to the position which it occupies. The parties are, first, the inspired writers to whom the revelations were made; second, those who were present when such revelations were made, and witnessed the phenomena that accompanied them; and, third, those who were not present, because living in a different locality, or in a different age.

The party inspired had an inward evidence that was peculiar and satisfactory to themselves, and which none but God could give; and this was accompanied and corroborated by outward phenomena of which God only could be the author. For instance, Moses had such evidence at the burning bush, in Egypt, at Sinai, and on many other occasions. Joshua, too, had similar evidence, not only while Moses lived, but also after he died. See first chapter of Joshua, also fifth chapter and thirteenth and following verses. Read also the history of Samuel and others during the period of the Judges, who were quite familiar with such divine communications, being so frequently under the divine inflatus, and who were known by the whole nation to "*speak the word of the* LORD." Read, too, Isaiah vi. 1–8. Also, the first chapter of Jeremiah. It will be well, too, to study, and study carefully, the visions of Ezekiel by the river Chebar, where, we are told, "The word of the Lord came expressly unto Ezekiel the priest, the son of Buzi, in the land of the Chaldeans by the river Chebar; and the hand of the Lord was there upon him." See the first three chapters of Ezekiel. Read also the book of Daniel, particularly the tenth chapter. And, in the New Testament, it will suffice to read the second chapter of the Acts of the Apostles, the twelfth chapter of Second Corinthians to the ninth verse; and the first chapter of Revelation, particularly from the tenth verse. In a word, they all had that peculiar inward assurance which none but God could give, corroborated by phenomena of which none but God could be the author. They also, in many instances, had evidence from the fulfilment of their own prophecies; indeed, most of the miracles were the fulfilment of predictions that preceded them. In addition to the instances already given take the following: In 1 Samuel xii, 16–18, we read thus: "Now therefore stand and see this great thing, which the LORD will do before your eyes. Is it not wheat harvest today? I will call unto the LORD, and he shall send thunder and rain; that ye may perceive and see that your wickedness is great, which ye have done in the sight of the LORD, in asking you a king. So Samuel called unto the LORD; and the LORD sent thunder and rain that day: and all the people greatly feared the LORD and Samuel." The prediction of Elijah and the long drought that followed are well known. Also his prayers in answer to which the copious rains descended at one time, and consuming fire at another. In connection with this read Jer. v. 24, x. 13, and xiv. 22, and you will see that the God of the Bible claims that he only has power to send and withhold the rain. "Are there *any* among the vanities of the Gentiles that can cause rain? or can the heavens give showers? Art not thou he, O LORD our God? therefore we will wait upon thee: for thou hast made all these *things*." Similar instances abound in the New Testament. The death of Ananias and Sapphira his wife, the blindness of Elymas the sorcerer, and the predictions of Peter and Paul, which preceded those events, are also well known: they are only two out of numerous instances of a similar kind in which miracle and prophecy are connected. These may be considered specimens of what Paul calls "the signs of an apostle," and by which he vindicates his claims to inspiration. "Truly," he says, "the signs of an apostle were wrought among you in all patience, in signs and wonders, and mighty deeds." Any one who will carefully read the above and similar scriptures, will see that the inspired writers had abundance of evidence that God spake to and by them; such evidence as none but God could give, and such as rendered mistake simply impossible."

The second party heard the inspired writers proclaim their divine and well-attested messages, and sometimes heard God himself, and were *eye* and *ear* witnesses of the wonderful phenomena, as at Sinai, at the baptism of our blessed Lord, and at the outpouring of the Spirit on the day of Pentecost. And the thousands in the wilderness were not only permitted to see and hear while Jesus spake, and the bread and the fish increased in his creative grasp before their eyes, but did also eat thereof, and were satisfied. This party were also, for the most part, acquainted with the life and character of the parties claiming to be inspired. They knew them to be persons of good judgment and unblemished character; they also were witnesses of what accompanied and followed the promulgation and reception of Scripture truth; and in addition to all this, they had, in common with all others, the evidence afforded by fulfilled prophecy.

The third party have the well-authenticated FACTS recorded in the Bible,* and interwoven with the histories of

* See "Leslie's Method with the Deists," at the end of the book.

all the ancient nations, as given by their own historians and principal writers. The *facts*, for instance, that the prophets, apostles, and Jesus Christ lived, wrote, spoke, and acted as is recorded of them in the Bible; that their claims to inspiration were attested by the miracles recorded, and under the circumstances and in the presence of the spectators specified. They have also the indisputable facts, that many of the events which the inspired writers declared would take place, have taken place precisely as predicted. Now all these facts are inseparably connected with the doctrines and morals of the Bible. In other words, with the *teachings* of the Bible. To deny the *facts*, is folly in the extreme; and to admit them, is to admit that the teachings of the Bible are the teachings of the God of the Bible. For these *facts* involve the exercise of attributes which belong only to God Almighty; and they were exerted to prove this very thing, namely, that these teachings are the teachings of the God of the Bible. Mark, I do not say to prove the existence of a Supreme Being, but to prove the being of that very God whom the inspired writers represent as clothed with infinite attributes, from whom they received their teachings, and beside whom they declare there is not another! "Hear, O Israel: The LORD our God is one LORD." "There is NONE ELSE beside him." "Thou art God ALONE."

It follows, that our belief, as to the inspiration of the Scriptures, rests upon numerous and indisputable FACTS, and these facts of such a nature, that they are obviously the offspring of God's *wisdom*, *power*, *omniscience*, *goodness*, and *justice*. Prophecies demonstrate his omniscience; miracles, by which the heavenly bodies and the earth are arrested in their motions, as when the sun and moon are said to have stood still; miracles, by which the lights of heaven are extinguished, and the earth wrapt in darkness at midday; miracles, by which the laws of nature, as they are called, are suspended, thrown aside, or even reversed; as in raising the dead, dividing the sea, throwing the stream of Jordan backward, or at least arresting it at a given point, controlling the winds and the waves in a moment; I say miracles such as these, and others recorded in Scripture, certainly indicate the exercise of a power that controls the universe, and that power must be the power of the omnipotent God; his signal judgments on the wicked, as in the case of the antediluvian world, and the overthrow of the cities of the plain, as also the death of Jesus Christ, are striking proofs of his justice; while the end obviously aimed at in the work of creation and redemption, together with the marvellous economy of grace and providence, which includes miracles and prophecy, alike prove his wisdom and goodness. Thus the *inspiration* of the Scriptures, the *power*, *omniscience*, *justice*, *wisdom*, and *goodness* of God, are established with all the certainty of FACTS, which facts are as indisputable as our very being. Such is the book which we claim to be *complete in itself*, and such are some of our reasons for so doing. Yet we are sent to the masses of gross matter with which we are surrounded to prove from thence the being and attributes of an Almighty Spirit, and are confidently assured that, if we cannot do that, "there can be no proof that the Bible is of God." Do the philosophers who teach thus really know that this is the triumphant utterance of almost every young sceptic and old infidel in the land? Do they know that the assumed sufficiency of the book of nature, of the human reason, of the human conscience, together with the assumption that the Bible does not contain evidence of "the existence of a God," does not contain evidence that "it is a

7*

revelation from God," are the reasons assigned by such young sceptics and old infidels, for absenting themselves from public worship, crying out priestcraft, and rejecting the whole system of Christianity? Do they know that such teachings are increasing the number of such sceptics continually? Do they know that between such teachings and infidelity there really is no ground upon which a man can stand? I say do they know all this? If they do not, they are seriously defective in knowledge, especially as public teachers. And if they do, their professed fidelity to the Christian system is more than questionable.

But there is another way in which any man may prove, not only that there is a God, but also, that the Bible is a revelation from God. The way is very easy, and very simple, so much so, that it is within the reach of all who can hear the word of the LORD, for this way is only known by a revelation from God, even the God of the Bible, who makes it known in these words: "Call unto me, and I will answer thee, and show thee great and mighty things, which thou knowest not." "The LORD is nigh unto all them that call upon him, to all that call upon him in truth." "If any man will do his will, he shall know of the doctrine whether it be of God." "Whosoever shall call upon the name of the LORD shall be saved." "All things whatsoever ye shall ask in prayer, believing, ye shall receive." "I say unto you, what things soever ye desire when ye pray, believe that ye receive *them*, and ye shall have *them*." Now any man may test the truth of this doctrine, even though he never saw the material world, though he had been born blind! And, remember, to establish the truth of this doctrine, is to establish the truth of every doctrine in the Bible. This statement is so evidently true that we think it entirely unnecessary to stop here to prove it. And it would be still more a work of supererogation to stop to prove that prayers offered to the God of the Bible, by the children of men, have been answered. Concerning the last of the promises, quoted above, that holy woman, Mrs. Hester Ann Rodgers, records the following testimony: "I have proved it in a thousand instances, and never knew it to fail in one." This is but one out of millions of testimonies to the truth of this blessed doctrine, that the God of the Bible hears and answers the prayers of the children of men when they offer them as the Bible teaches. And to show that the most ignorant and helpless of the poor fallen children of Adam may comply with that teaching, and, consequently, do that very thing which Watson's opponents say cannot be done, I will give a single instance, which I had from an eminent minister of the Gospel, who some years ago went to his reward. He said he was visiting in a certain hospital where he found a poor woman so ignorant that he despaired of reaching her judgment with the truth he desired to communicate, she being entirely unacquainted with Bible teaching, and quite uneducated. He, however, adopted this method: he obtained her promise that she would offer to the God of the Bible the following prayer, repeating it frequently till he should return again: "O God, show me my heart, for Christ's sake. Amen." He left her repeating this prayer, and on returning a short time after, found her deeply penitent, exclaiming, "O sir, God has showed me my heart, and it is so bad! What will I do?" These are the words, as near as I can remember. He then gave her this prayer: "O God, pardon my sin, and give me a new heart, for Christ's sake." He left her repeating this prayer, and on returning some time after he found her rejoicing, and rejoiced with her, while she declared that God had both pardoned her sin and given her a new heart. Oh, how much better it was to adopt this method than to leave this poor woman to "the facts of the material universe, and the intuitions of her mind," to prove the being of a God, giving as the reason that, "if there be no prior proof of God's existence *out of the Bible*, there can be no proof that the Bible is of God." My dear sir, here is proof without the slightest reference to anything out of the Bible. This poor woman obeys one single command of the Bible, by praying to the God of the Bible, and she receives a direct answer to her prayer, an unmistakable answer, and such as none but God Almighty could give; and that answer consisted in her receiving the very blessings which she requested. Now if those philosophers, so called, who reject the Bible, should affect to despise this proof because of its simplicity, surely they will not do so who profess to believe and teach the Bible; seeing they cannot slight this kind of proof without slighting both the Bible and its author. The following is one of the instances in which the Bible tells us this kind of proof was adopted, and adopted with glorious success: "And Elijah came unto all the people, and said, How long halt ye between two opinions? If the LORD be God, follow him: but if Baal, then follow him. And the people answered him not a word. Then said Elijah unto the people, I, even I only, remain a prophet of the Lord; but Baal's prophets *are* four hundred and fifty men. Let them, therefore, give us two bullocks; and let them choose one bullock for themselves, and cut it in pieces, and lay it on wood, and put no fire *under*: and I will dress the other bullock, and lay it on wood, and put no fire *under*. And call ye on the name of your gods, and I will call on the name of the LORD: and the God that answereth by fire, let him be God. And all the people answered and said, It is well spoken." Prayer was offered to Baal by his worshippers from morning till noon, and continued even "till the time of the offering of the evening sacrifice," but "there was neither voice, nor any to answer, nor any that regarded." Then Elijah having "built an altar in the name of the LORD," drew near and said, "Hear me, O LORD, hear me, that this people may know that thou art the LORD God, and *that* thou hast turned their heart back again. Then the fire of the LORD fell, and consumed the burnt-sacrifice, and the wood, and the stones, and the dust, and licked up the water that was in the trench. And when all the people saw it they fell on their faces; and they said, The Lord, he is the God; the LORD, he is the God." Now we simply call attention to the following particulars: First, the God of the Bible is rejected, and Baal, that is, a dumb idol, is substituted in his place, and almost an entire nation bow down to, and worship him, according to the "intuitions of their pure reason," and in defiance of "the facts of the material universe," with which they were surrounded: here are ignorance and indolatry in some of their worst forms, and that in the land of Israel! Second, it is proposed that, to find out the true God, prayer shall be offered: and it is agreed on all hands that "the God that answereth by fire" shall be recognized and worshipped as the true God. To this "all the people answered and said, It is well spoken." This kind of test had not occurred to the people, but as soon as it is presented to the mind, accompanied of course by the supernatural light and power that always accompany revelations from God, their common sense at once approves of it; there was not one transcendentalist, as far as we know, found among them; not one to say: "If we owe our knowledge of the existence of God to revelation alone, then it is impossible to prove, logically, the existence of God;" not one to say: "If we owe the knowledge of the existence of God to revelation alone, then we cannot, by human reason, prove that the Bible is a revelation from God." Such conclusions have no countenance, on this occasion, either from God, his prophet, or the people: they all agree, that a direct and unmistakable answer to prayer, will be proof sufficient, without any "prior proof of God's existence out of the Bible." And well they might, for it was an indisputable fact, that despite all such proofs, be they great or small, conclusive or inconclusive, the people were ignorant of the true God, so ignorant that they were gross idolaters. The sun, beautiful as is that heavenly body, was so far from demonstrating to that people the being and attributes of the true God, that they worshipped the sun itself! Third, this proof, as might be expected, answers the end proposed; for as soon as Elijah's prayer was answered, "all the people fell on their faces; and they said, The Lord, he is the God; the Lord, he is the God." Fourth, this God, who "is plenteous in mercy," confirms the faith of this deluded, but now believing people, by another gracious and wonderful answer to prayer, offered by the same man—the man who more than three years before had publicly said, "As the Lord God of Israel liveth, before whom I stand, there shall not be dew nor rain these years, but according to my word," now calls again upon this prayer-answering God, "The Lord God of Israel," who answered the former prayer by fire, but who answers this prayer by sending a copious rain upon the thirsty land; and thus blessing the people whose departure from the true God had caused the long drought, but who have now returned to him, even to the God who answereth prayer. Fifth, it is evident that the God who answered these prayers has complete control of mind and matter—has absolute control over all worlds, the invisible as well as the visible; for if wicked spirits, who are opposed to all good, could have sent either fire or rain, they would certainly have done so, and thus have frustrated the designs of God and his prophet. But they could do neither the one nor the other. They could do just nothing at all beyond what the God of Elijah saw fit to permit. If he says there shall be no rain, there can be none. If he says the fire shall not fall upon that idolatrous altar, all the devils in hell cannot communicate a single spark to it, much as they have to do with the fiery regions. If he commands the fire and the rain to fall, they come down, and there is no power that can possibly prevent it. The people saw this; they could not but see it; hence they cry out, "THE LORD, HE IS THE GOD; THE LORD, HE IS THE GOD." Thus, what God demonstrated by miracles in the land of Egypt, that same he demonstrated in the land of Israel by answering prayer, even that he is God, and beside him there is not another! So clear it is that revelation is complete in itself—carries its own evidence with it. God, by revelation, says to man, "Call upon me and I will answer." Man calls, and the direct answer is received. And the answer is such that it proves these two points, first, that it comes from the God to whom the prayer was offered; second, that this God has absolute control over all worlds, beings, and laws, at least as far as our knowledge extends. And these two points being proved, it follows, of course, that this God is worthy of our confidence and trust, and he only, and that the revelation which taught us to pray, must be from him who answered our prayers. Thus, again, we see, that revelation imparts perfect teaching, and perfect evidence that its teaching is the teaching of God Almighty. And these two particulars, it is evident, comprehend everything; these being true there, is absolutely nothing wanting. It is strictly true that, "The law of the LORD is perfect: the testimony of the LORD is sure, making wise the simple."

The following quotation from Watson's sermon on "The Excellency of the Knowledge of Christ Jesus" will, we think, be in place here: "Christianity appeals to experience. It declares that certain supernatural results shall follow upon the use of particular means. The weary and heavy laden who come to Christ shall find rest unto their souls. Peace and joy are consequent upon believing in him. The heart is purified by faith. The prayer of faith shall be answered. The way of practical holiness is a way of pleasantness and peace. What, then, is the fact? Let the appeal be made to sincere Christians in every age and place. Have they used the remedy in vain? Does the gospel describe a state of heart which they have never found? Has their prayer never been answered? Do wisdom's ways answer the description given of them? Speaking of his Father, our Lord said: "If any man will do his will, he shall know of the doctrine whether it be of God, or whether I speak of myself." By prophecy, miracles, and the unanimous testimony of experienced Christians, the gospel is confirmed to us as the sure word of God. O blessed knowledge, so assured! Tossed on a sea of doubt,

'Here is firm footing, here is solid rock.
This can sustain us: all is sea beside.'"

He had previously spoken of miracles and prophecy, in proof of revelation; here he adduces experience for the same purpose, and one of the particulars included in the Christian experience is the answer to prayer offered to the God of the Bible in the name of Jesus Christ. That the miracles of the Bible, the fulfilled prophecies of the Bible, and the fulfilled promises of the Bible, in answer to prayer, prove the truth of revelation, is Watson's position. And, with him, we have attempted to defend this position, and our defence is before the reader. Dr. Dempster, however, as well as Watson's reviewer, maintains that "if there be no prior proof of God's existence *out of the Bible*, there can be no proof that the Bible is of God."

CHAPTER V.

As this is a defence of "Watson's Theological Institutes," and as the design of Dr. Dempster is one with that of Mr. Cocker, it seems necessary that we should quote the doctor more at length, both in justice to him and in justice to Mr. Watson.

The doctor says, "Deductions from the mind's own first principles constitute *à priori* reasoning." These principles he variously denominates, at different times, "mental intuitions," "primary truths," "primary judgments," "intuitive truths," "first truths," "verities," "axioms." And concerning them he reasons thus: "As the rejection of these is the sole ground on which the theistic *à priori* argument is pronounced impossible, the necessity of these must restore that argument to its primary place in this discussion. How else can *proof* of the Divine existence be furnished? Is this proof ever attempted in revelation? If not, where and when has it ever been attempted? Is it susceptible of proof, or is it not? Is it merely a *fact* that God's existence is not proved in revelation? or is it a *necessity* that it is not? If it cannot be proved without revelation, evidence will appear invincible that it cannot by revelation; and if it cannot be proved by revelation or without revelation, it cannot be proved at all. This is exactly the conclusion reached by Kant and his followers, by Hamilton and his school, by Mansel and his admirers, and, we regret to add, by Mr. Watson and that entire class of divines who deny the possibility of NATURAL *Theology*. What would be the response of those learned rejectors of natural religion, should it be shown that revelation is *unsusceptible of proof of its Divine Author?*" * * * * "Our position is, that an authoritative revelation cannot be authenticated until prior evidence has proved its author." * * * "There is either proof of him without revelation, or there can be no proof of revelation." ("N. W. C. A.," Dec. 17, 1862, article No. 2.)

As the doctor's first article, which will be found in the issue of the previous week, is little more than a rehearsal of what Mr. Cocker had said, we had concluded not to quote from it, but we now see reasons for giving the following quotation from it: one reason is, he is pleased to construct certain arguments for his opponents, which they beg to say are not theirs, and would much prefer to construct their own arguments.

After speaking of what he calls "the sensational scheme," "the materialistic theory," "that of innate ideas," and of that which declares "that there are specific forms into which thought develops itself, as the acorn into the oak;" and, after speaking of certain "profound divines" who "deny the possibility of NATURAL THEOLOGY;" and after earnestly deprecating the terrible and "far-reaching consequences" of all this, he thus proceeds:

"Then arises the startling inquiry, if no utterance of him comes from these sources ['the mind's own first principles' and the material world], can there be any from revelation? Is it promptly answered 'that the miracles of revelation prove the infinity of their author?' But if ten thousand divine manifestations in nature fail to indicate him, how can the few that signalize the Scriptures manifest him? Has revelation ever attempted to *prove* a God? Where there is the least appearance of such attempt, is it not by an appeal to nature? Is it not thus based on the foundation of natural theology? Was not nature equally significant prior to all such appeals? But, if it had no such significancy, how could the Bible truthfully appeal to it for such purpose? How can a mere declaration prove his existence?. Not unless something of him was previously known. If profoundly ignorant of their author, how can miracles assure us of the divinity of their author? How could they delineate his character? Is the reply, that they were benignant in their nature? Be it so. But how many deceivers have showed kindness in order to inveigle their victims? If this stupendous creation and our wondrous constitution of mind are utterly silent of their great Creator, how can mere words, uttered by, we know not whom, reveal him? How can a few isolated miracles do this if all that have conspired to construct the creation fail to do it?"

The reader has now a faithful exhibit of the doctor's position in this controversy, and of the arguments by which he attempts to establish that position. Of what the doctor calls "the mind's own first principles," and the "deductions" therefrom, which he says "constitute *à priori* reasoning," we have already spoken at some length in a former part of this defence, and, consequently, have nothing to say here on these points. That the Bible is complete in itself, in *evidence* as well as teaching, has already been shown, so that what the doctor says to the contrary, in the above quotations, needs no further notice, though, even on these points, we may take occasion to notice the weakness of some of his remarks.

Copying after the example of Mr. Cocker, it would seem, the doctor connects Mr. Watson with what he calls "the sensational scheme," the "materialistic theory," and includes him amongst certain "profound divines," and "learned rejectors of natural religion," whom he represents as teaching that the existence of a God "cannot be proved by revelation or without revelation," and therefore not at all. "This," he adds, "is exactly the conclusion reached by Kant and his followers, by Hamilton and his school, by Mansel and his admirers, and we regret to add, by Mr. Watson and that entire class of divines who deny the possibility of NATURAL *theology!*" Mr. Cocker represents Watson as teaching what "must inevitably land in pure materialism," and Dr. Dempster represents him as teaching that "it," God's existence, "cannot be proved at all;" so that, according to the doctor, his teaching must land in atheism, while, according to Mr. Cocker, it "must inevitably land in materialism." To find evidence of these dreadful charges the latter refers us to "the chapters on the presumptive evidence," * * * * "on the moral law," and "on the existence of God." But the latter is pleased to give us his simple *assertion* to that effect, without quoting so much as one syllable from Watson's writings in proof of his *assertion!* As our reply to Mr. Cocker is a reply to the doctor on this point, we have only to add that it seems to us very wrong for the Methodist Episcopal Church to make the candidates for her ministry study "Watson's Theological Institutes" for four years, and, at the same time, by her periodicals and theological teachers represent them as above! We submit, with all deference, whether she should not either exclude "The Institutes" from "the course of study," or effect some change in her editorial and theological departments. The doctor goes on: "Is it promptly answered, 'that the miracles of revelation prove the infinity of their Author? How can a few isolated miracles do this, if all that have conspired to construct the creation fail to do it?" I will tell you, doctor. "All that have conspired to construct the creation," do not and cannot prove *that Moses and the other writers of the Scriptures were teachers sent from God;* BUT MIRACLES DO THIS; even though they were few; but they are not few, THEY ARE VERY MANY! AND VERY GREAT!—so much so as to demonstrate that their Author has absolute control of the heavens above, and of the earth beneath, and of all that therein is; so far as our observation extends, beyond which, of course, we know nothing, save by testimony; and that testimony we have from the writers of the Scriptures, whose claims are established by *miracles*, *prophecy*, and *answers to prayer*. The testimony asserts the being of an eternal God, clothed with infinite attributes: and the *phenomena* by which the truthfulness of that testimony is sealed to us, demonstrate their Author to be UNCONTROLLED and UNCONTROLLABLE! So that, if the testimony be not true, that UNCONTROLLED and UNCONTROLLABLE BEING *has set his seal to a lie!* And if it be true, then it is certain that the Bible is complete in itself, both as to its teaching and as to the evidence by which that teaching is proved to be from the True God, besides whom there is not another! In a word, *the teaching, and the phenomena by which that teaching is sealed, evidently originate in the same Being, and the phenomena prove that Being to be* WHAT THE TEACHING SAYS HE IS! Thus the teaching and the phenomena of the Bible make the Bible a perfect book. Nothing can be added to it; let nothing be taken from it. Neither miracles, nor the facts of the surrounding worlds, taken alone, can prove the being of the God of the Bible, simply because the *limited* cannot prove the *unlimited*, because the *finite* cannot prove the *infinite*, because nothing can *impart* what it does not *possess!* But *miracles and testimony such as the Bible* presents, and in the connection in which it presents them, do most conclusively prove the being of that very God. It is in this connection "that the miracles of revelation prove the infinity of their Author." It is for want of attending to this connection, it is because the doctor does not observe this connection, that he asks the question under consideration; and it is for the same reason that he asks, "How can a mere declaration prove his existence?" No, doctor; "a mere declaration" proves nothing at all, much less the being of a God, unless, indeed, that in some instances, "a mere declaration," or assertion, proves the folly of its author! But the declarations that are proved to be the declarations of God Almighty, as are the declarations of the Bible, prove something! Such declarations are infinitely reliable, they are "true and righteous altogether," for "God cannot lie."

"Has revelation ever attempted to *prove* a God?" continues the doctor. "Is it merely a *fact* that God's existence is not proved in revelation? or, is it a *necessity* that it is not." With all deference to the doctor we deny both the "*fact*" and the "*necessity*" here alleged. The sacred writers not only prove the being of a God, but, what is far more, they prove the being of THAT GOD whose infinite perfection they set forth in strains the most glowing and rapturous, and in the use of terms the most sublime and expressive, the most elevated and glorious, and which, though they express so much, suggest infinitely more, leaving the mind rapt in adoring wonder, and lost in the Infinite! And the proofs which the sacred writers give us of the being of this God are as extensive as are the *miracles*, the *prophecies*, and the *answers to prayer* which they record, and these run through the whole book from Genesis to Revelations. It is thus that "the Bible shows its trustworthiness." But the doctor inquires, "What would be the response of those learned rejectors of natural religion, should it be shown that revelation is unsusceptible of proof without prior proof of its divine Author?" And again, "How can a mere declaration prove his existence?" And yet again, "How can mere words, uttered by we know not whom, reveal him?" To such inquiries, doctor, there can be but one response, namely this: "a mere declaration," and "mere words uttered by we know not whom," prove just nothing at all, unless, as we said before, they prove the folly of those who uttered them. But to represent the Bible as containing mere assertions without a known author is marvellous in the extreme, especially when this is done by a doctor of divinity, a theological tutor! If this be the character of the Bible it is utterly unworthy of confidence, and the confidence hitherto placed in it has been entirely misplaced. Nor do we wonder that the doctor, while these are his views, should seek another book in which to place confidence. For our part, did we entertain these views of the Bible, we would at once turn to the book of nature, and take our texts from thence, or cease preaching altogether; for we certainly would not preach any more from the Bible, while entertaining these views. And even though we should admit that the book of nature teaches all the doctor claims, and much more; what then? Would it follow that a book containing "mere words, uttered by we know not whom," is the Book of God? We certainly can see no such consequence; nor do we see any connection whatever between such premise and such conclusion. If the heavenly bodies were a thousand times more numerous and glorious than they are, and the dance of the spheres ten thousand times more enrapturing than at present; and the mental and moral faculties of man a thousand times better than they are, still, even that would not prove that the unknown authors of certain assertions were teachers sent from God. On the other hand, if the book of nature were a thousand times less expressive than it is, still teachings sealed, as are those of the sacred writers, with *miracles*, *prophecy*, and *answers to prayer*, would be as obviously the teachings of that God whose they claim to be, as they are at present. It follows that the assertion that "if there be no prior proof of God's existence *out of the Bible*, there can be no proof that the Bible is of God," is utterly without foundation, and indicates a strange want of discrimination.

But the doctor assumes that those who differ from him rest their cause upon the benevolence of "a few isolated miracles," and then proceeds to invalidate his own assumption thus: "But how many deceivers have showed kindness in order to inveigle their victims?" That many of the miracles recorded in Scripture, especially those wrought by Jesus Christ, are characterized by godlike benevolence, is quite certain; but the doctor has no right to assume that it is upon their benevolence alone that his opponents rest their cause. Those miracles which indicate the just displeasure of their author, as well as his absolute sovereignty, afford their quota of evidence as well as those which are characterized by benevolence. Hence Mr. Watson says: "The flood, being so awful and marked a declaration of God's anger against the violation of the laws of this primitive religion, would give great force and sanction to it, as a religious system, in the minds of Noah's immediate descendants." And then, after specifying the principles of that system, and making some further remarks, he adds:

"The destruction of the wicked by the flood put the *seal of heaven* upon the religious system transmitted from Adam; and under the force of this divine and unequivocal attestation of its truth, the sons and descendants of Noah went forth into their different settlements, bearing for ages the deep impression of its sanctity and authority."

That the deluge and the prophetic warnings which preceded it, and which were fulfilled by it, must be attributed to the Omniscient and Sovereign Ruler of heaven and earth is so evident, we think, as to render an attempt to prove it unnecessary and superfluous; nor is it less evident that this terrible judgment was characterized by the justice as well as by the power and omniscience of its author. Nor will the doctor contend, we think, that the "kindness" manifested by its author was manifested simply "in order to inveigle" his "victims," for the kindness shown to Noah and his family was certainly sincere in its nature, and happy in its results. And, as to the rest of mankind, alas! the terrible judgment, though just, but too plainly indicated that God's "mercy was clean gone," and that he had "forgotten to be gracious." The opening of the windows of heaven, the breaking up of the great deep, the universal deluge, and the universal destruction of an apostate world, certainly leave little room for philosophers to speculate upon the kindness herein shown. We think it would be much wiser to imitate the thoughtful and pious example of Mr. Watson, as indicated in the quotations given above, or to exclaim with Paul, "It is a fearful thing to fall into the hands of the living God." The reader can easily extend these remarks to other and similar displays of the divine justice and power, in the miraculous judgments with which apostate men have been visited from time to time, and which are recorded in holy writ. Such as the destruction of Sodom and Gomorrah, and the other cities of the plain, and the equally miraculous destruction of Korah, Dathan, and Abiram, when "the earth opened her mouth and swallowed them up," and the not less miraculous destruction of the fourteen thousand and seven hundred by "the plague," on the same occasion. These and similar miracles afford conclusive and fearful evidence of the truth of the Scriptures. And there certainly is no room to conclude that their author designed to deceive by the kindness therein manifested! And, although the miracles of Jesus Christ are altogether characterized by the godlike benignity of their author, it would be both absurd and blasphemous to suspect for a moment that the author of these miracles designed by this manifested kindness to *deceive* and *inveigle* the poor, helpless, and miserable children of men! Certainly he who could say to the winds and to the sea, "Peace, be still, and there was a great calm;" he who by a word gave sight to the blind, hearing to the deaf, utterance to the dumb, and made the lame to leap with all the joyful activities of the village youth in their evening sports; he who by his creative power supplied the hungry thousands with abundance of food; he who could control the fish, as well as the waves, of the sea, and cause one of them to wait upon him with the exact sum of money demanded for tribute, and that at the moment required, with all the promptness of a faithful servant; he who, with or without a word, "healed all manner of sickness and all manner of disease among the people," cleansed the leper and raised the dead; he, I say, certainly had no need to *deceive* and *inveigle* the wretched and helpless children of men either to obtain their favor or to do them an injury! The very thought is so intolerable I will not, I cannot, longer dwell upon it! The fact is, the more I investigate the subject the more I am convinced that the supernatural phenomena of the Scriptures demonstrate their author to be what the Scriptures say he is. Every attempt to establish a contrary conclusion will, I am convinced, terminate in absurdity or worse. I say SUPERNATURAL phenomena, for all the phenomena of which we speak are purely supernatural. To say nothing further of miracle and prophecy, let us for a moment reflect on *answers to prayer*. At this moment, perhaps, millions of human spirits, scattered all over the earth, offer prayer to God in the name of Jesus Christ; perhaps for the most part these prayers are the simple desires of the soul, only expressed by the falling tear or the unutterable sigh, yet all these prayers are answered! And this is being done every moment, for these praying ones " cry day and night," they " pray without ceasing," and because their prayers are answered they " rejoice evermore, and in everything give thanks." Now to me it is as clear as a sunbeam that the Being who reads and understands all these praying hearts, and returns an answer to each prayer, according to the desire of the heart, which desire was only expressed by a sigh or a tear, or perhaps by neither; the Being who reads all the grateful feelings, as well as the prayerful desires, and hears and accepts all the thanksgivings of the heart; I say to me it is as clear as a sunbeam that this Being must be *omniscient, omnipresent, and omnipotent.* In a word, he must be all that the Bible says he is. *For to read all these hearts, and answer all these prayers, he must not only be present to* HEAR, SEE, *and* HELP, *but he must have* POWER *and* WISDOM *to control* ALL WORLDS, POWERS, *and* CONTINGENCIES. For it were to no purpose that he searched their hearts, and heard their prayers, if there were any *powers*, *laws*, or *contingencies* that could prevent his returning an answer. So sure, then, as the God of the Bible hears prayer, and returns an answer "to all that call upon him in truth," so sure all who hear the teachings of the Bible can prove to their utmost satisfaction the being of the God of the Bible; can prove "that he is a rewarder of them that diligently seek him;" and all this without first proving his being from the material world, all this independent of any such previous proof; even the man that was born blind, and, therefore, never saw the material world, can in this way prove the being of the God of the Bible. It must be admitted that in his case, at least, "faith cometh by hearing the word of God." But, according to Dr. Dempster, such persons could not have faith at all, for it certainly could not come by seeing! and the doctor says it cannot come by hearing!

We now return to Mr. C. who closes his review of Watson's Institutes thus: "The science of natural theology is recognized by the master mind of Paul: 'That which may be known of God *is manifested in their hearts;* God himself having shown it unto them, for his eternal power and godhead, though they be invisible, yet are they seen ever since the world was made, *being understood by his works*, that they might have no excuse.'" (Romans i, 19, 20. Conybeare and Howson's translation).

Just here we ask two questions—first, does the above text establish the reviewer's position? Second, is it opposed to Watson's position? To both these questions we answer, no. And if not, the text is quoted to no purpose. The reader, we doubt not, will see the correctness of our negative to these questions when we present again, as we have done before, the position of Watson, and that of his reviewer; for it is necessary that the reader should have these positions clearly in view in connection with the above text and the claims of the reviewer.

Watson's position is simply this: he claims that man, originally, had the knowledge of God's being and attributes by direct revelation from God himself. See his definition of a revelation. He claims that the human family were never without the knowledge thus received. He also claims that when any of the human family lost that knowledge they never obtained it again without supernatural assistance. And after giving numerous reasons for these claims, he thus concludes: "Matter of fact does not therefore support the notion that the existence of God is discoverable by the unassisted faculties of man: and there is, I conceive, very slender reason to admit the abstract possibility." He then adds: "The abundant rational evidence of the existence of God, which may now be so easily collected, and which is so convincing, is therefore no proof that without instruction from heaven the human mind would ever have made the discovery." Now we ask, do the words of Paul, quoted above, contradict what Watson says in the quotations here given? Do these words of Paul prove that "the unassisted faculties" of fallen man can derive a knowledge of the God of the Bible from the material world? Do they prove that "the human mind" without supernatural assistance could do this? Does "matter of fact support this notion?" Is there more than "slender reason to admit the abstract possibility" of this? And though man "can now collect abundant rational" and "convincing evidence," does it follow that he could have done so by his *natural powers* without *supernatural assistance?* If the text under consideration proves the affirmative of these questions, then the evidence, or reason, for "admitting the abstract possibility" of this is not as "slender" as Watson supposed it to be. That is all! But if the text does not prove the affirmative of these questions, then this last attempt to criminate Watson proves as unsuccessful as all the preceding. When the reviewer shall show that it does establish the affirmative of these questions, then, and not till then, will he have shown that Watson is mistaken; though it certainly would not follow that his teachings, for this simple reason, "must inevitably land in pure materialism," much less would it follow that the reviewer's position is right. Hence the necessity of inquiring, not only whether the text is opposed to Watson's position, but also whether it supports the reviewer's position, which has nothing to do with the question as to what man *is*, or *may be*, GRACIOUSLY; nothing to do with the question as to what man *knows*, or *may know*, by SUPERNATURAL ASSISTANCE, for, as we have shown in a former part of this defence, there can be no dispute with Watson on these points. The question is as to what man *is* and *knows*, *naturally*, *necessarily*, and *universally*, what he is "constituted by the great Architect of his mental being," what he *is*, and *knows*, after and despite the fall, independent of the *gracious* or *supernatural* help. The reviewer says: "Instead, then, of our knowledge of God resting upon revelation alone, we regard the idea of God as a phenomenon of the universal human intelligence. It is in all minds in which reason is in any considerable degree developed, and is there as a necessary truth." In support of this view he quotes the following words of McCosh: "The idea of God, the belief in God, may be justly represented as native to man." Nor is this all, for it is claimed that "we immediately apprehend the moral quality of actions. The mind intuitively apprehends them as right or wrong, and spontaneously approves or condemns them." And "this distinction in the quality of moral actions is felt to be independent of the mind which perceives it and of any mutable condition of things. Good and evil, right and wrong, are *immutable.* The distinction between them must be the same everywhere, at all times, and to all beings—to God, to angels, and to men. It is as impossible to conceive that there are intelligences to whom falsehood can appear a virtue, and justice a vice, as that there are intelligences to whom two and two equal five, or to whom the properties of the triangle can be more or less than they are to us. Accompanying this perception of the immutable distinction between virtue and vice, we have the consciousness of its being our DUTY to avoid the one and perform the other. We feel upon us an OBLIGATION which is imperative. We have also an abiding conviction that moral good is *rewardable,* and that vice merits *punishment.* And, finally, we have a conscious apprehension of a future *retribution.*"

As we quoted much more of this kind formerly, this will suffice for our present purpose. This is a specimen of what the reviewer calls "the science of natural theology," and which he says "is recognized by the master mind of Paul." The amount is, *every child of man, in every age and country, without a single exception, has a knowledge of God, of moral good and evil, and of a future retribution. And this knowledge is as natural, and as inevitable, as is our knowledge of obvious and unmistakable numbers!* Every man has the "abiding conviction" of all this! And we are confidently assured that all this is fully supported by the nineteenth and twentieth verses of the first chapter of Romans; though the apostle, in the following verses, speaks of certain "fools" who "changed the glory of the uncorruptible God into an image made like to corruptible man, and to birds, and to fourfooted beasts, and creeping things." And he even tells us that they "changed the truth of God into a lie, and worshipped and served the creature rather than the Creator." I do not see that these "fools" are any better than that other "fool" who, according to the psalmist, "said in his heart that there is no God:" nor are they much better who, when they "kill" God's people, "think that they do God service." Watson's reviewer, however, finds no such people in this or in any other age; every individual of the human race, according to his showing, is almost equal to an angel, if not entirely so! We still believe, however, that the sacred writers have not misrepresented the children of men, and so long as we believe this we cannot possibly believe the above and similar teachings of the reviewer: for certain it is that the ψυχικος ἀνθρωπος, the natural man, as described by the sacred writers, is the very reverse of the man described by the reviewer, as we have shown in a former part of this defence, and this showing we will support in due time by the facts of human history. In the mean time, it is worthy of remark that while these teachers of natural theology represent *the natural man* as being almost, if not entirely, on a level with the angels, they, nevertheless, confidently assert that this same man cannot discover God in his own word, not, at least, till he first proves his being and attributes from the facts of the material universe. The fact is, according to the showing of Watson's reviewer, the natural man is a very wise man; while, according to the showing of the sacred writers, he is a "fool," and in support of this painful conclusion they adduce the most terrible facts; these facts, however, are all ignored, and, impliedly at least, denied by Watson's opponents.

Although it is quite sufficient for our purpose to have shown, as we trust we have, that the text in question neither contradicts the teaching of Watson nor confirms that of his reviewer, yet we will endeavor to show what the text does teach.

Observe, then, the apostle is not speaking of the *knowledge* of the Gentiles at the time he wrote the passage under consideration, but of their *ignorance* at that time, and for a long time previous. So ignorant were they that they substituted the creature for the Creator, and worshipped the former instead of the latter. Nor did they choose the most noble creatures. But, having worshipped "an image made like to corruptible man," they finally worship "birds, and four-footed beasts, and creeping things"—ἑρπετων; "that is," say Bloomfield and others, "reptiles of every kind, not only serpents, but crocodiles and fishes." Such were some of the creatures which these blind, stupid, idolatrous Gentiles substituted for the living God. This last kind of idolatry mentioned was practised more especially in Egypt; and this shows us that the apostle is here taking a view of the whole Gentile world, at that and every previous period of its apostasy.

But there was a time "when they knew God,"—a time when "that which may be known of God" was actually known in the Gentile world. But how was this made "manifest to them" originally? The apostle answers: "God hath showed it unto them." How did he show it unto them? "By the light," says Mr. Wesley on the place, "which enlightens every man that cometh into the world." Observe, the knowledge of God, according to our apostle, was originally from God himself. "God hath showed it unto them." And it came, not in the natural order, but in the supernatural order; it came through Jesus Christ, who "is the true light which lighteth every man that cometh into the world." So far all is clear, and so far natural theology has plainly no place in the teachings of the apostle. But this knowledge of God which the Gentile world once had, and which they obtained in the way here specified, they lost; and the apostle tells us how they lost it. " When they knew God, they glorified *him* not as God, neither were thankful, but became vain in their imaginations, and their foolish heart was darkened. Professing themselves to be σοφοι," that is, philosophers, as such men still call themselves, "they became fools." * * * " And even as they did not like to retain God in their knowledge, God gave them over to a reprobate mind [margin: a mind void of judgment], to do those things which are not convenient, being filled with all unrighteousness." Intellectually and morally, all was wrong. They were "void of judgment," "without understanding," " without natural affection," and "filled with all unrighteousness." Emptied of all that is good, and filled with all that is bad, they were more vile than the reptiles which they worshipped! Good God, what a picture! And as though his inspiration were not a sufficient guarantee for its truthfulness, the apostle adduces facts as indisputable as they are shocking. Yet of these very same degraded creatures Watson's reviewer gives us a picture so lovely that the best man on earth need not be ashamed of it! And he "can ill conceal" his "regrets because Watson degrades the reason!" My dear sir, Watson never had the ability, even if he had the disposition, to give a more degrading picture of fallen man than that which Paul gives us in the above and other passages which we have quoted. So that if there is any cause for these regrets, it is Paul, not Watson, that must bear the blame. nd, even suppose neither Watson nor Paul had ever written a line on the subject, what then? Still we have matter of fact staring us in the face! Nor will our regrets alter these facts in the least.

But, for this ignorance, and all the other things here specified, the apostle says, "they are without excuse," not only because God revealed himself to man from the beginning, and "spake to the fathers by the prophets," and "lighteth every man that cometh into the world," but, also, because "the invisible things of him from the creation of the world are clearly seen, being understood by the things that are made, even his eternal power and godhead." To this and the preceding verse I find different critics give different renderings, at least to some of the words which we will notice. And this arises, doubtless, from the fact that these sentences are differently constructed in different Greek Testaments. In verse 19, some translate "to them," some "in them," some "among them," and some "in their hearts." "'Εν αὐτοις, *in them*, says Olshausen, "refers to the internal nature of the knowledge of God." The same writer says: "The expressions γνωσις, or ἐπιγνωσις του Θεου, *knowledge of God*, denote, however, in the language of the New Testament, that absolute knowledge of God which is conveyed to man by means of the manifestation of God in Christ; from which we may assume that the form το γνωστον του Θεου was purposely chosen by the apostle, in order to designate that lower degree of acquaintance with God, which was given to men on the footing of the Gentiles, and which was only gradually obscured by sin." In the 20th verse, the words, which are differently rendered, are ποιημ and θειοτης. This last word is translated godhead in the common version, but Bengel, Doddridge, Olshausen, and, I think, most critics, render this word *divinity;* for in Col. ii, 9, the word translated godhead is different, being θεοτητος. Doddridge observes that Augustine "nicely distinguishes" between these words, and seems to approve of the distinction made by that father. Olshausen translates, *his eternal power and divinity*, and says, "The 'eternal power' is very definite and easy to understand." * * * * "On the other hand, the expression θειοτης, is both striking and obscure, since Θεου is necessarily supplied. But doubtless the apostle, by this word, as above, by choosing γνωστον, intended to mark the incompleteness of their knowledge." Bengel, after defending the above translation of the word *theiotes*, says, the invisible things of God would certainly become visible at the creation, if ever;" and then, after some further remarks, adds: "So that the understanding of the fathers from the creation of the world may condemn the apostasy of the Gentiles."

Dr. Bloomfield, in his Greek Testament with English notes, translates the words τοις ποιημασι νοουμενα, "being comprehended by the things which he hath created and ordered," and adds, "for we may extend ποιημ, with Kypke, to the operations of God's providence as well as to creation." I do not see, however, where the doctor gets the word *created*, for certainly the word ἐκτισεν is not here in any of its forms. As to the word ποιημ, in its different forms it has very many different shades of meaning. For instance, in Matt. xii, 33, its meaning, as given in Greenfield's Greek Lexicon, is, "to bring to pass, cause to take place, do, accomplish," &c. Understanding the words thus, the apostle's meaning would be: *His eternal power and divinity are clearly seen, being understood by the things which he has brought to pass, accomplished, caused to take place.* This would comprehend the whole work of Providence, including miracles, the fulfilment of prophecies, threatenings, promises, and answers to prayer. And this he certainly has been accomplishing and bringing to pass "from the creation of the world." And this agrees perfectly with what our apostle says elsewhere, when he specifies some of "the things" comprehended in the term under consideration. For instance, when preaching at Lystra, he says, "We also are men of like passions with you, and preach unto you, that ye should turn from these vanities unto the living God, which made heaven, and earth, and the sea, and all things that are therein; who in times past suffered all nations to walk in their own ways. Nevertheless he left not himself without witness, in that he did good, and gave us rain from heaven, and fruitful seasons, filling our hearts with food and gladness." Such are some of "the things" which are God's *witnesses*, and which left the heathen "without excuse," even when "He suffered all nations to walk in their own ways." Nor were these and similar gracious providences God's only witnesses among the heathen, for he wrought his miracles and wonders in all the ancient Gentile nations—not only "in the land of Ham," but in the midst of the ancient Assyrians and Chaldeans, especially in Babylon and Nineveh, and, in short, in all the ancient nations, whether antediluvian or postdiluvian. Nor was this all, for he taught them his worship also. Hence we find the practice of offering sacrifice existing in all those ancient nations, yea, and of making formal prayer to God; and this knowledge they could not possibly derive from the works of either creation or providence, but must have had it directly from God himself. And this, the word of God assures us, was the fact. When Abraham first "sojourned in Gerar," he tells us he "thought surely the fear of God is not in this place," but he was mistaken. We are told "God came to Abimelech in a dream by night, and said to him, Behold, thou art but a dead man, for the woman which thou hast taken; for she is a man's wife." .... "Now, therefore, restore the man his wife; for he is a prophet, and he shall PRAY for thee, and thou shalt live: and if thou restore her not, know thou that thou shalt surely die, thou and all that are thine." .... "So Abraham prayed unto God: and God healed Abimelech, and his wife and his maid servants." Here let it be noticed, that this king receives instruction from the lips of the Most High on the subject of PRAYER, and on the other points specified in this history, that the whole comes as a law accompanied by its appropriate sanctions, that the king converses with God, calls him by his peculiar name JEHOVAH, appeals to him as the searcher of hearts, and receives this answer in reply: "I know that thou didst this in the integrity of thy heart;" and, finally, he gives evidence that he is acquainted with this God, and that he is familiar with such communications from him. (Genesis xx.) We find, too, that Job and his friends received *direct instruction* from the LORD on the subject of *prayer*, and on many other subjects. "Then the LORD answered Job out of the whirlwind, and said," &c. "And it was so, that after the LORD had spoken these words unto Job, the LORD said to Eliphaz the Temanite, My wrath is kindled against thee, and against thy two friends: for ye have not spoken of me the thing that is right as my servant Job hath. Therefore take unto you now seven bullocks and seven rams, and go to my servant Job, and offer up for yourselves a burnt offering; and my servant Job shall PRAY for you: for him will I accept; lest I deal with you after your folly." Here these men receive instruction *directly from the mouth* of the LORD on the two great subjects, *sacrifice* and *prayer*. Other quotations might be given, but these will suffice to show that God did not leave the ancient nations of the earth to derive a knowledge of his being and worship from the material universe, that instruction by direct revelation was not confined to Abraham and his posterity, that the advocates of natural theology have no right to assume that the human race was ever destitute of instruction by direct revelation from God. And we think it is highly presumable, were there no other evidence, that the revelations and supernatural phenomena recorded in the scriptures which we have quoted, and in others which might be quoted, are included by the apostle in "the things" which he declares to be God's witnesses, and which, in the scripture under consideration, he says left the Gentiles "without excuse" for their idolatry. If this be not the case, then the term *ποιημ*, or *ποιημασι*, in which he comprehends "the things" of which he speaks, must only mean the material universe, the works of creation. But in that case he would leave out the principal witnesses, i. e., all the miracles, fulfilled prophecy, fulfilled threatenings, and answers to prayer, and all those gracious providences which he elsewhere declares to be witnesses, and which we know God claims to be his witnesses, among the Gentiles as well as among the Jews. Moreover, if by "the things" which left the idolatrous Gentiles "without excuse," the apostle meant created things, why did he not use the word appropriate in that case, as he has done in the former part of the verse when speaking of "the creation"? There he uses the word *κτισεως*, here the word *ποιημασι*. It is perfectly true that "the heavens declare the glory of God," and so it is written. As these shining worlds sweep through the fields of space all around us, they "declare the glory" of *that God, that very God, made known to us by revelation:* that is far more than to say, "the heavens prove the being of a First Cause;" a Gentile philosopher might say that much, though, as we shall show, those philosophers were very slow to learn even that much: they talked, it is true, freely enough about an eternal power, but they recognized that power as belonging to matter, and as being too strong even for the gods; and both the matter and its power they declared to be eternal. But without a revelation no man ever said, no man ever could have said, "The heavens declare the glory of ELOHIM," for without a revelation that name never had been known! Hence this scripture is so far from proving what is claimed by Watson's opponents, that it proves just the reverse! It proves indisputably, that this is the utterance of one of those to whom the Great First Cause has revealed himself by NAME, and that NAME is ELOHIM, is JEHOVAH, and the NAME itself speaks volumes! Moreover, the author of this utterance speaks of "the law of Jehovah," which he declares to be "perfect," and which also is a revelation from this same LORD GOD, and could not possibly have been known but by revelation. Seeing, then, that "the heavens declare the glory of Elohim" to none but those who have an authenticated revelation from Elohim, it follows that this declaration cannot prove the knowledge of those who have no revelation; but this is the very thing assumed by the advocates of natural theology. Finally: *creation, revelation, and the supernatural phenomena which we have specified, bear a united testimony to the fact, that* JEHOVAH *is the author of* ALL, *and that beside* HIM *there is no* GOD! These three teachers distinctly and unitedly speak thus: *revelation* MAKES KNOWN; *and the supernatural phenomena prove revelation to be what it professes to be; while the magnificent works of creation bear a testimony that constantly illustrates and corroborates the whole!*

In closing our remarks upon the text in Romans, we cannot withhold from the reader Mr. Watson's views of that scripture, as given in his "Exposition." See the place.

"Human reason was never left to acquire, for the first

time, the knowledge of the existence of God from his works; but that doctrine being already in the world, the works of God made their constant appeal to the reason of man, presented to it an evidence of the most convincing kind, and opened courses of ennobling and sanctifying thought which, if they had taken the least delight in them, would have preserved men from all the degrading polytheism which followed." On the 20th verse he says: "Some include in the *τα ποιηματα* all the operations of God in his moral government, and the previous dispensation of grace; and it is certain that the word used is wide enough in its meaning to comprehend them. The argument, however, rather binds us to take it in its stricter sense of the creation and preservation of those things which are visible in the frame and constitution of the world. But it by no means follows from this, that the apostle intended to teach that the principles of God's moral government, his will, and our duties and hopes, in a word, all that has been termed natural religion, is to be learned by the study of physics, and that the visible world is a sufficient book for man. The apostle knew well that both among Gentiles and Jews, from the earliest ages, there had been communications of moral truth in direct revelations, and traditions of those revelations; that the world had never been without moral laws, or without promises of redemption; and what he knew to be fact, universally acknowledged by those to whom he writes, he assumes; and considers, therefore, that what proves the existence of that God, made known, as to his will and designs, in these early and widely diffused revelations, gave authority also to all the truth which had ever been connected with the doctrine. He assumes, in fact, what we see assumed throughout the Scriptures, that God communicated the knowledge of himself and his will originally to mankind; that this knowledge, though disregarded and darkened, was never wholly lost; that the visible creation was a standing *testimony* to it as existing, not the means of first revealing it, nor of recovering it through a process of reasoning, if, in any instance, entirely lost." Mark, Watson says, and understands Paul to say, that "the visible creation was a standing *testimony* to" what God had revealed. On the other hand, the advocates of natural theology claim that the visible creation *reveals*, as well as testifies to, "all that has been termed natural religion." In the one case, the *natural* is represented as bearing witness to the *supernatural;* in the other all is *natural*, and the *supernatural* is excluded. That is the difference.

CHAPTER VI.

To the teachings of Watson's reviewer, as to what man is *naturally*, *inevitably*, and *universally*, we will now oppose the *facts* of human history.

In an article published in "The Methodist Magazine and Quarterly Review," for January, 1838, entitled "Observations on Watson's Theological Institutes," by W. M. B., we have the following remarks: "The first particular, perhaps, which will strike the thoughtful reader as he proceeds, is the strange fatuity with which philosophers and theologians of old sought to develop the idea of God from the elements of human reason. As if the *reality* of divine revelation must be established by proving it unnecessary; as though it were to be demonstrated that God had revealed himself, by showing that we could have discovered him without revelation. First, in order of these attempts, came the doctrine of innate ideas; and the defender of divine truth asserted that the idea of God is congenital to the mind of man, and cannot be shaken off. Thus it was to be proved that the Scriptures revealed a high and important truth, in that they proclaimed to us a doctrine which we could not, from our very constitution, fail to know. But stubborn fact annihilated the chimera. Men were found who had no such idea, and the doctrine disappeared. Next appeared the baptized believers in natural religion. These did not maintain that the idea of God was born with us, but that the capacities born within us could, at the least, find a God in the things without us. Fact and reason, however, both overthrew the notion. For the *fact*, the idea never *was* discovered by man. For the *reason*, it does not appear that, without religion, the mind of man could, by any means, be brought to such a degree of elevation as even to entertain the question. The reasoning of Mr. Watson on this point is quite satisfactory." The reader will observe that where W. M. B. finds Watson "quite satisfactory," just there it is that Mr. C. finds the error that "landed, as indeed it must inevitably land, in pure materialism." It is a mistake, however, to suppose that "the strange fatuity, the chimera, of philosophers and theologians of old," and of "baptized believers," has "disappeared;" or, if it had disappeared, it certainly has appeared again, and again it must be opposed, if not "annihilated," by "stubborn fact;" for nothing but "stubborn fact," it seems, will drive "baptized believers" from this strange fatuity," this marvellous "chimera."

In evidence of the *innate ideas*, the *natural theology*, of the ancient Egyptians, we will give a single quotation from the satirist Juvenal, as some will believe him sooner than Paul:

Who has not heard, where Egypt's realms are named,
What monster gods her fertile sons have framed?
Her Ibis, gorged with well-grown serpents, there
The crocodile commands religious fear;
Where Memnon's statue magic springs inspire
With vocal sounds that emulate the lyre;
And Thebes—such, fate, are thy disastrous turns—
Now prostrate o'er her pompous ruins mourns;

A monkey god, prodigious to behold!
Strikes the beholder's eye with burnish'd gold:
To godship here blue Triton's scaly herd,
The river progeny is there preferr'd;
Through towns Diana's power neglected lies,
Where to her dogs aspiring temples rise:
And should you leeks or onions eat, no time
Would expiate the sacrilegious crime.
Religious nations, sure, and bless'd abodes,
Where every orchard is o'errun with gods.

This "natural religion" of the Egyptians was a little too bad even for Juvenal, immoral and sceptical as he was.

The Carthaginians, Tyrians, Phœnicians, Philistines, and Canaanites were little, if anything, better than the Egyptians. Hercules, the Moon, and Saturn seem to have been the principal deities of the Carthaginians; it was to the latter they offered human sacrifices, which were common among them. It is this probably that gave rise to the fable of Saturn's having devoured his own children. The idolatrous practices of the other nations mentioned above being specified in Scripture, it is not necessary to mention them here. Tertullian says that children were sacrificed to Saturn, or Moloch, down to the proconsulship of Tiberius, who hanged the sacrificing priests themselves upon the trees which shaded their temple. Diodorus says that "when Agathocles was going to besiege Carthage, the people, seeing the extremity to which they were reduced, imputed all their misfortune to the anger of their god, Saturn, because that, instead of offering up to him children nobly born, he had been fraudulently put off with the children of slaves and foreigners. To atone for this, and appease the anger of this god, two hundred children of the best families in Carthage were offered in sacrifice on this occasion, and as many as three hundred of the citizens voluntarily went into the fire and sacrificed themselves without compulsion."

It is well known that the Assyrians and Chaldeans were gross idolaters. The following from Eusebius will convey an idea of their "intuitions of pure reason": "Ur, which signifies fire, was the idol they worshipped, and, as fire will, in general, consume everything thrown into it, so the Assyrians published abroad that the gods of other nations could not stand before theirs. Many experiments were tried, and vast numbers of idols were brought from other parts, but they being of wood, the all-devouring god Ur, or fire, consumed them. At last an Egyptian priest found out the art to destroy the reputation of this mighty idol, which had so long been the terror of distant nations. He caused the figure of an idol to be made of porous earth, and the belly of it was filled with water. On each side of the belly holes were made, but filled up with wax. This being done, he challenged the god Ur to oppose his god Canopus, which was accepted of by the Chaldean priests; but no sooner did the wax which stopped up the holes in the belly of Canopus begin to melt than the water burst out and drowned the fire." Adramelech was another god of the Assyrians; Nisroch, too, was in high repute among them, especially at Nineveh. Milton, who very properly recognized idols as the mere representatives of devils, speaks of this idol, or rather of the demon which it represented, thus:

> ———In the assembly next upstood
> Nisroch, of principalities the prince.

Both the Assyrians and Chaldeans sacrificed their children to their idols. In the province of Sepharvaim the people are said to have been "most horrid and barbarous idolaters."

Of the Medes and Persians we are told that, "In consequence of the veneration they paid the sun, they worshipped fire, and invoked it in all their sacrifices. But their adoration was not confined to the sun; they worshipped the water, the earth, and the winds as so many deities. Human sacrifices were offered by them, and they burnt their children in fiery furnaces appropriated to their idols." Two notable gods among them were Arimanius and Oromasdes. "Some ancient writers have given us a very odd account of this god Arimanius, which may serve to point out their ignorance of divine things. Oromasdes, say they, considering that he was alone, said to himself, If I have no one to oppose me, where then is all my glory? This single reflection of his created Arimanius, who, by his everlasting opposition to the will of Oromasdes, contributed to the glory of the latter. We are told by Plutarch that Oromasdes created seven inferior gods, or genii, such as wisdom, goodness, justice, truth, the comforts of life, and all lawful enjoyments. On the other hand, Arimanius created as many devils, such as lies, wickedness, and all sorts of abominations. The former likewise created twenty-four devils, and enclosed them in an egg; the latter broke the egg, and by that means created a mixture of good and evil." Thus it was that "the intuitions of pure reason" perverted the Scripture account of the creation and fall of angels and men. Nor do we find that the heathens of more modern times are any better; in the writings of some of the nations, or tribes, within the bounds of the great Mogul Empire, we are told that "in the beginning God created a woman, whose name was Paraxacti, which signified sublime power, and this woman had three sons, the first of whom was born with five heads, and was called 'Bruma,' which signifies knowledge, and he was endued with the power of creating all inferior beings. The name of the second son was Vixnu, and he was to be the lord of providence, by preserving all things as they came from the hands of 'Bruma.' The third son was named Rutrem, and he had power given him to destroy all things which his other two brothers had made and preserved. This Rutrem, like his brother Bruma, had five heads, and the three brothers agreed to marry their mother,"the result of which was another monster progeny, and all gods, of course, having splendid temples built for them, and in which they are worshipped according to "the intuitions of pure reason." These gods, according to the showing of their worshippers, continued to increase; but they are such monsters, and their history so absurd and so vile, that we must not quote further. See Bishop Hurd's "History of Religions," to which we are indebted for the above quotations.

The following extracts are from a tract published by the M. E. Church, and entitled "A Catechism for the Deist:" "The inhabitants of Ceylon worship devils." "When the missionaries landed in Bengal in the year 1793 they found the inhabitants sunk in the grossest idolatry, acknowledging, at least, three hundred and thirty millions of gods. What was the nature of their worship at that time? It was blind adoration of a senseless idol; devotion to a monkey, a serpent, or a log of wood, mixed with many acts of impurity. What ideas had they of futurity? Nothing more than eternal transmigration, or absorption into the soul of the universe. They believed that when a man died he rose again either in the form of a cat, or a dog, or a worm, or some other reptile." Rev. Mr. Ward, who has been a long time a missionary in India, says: "I have never known one man among them, previously to his conversion to Christianity, who appeared to fear God and work righteousness. The *impurity* of their conversation is beyond all description. They are finished adepts in the art of *deception.* For *slander* and *abuse* they stand unrivalled, even among the most degraded of mankind! What is the practice of heathen mothers in India respecting their children? When the *first-born* is two or three years old, the mother takes it to the river, encourages it to walk in the stream, and then abandons it to the cruelty of the terrible alligator: this she does in hopes of having a numerous offspring. " Such are some of the "deductions from the mind's own first principles," some of those "primary judgments" of which our transcendental philosophers speak! To those who have such exalted views of *the natural man* and of *natural religion,* we would recommend a careful perusal of this little tract, also of what Mr. Wesley says on the same subject in vol. v of his Miscellaneous Works, p. 496, &c. A few short quotations just here may be useful.

"Shall we turn our eyes for a moment from the scriptural to the profane account of mankind in the earliest ages? What was the general sentiment of the most polite and knowing nation, the Romans, when their learning was in its utmost perfection? Let one, who certainly was no bigot or enthusiast, speak for the rest. And he speaks home to the point:

'Full many a war has been for women waged
Ere half the world in Helen's cause engaged;
But, unrecorded in historic verse,
Obscurely died those savage ravishers,
Who like brute beasts the female bore away,
Till some superior brute re-seized the prey:
As a wild bull, his rival bull o'erthrown,
Claims the whole subject herd, and reigns alone.'

I doubt he who gives this, not as his peculiar opinion, but

as what was then a generally received notion, would scarce have allowed even as much as Juvenal:

> 'Chastity did once, I grant, remain
> On earth, and flourish'd in old Saturn's reign;'

unless one should suppose the reign of Saturn to have expired when Adam was driven out of paradise. I cannot forbear adding another picture of the ancient dignity of human nature, drawn by the same masterly hand. Before men dwelt in cities, he says:

> 'The human herd, unbroken and untaught,
> For acorns first, and grassy couches fought;
> With fists, and then with clubs maintained the fray,
> Till, urged by hate, they found a quicker way,
> And forged pernicious arms, and learn'd the *art* to slay.'

What a difference there is between this and the gay, florid accounts which many moderns give of their own species!" And, we may add, what a difference between this and the accounts given by Watson's reviewers!

As the teachings which called forth this defence are a mere revival of those opposed by Wesley and Watson, in their day, we must beg leave to give yet another quotation from the former; we take it from page 503:

"Would we know, then, what manner of men the heathens in Africa were two or three thousand years ago? Inquire what they are now, who are genuine pagans still, not tainted with either Mohammedanism or Christianity. They are to be found in abundance either in Negroland or round the Cape of Good Hope. Now what measure of knowledge have the natives of either of these countries? I do not say in metaphysics, mathematics, or astronomy. Of these it is plain they know just as much as their four-footed brethren; the lion and the man are equally accomplished with regard to this knowledge. I will not ask what they know of the nature of government, of the respective rights of kings and various orders of subjects: in this regard, a herd of men are manifestly inferior to a herd of elephants. But let us view them with respect to common life. What do they know of the things they continually stand in need of? How do they build habitations for themselves and their families; how select and prepare their food; clothe and adorn their persons? As to their habitations, it is certain, I will not say our horses (particularly those belonging to the nobility and gentry), but an English peasant's dogs, nay, his very swine, are more commodiously lodged; and as to their food, apparel, and ornaments, they are just suitable to their edifices:

> Your nicer Hottentots think meet
> With guts and tripe to deck their feet;
> With downcast eyes on Totta's legs,
> The love-sick youth most humbly begs,
> She would not from his sight remove
> At once his breakfast and his love.

Such is the knowledge of these accomplished animals, in things which cannot but daily employ their thoughts; and wherein, consequently, they cannot avoid exerting, to the uttermost, both their natural and acquired understanding."

Once more: speaking of the glowing representations which some have given of the Chinese, and of their own high opinion of themselves, as expressed in the following proverb: "The Chinese have two eyes, the Europeans one, and other men none at all," and after giving evidence of the ignorance and degradation of the masses, he says, page 506: "But in order to see the true measure of their understanding in the clearest light, let us look, not at women, or the vulgar, but at the nobility, the wisest, the politest part of the nation. Look at the mandarins, the glory of the empire, and see any, every one of them at his meals, not deigning to use his own hands, but having his meat put into his mouth by two servants, planted for that purpose, one on his right hand, the other on his left! Oh, the deep understanding of the noble lubber that sits in the midst, and

'Gapes, as the young swallow, for his food.'

Surely an English ploughman, or a Dutch sailor, would have too much sense to endure it. If you say, 'Nay, the mandarin would not endure it, but that *it is a custom;*' I answer, undoubtedly it is; but how came it to be a custom? Such a custom could not have begun, much less have become general, but through a general and marvellous want of common sense."

Such are some of the facts of human history, as to whole nations, both ancient and modern; and facts much worse than any we have mentioned have been omitted, because too bad to mention; nor would we have copied some of the above testimonies were it not that we considered it necessary in view of the confident assertions we design to refute. Presuming that the reader is satisfied with, as well as sick of, the dark picture here given, we will now turn from nations to individuals; nor will we select the most ignorant and degraded, but the brightest luminaries of the ancient heathen nations, especially those of Greece and Rome, and that in their palmiest days. Watson has adduced numerous testimonies for the same purpose, but we choose to quote from other sources, and thereby increase the evidence.

The following quotations are from Grotius on "The Truth of the Christian Religion."

Aristotle, it is well known, asserted the eternity of the world, both in matter and form; yet he says, very candidly: "There are some questions against which very good arguments may be brought; it being very doubtful which side is in the right, there being great probability on either hand, we have no certainty of them. And though they be of great weight, we find it very difficult to determine the case and manner of their existence. As, for instance, whether the world were from eternity or no; for such things are disputed." Speaking of the generation of animals he uses these words: "It would not be a foolish conjecture concerning the first rise of men and beasts, if any one should imagine that of old they sprung out of the earth in one of these two ways: either after the manner of maggots, or to have come from eggs." Finally, after weighing the probabilities for and against each of these conjectures, he concludes thus: "If therefore animals had any beginning, it is manifest, it must be in one of these two ways." Such are "the primitive judgments" of this philosopher. He was not sure whether "animals had any beginning," but if they had, "it must be after the manner of maggots, or from eggs!"

Diodorus Siculus, after supporting the maggot theory at great length, thus concludes: "Now the earth being very much dried and hardened, by the heat of the sun, and by the wind, was no longer able to bring forth living creatures, but they were afterward begotten by mixing with each other." "Euripides" says Grotius, "seems not to contradict this account, for he says in his Menalippe:

'Heaven and earth at first were of one form,
But when their different parts were separate,
Thence sprung beasts, fowls, and all the shoals of fish,
Nay, even men themselves.'

This, therefore, is the account we have received of the original of all things. And if it should seem strange to any one, that the earth should in the beginning have a power to bring forth living creatures, it may be further confirmed by what we see comes to pass even now. For at Thebais, in Egypt, upon the river Nile's very much overflowing his banks, and thereby moistening the ground, immediately by the heat of the sun is caused a putrefaction, out of which arises an incredible number of mice. Now, if after the earth has been thus hardened, and the air does not preserve its original temperature, yet some animals are, notwithstanding, produced from hence, it is manifest that in the beginning all sorts of living creatures were produced out of the earth in this manner!" According to the "intuitions" of this philosopher *men* and *mice* had the same origin! And so had all "living creatures;" they were produced from *marshy* and *putrid* places, by the heat of the sun, and after the earth became too hard and dry for such purposes, "they were afterward begotten by mixing with each other." These philosophers preferred this to the egg theory, doubtless for this obvious reason: they could not tell where the egg came from! For the same reason it is, no doubt, that Aristotle does not say a word about the origin of the egg; that was too much for his "primitive judgments." The gods, too, it would seem, they supposed to have originated in the same way, for in the hymns ascribed to Orpheus, it is said:

"All things that are, sprung from chaos vast."

The same sentiment is thus expressed by Epicharmus:

"'Tis said that chaos was before the gods."

"And Aristophanes," says Grotius, "in his play called the *Birds*, in a passage preserved from Lucian, in his *Phi-*

lopatris," thus accounts for the origin of gods, men, and all animals:

> "First of all was chaos and night, dark Erebus and gloomy Tartarus;
> There was no earth, nor air, nor heaven, till dusky night,
> By the wind's power on the wide bosom of Erebus, brought forth an egg,
> Of which was hatched the god of love (when time began), who with his golden wings
> Fixed to his shoulders, flew like a mighty whirlwind, and mixing with black chaos,
> In Tartarus' dark shades, produced mankind, and brought them into light.
> For, before love joined all things, the gods themselves had no existence;
> But upon this conjunction, all things being mixed and blended, æther arose,
> And sea and earth, and blessed abodes of immortal gods."

"These," adds Grotius, "appear, upon a very slight view, to be taken from the tradition of the Phœnicians, who held an ancient correspondence with the inhabitants of Attica, the most ancient of the Ionians." We have the same sentiment expressed in the following words, quoted from Parmenides:

> "Love was the first of all the gods."

Orpheus, too, in his hymn to night, says:

> "I sing the night, parent of men and gods."

And Zeno, too, who was a Phœnician, gives us his views in the following words: "The chaos in Hesiod is water, of which all things were made; the water subsiding made mud, and the mud congealing made solid earth."

Thus it is that those great men, the brightest lights of the ancient heathen nations, attempted to account for "the origin of all things." Some commence with *water*, some with *putrid mud*, and some with *an egg;* but where the water, the mud, or the egg came from, they do not attempt to tell, except Aristophanes, who tells us that the "egg was brought forth by the wind's power on the wide bosom of Erebus," and of this egg, whose mother was Erebus, or dusky night, and whose father was the wind, "was hatched the god of love." Whether this attempt to account for the origin of the egg was better than no attempt at all we leave the reader to decide; only, we must not lose sight of the fact, that "the primitive judgments" of these sapient ones, *give a common origin to maggots, mice, men, and gods!* Nor let it be supposed that these are the mere flights of poetic minds, or the mere whims of certain eccentric philosophers; for the best schools of antiquity, the schools of the philosophers, have done no better. Dr. Thomas Burnet, as quoted by Watson, says: "The Ionic, Pythagoric, Platonic, and Stoic schools, all agreed in asserting the eternity of matter, and that the doctrine that matter was created out of nothing seems to have been unknown to the philosophers, and is one of which they had no notion." Dr. Doddridge, too, speaking of the Epicureans and Stoics, says: "But I think Dr. Benson has expressed himself, on the whole, in a very impartial and judicious, as well as comprehensive, manner, when he tells us, 'They held that matter was eternal, god corporeal,' that is, a fiery substance, 'and they,' generally, 'looked upon all things as subject to an irresistible fatality, and that virtue was its own sufficient reward. And they fluctuated exceedingly as to their belief of future rewards and punishments, though they had some expectations of a future state, as well as of the conflagration and renovation of the world;' with relation to which, several of them seem to have expected a continual revolution of exactly similar events at equally distant periods of time. The attentive reader will easily see how opposite the genius of each of these sects was to the pure and humble spirit of Christianity, and how happily the apostle levels his incomparable discourse at some of the most distinguishing and important errors of each." See the doctor's notes on Acts xvii, 18. It will be seen that Doddridge observes, very properly, not only that the teachings of those philosophers were deficient, but that they were directly "opposite" to those of the inspired writers. They were not only ignorant of God and of themselves, but when Paul proclaimed to them the truth in each case, they treated it with contempt, and called him a *babbler*, or, *a base fellow*, as it is in the margin. No wonder that the city of Athens, under the teaching of such philosophers, was "wholly given to idolatry," or, as it is in the margin, "full of idols." It is only necessary to observe, that the silly accounts given by those different philosophers, of "the origin of all things," are only so many perversions of the history of the creation and formation of the world, as given in the first chapter of Genesis, especially of the second verse. And all this goes to show that the light of revelation had reached them, but they had closed their eyes to it, and perverted its teachings, as Watson shows.

Speaking of the facts, that the light of revelation had reached the heathen, and that they had perverted the teachings of revelation, Grotius says, "Which of the poets is it in which we do not find mention made of the attempt to climb the heavens?" And speaking of Ham, the second son of Noah, he says, "This person is transformed, not only by the Libyans, but also by many other nations, into the star Jupiter, as a god." In proof of this he gives the following quotation from Lucan, book ix:

"Jupiter Ammon is the only god
Amongst the happy Arabs, and amongst
The Indians and Ethiopians."

Le Clerc, too, gives us a perverted account of the deluge from Abydenus' history of Assyria, as quoted by Eusebius. Many similar accounts of the deluge are furnished by Grotius, from Berosus, Plutarch, Lucian, and others. He also says: "The history of Jonah's being three days in the whale's belly is in Lycophron and Eneas Gazeus, only under the name of Hercules; to advance whose fame everything that was great and noble used to be related of him, as Tacitus observes." Calmet says: "Many of the ancient fathers maintain, that the ancient heathen philosophers had nothing valuable but what they borrowed from the Hebrews; that they had drawn from the fountain of the prophets; that by the subtile artifice of the devil, some principles of truth slipped into their writings, in order to undermine the truth at such time as God should manifest it to the world. Eusebius has devoted two entire books (lib. xi, xii) of his great work of the Gospel Preparation, to show that Plato had taken the principal things of his philosophy and theology from the sacred books of the Jews." "Porphyry," says Le Clerc, "acknowledges that Plato took many things from the Hebrews, as Theodoret observes in his first discourse against the Greeks." Josephus, in what is called his first book against Apion, when speaking of the ancient philosophers and teachers among the heathen being acquainted with the teachings of the sacred writers, says of Pythagoras, that "it is plain that he did not only know our doctrines but was in a very great measure a follower and admirer of them;" and as one proof of this he gives the following quotation from Hermippus, who wrote the history of Pythagoras: "This he did and said in imitation of the doctrines of the Jews and Thracians, which he transferred into his own philosophy." To this declaration of Hermippus Josephus adds: "for it is very truly affirmed of this Pythagoras, that he took a great many of the laws of the Jews into his own philosophy." And after giving numerous instances of a similar kind he sums up thus toward the close of his second book against Apion: "We have already demonstrated that our laws have been such as have always inspired admiration and imitation into all other men; nay, the earliest Grecian philosophers, though in appearance they observed the laws of their own countries, yet did they, in their actions and philosophic doctrines, follow our legislator." And a little after he adds: "Our law hath no bait of pleasure to allure men to it, but it prevails by its own force; and as God himself pervades all the world, so hath our law passed through all the world also." Clearchus, too, the scholar of Aristotle, acknowledges the indebtedness of his master to the Jews for much of his knowledge, and gives us, in what he says are Aristotle's own words, a conversation which his master had with a learned Jew. He represents Aristotle as saying: "Now, for a great part of what this Jew said, it would be too long to recite it; but what includes in it both wonder and philosophy, it may not be amiss to discourse of." Clearchus finally closes with these words: "but as he [the Jew] had lived with many learned men, he communicated to us more information than he received from us." What this Jew communicated to Aristotle had in it, says that philosopher, "both wonder and philosophy." See this account as given by Josephus in the first book of his "Antiquity of the Jews," from which many more quotations might be given to show that what is valuable in the teachings of those philosophers, at least in matters of religion, they had from the Jews directly, or indirectly through the Chaldeans and others, as Mr. Watson observes, and this is still further confirmed by Josephus, who, when speaking of the Greeks, says: "Those who first introduced philosophy and the consideration of things celestial and divine among them, such as Pherecydes the Syrian, and Pythagoras, and Thales, all with one consent agree that they learned what they knew of the Egyptians and Chaldeans," who had their knowledge of divine things from the Jews.

But these philosophers, as Mr. Watson observes, and as Josephus proves, seldom acknowledged their indebtedness to revelation, or preserved in its purity the knowledge which they obtained from thence. "Some of the philosophers," says Josephus, "have been insolent enough to indulge such contradictions, while some of them have undertaken to use such words as entirely take away the nature of God; while others of them have taken away his providence over mankind." How correct is this statement! They denied the providence of God [the same fact is stated by Watson], and used words which excluded everything essential to the nature of God. Such were the corrupt teachings which they imparted to the people under the imposing title of philosophy, while they withheld from them those correct ideas of the true God which, from time to time, they obtained from sacred sources. Not only are these facts asserted by Josephus, but some of their reasons for so doing are thus assigned: "Pythagoras, Anaxagoras, Plato, and the Stoic philosophers that succeeded them, and almost all the rest are of the same sentiments, and had the same notions of the true God; yet durst not these men disclose those true notions to more than a few, because the body of the people were prejudiced with other opinions beforehand." And again, a few pages after, he says: "Nay,

Plato himself confesseth that it is not safe to publish the true notion concerning God among the ignorant multitude." No doubt these considerations had their influence in leading the philosophers to conceal from the people correct, and impart erroneous, ideas of God; yet the fact must not be overlooked, namely, that, if "the body of the people were prejudiced with other opinions beforehand," they were indebted to their teachers for the erroneous opinions which produced such bad effects; and those teachers, still depending upon the *natural* and rejecting the *supernatural*, could not correct the people when they would! Hence two facts are still to be accounted for, namely, Why had the philosophers taught the people those erroneous views of God and religion? And why did the people still hold to the error, and reject the truth when it was presented? For an answer to each of these questions we must return to the inspired penman; nor will we fail to find a satisfactory answer in the following inspired declarations: "The natural man receiveth not the things of the Spirit of God, for they are foolishness unto him; neither can he know them, for they are spiritually discerned." He cannot know them while he depends upon the natural, and rejects the supernatural remedy. "The carnal mind is enmity against God; it is not subject to the law of God, neither, indeed, can be," till the supernatural remedy, for its destruction, is applied and accepted. That occasional correct and even sublime ideas of God should be found in the writings and sayings of the ancient philosophers, in connection with so much that is directly the opposite, and even absurd, in the last degree, can only be accounted for by the facts here noticed. They had those ideas, as has been shown, from the teachings of revelation, but did not acknowledge the fact. Moreover, their unbelief, pride, and the other causes specified, led them, for the most part, to corrupt or reject the truth thus received. Or, as Paul expresses it, "they did not like to retain God in their knowledge," but "changed the truth of God into a lie, and worshipped and served the creature more than the Creator." In proof of this, and in opposition to the assertions of Watson's opponents, we will still further quote the facts of human history. And as Josephus is still before us we will just here favor the reader with a few samples of the gods worshipped by the ancient heathen, while yet those renowned philosophers, of which we have been speaking, were their teachers. The samples are furnished by the great Jewish historian in what is called his second book against Apion; but it is improperly so called, for it is a very able exposure of heathenism and the vain pretensions of heathen philosophers and historians, and a defence of the religion of his fathers, and of the writings of the prophets, particularly those of Moses. As for "the Egyptian Apion," as he calls him, he takes his leave of that writer on the fifth page of this book, as hardly worthy his notice.

Here, then, are a few of the samples, as furnished by our historian, and only a few, for they are so numerous, and most of them so vile, that we can only select a few of the best of them:

He charges "the most famous poets and the most celebrated legislators" with "spreading such notions originally among the body of the people concerning the gods; such as these: that they may be as numerous as the people have a mind to have them; that they are begotten one by another, and that after all the kinds of generation you can imagine. They also distinguished them in their places and ways of living, as they would distinguish several sorts of animals; as, some to be under the earth, some to be in the sea, and the ancientest of them all to be bound in hell; and for those to whom they have allotted heaven, they have set over them one who, in title, is their father, but a tyrant and a lord; whence it came to pass that his wife, and brother, and daughter (which daughter he brought forth from his own head) made a conspiracy against him to seize upon him and confine him, as he had himself seized upon and confined his own father before." They also taught that "some of the gods were beardless and young, and that others of them were old, and had beards accordingly. Also that some are set to trades; that one god is a smith, and another goddess is a weaver; that one god is a warrior, and fights with men; that some of them are harpers, or delight in archery; and, besides, that mutual seditions arise amongst them, and that they quarrel about men, and this so far that they not only lay hands upon one another, but that they are wounded by men, and lament and take on for such their afflictions. But what is the grossest of all are those unbounded lusts ascribed to almost all of them, and their amours. Moreover, the chief of all their gods, and their first father himself, overlooks those goddesses whom he had deluded, * * * and suffers them to be kept in prison or drowned in the sea. He is also bound up by fate, that he cannot save his own offspring, nor can he bear their deaths without shedding of tears. These are fine things indeed! as are the rest that follow." * * * "Nay, others there are that have advanced a certain timorousness and fear, as also madness and fraud, and any other of the vilest passions, into the nature and form of gods, and have persuaded whole cities to offer sacrifices to the better sort of them." * * * * "They also endeavor to move them, as they would the vilest of men, by gifts and presents, as looking for nothing else than to receive some great mischief from them unless they pay them such wages." It is well known that the aborigines of this country offer all their gifts to just such gods, and for precisely the same reason. The Rev. P. O. Johnson, for many years a missionary among the Indians, told me that, being overtaken by a storm while out upon a certain lake in an open boat, an Indian who was in the boat with him concluded that his god was angry, and was about to appease him by throwing him his blanket, but Mr. J. forbade his doing so. However, as the storm continued, and they were in imminent danger, the Indian attempted to throw out his blanket several times, asserting that this was the only way they could be saved. But the missionary, knowing that if the blanket were thrown out, and they should afterward reach land, the poor Indian would give his god credit for their deliverance, and be, perhaps, hopelessly confirmed in his idolatry, interposed his authority, and confidently affirmed that the Christians' God would bring them safe to land, and not ask his blanket either. And so he did, and thus gave evidence to this poor idolater that the Christians' God is the true God, and besides him there is not another. Such were "the intuitive beliefs" of the *natural man* in ancient Greece, and such are his "intuitive beliefs" to-day as he wanders through the unbroken woods of America, the wilderness his home, the skin of a wild beast his covering, and an idol or a devil his god; nor does he discover the slightest evidence of an ability to raise himself in any sense of the word; on the contrary, he continues to sink deeper and deeper in ignorance, indolence, and misery, till the lion, the wolf, and the deer would, in many respects, be degraded by being compared with him. These are indisputable facts, before which the teachings of transcendentalism, respecting the natural man, cannot stand for a moment.

After describing the ignorance and idolatry of the ancient heathen, as above, Josephus has the following reflections, which we think worthy of notice: "Wherefore, it deserves our inquiry what should be the occasion of this unjust management, and of these scandals about the Deity. And truly I suppose it to be derived from the imperfect knowledge the heathen legislators had at first of the true nature of God; nor did they explain to the people even so far as they did comprehend of it; nor did they compose the other parts of their political settlements according to it, but omitted it as a thing of very little consequence; and they gave leave both to the poets to introduce what gods they pleased, and those subject to all sorts of passions, and to the orators to procure political decrees from the people for the admission of such foreign gods as they thought proper. The painters, also, and statuaries of Greece had herein great power, as each of them could contrive a shape [for a god], the one to be formed out of clay, and the other by making a bare picture of such a one. But those workmen that were principally admired had the use of ivory and gold as the constant materials for their new statues." The amount is this: poets, painters, and statuaries invented gods at pleasure, fixed their shape, and ascribed to them the vilest passions; while the mechanic made them of such material as he could procure; and this would vary from wood to gold, according to his means and the taste and means of the purchaser. But all the designers and mechanics in Greece could not invent and make gods enough to meet the demands of the people; hence the orators had a chance to exert their oratorical powers, which they did, and obtained decrees from the people to import foreign gods to meet the increasing demands of the people! This terrible state of things among the masses of the people, Josephus attributes to the ignorance and dishonesty of their teachers and rulers. The blind led the blind, and both fell into the ditch, the horrible ditch of idolatry, the vilest impurity, and the deepest misery; nor did they ever rise from thence, only so far as they accepted the *supernatural* remedy provided by the merciful Father of the spirits of all flesh.

CHAPTER VII.

As the views we oppose are asserted with great confidence, and as many cling to them with great tenacity, especially the sceptical classes, we must be permitted to dwell yet longer on the facts of human history. We desire especially to show that this ignorance of God was not confined to the uninstructed and unthinking masses. We will gather a few more of the facts of history from Grotius. Speaking of Moses, Strabo says: "He both said and taught that the Egyptians did not rightly conceive of God when they likened him to wild beasts and cattle; nor the Libyans, nor the Greeks, in resembling him by a human shape; for God is no other than that universe which surrounds us; the earth, and the sea, and the heaven, and the world, and the nature of all things, as they are called by us." Poor Strabo! he could not worship the gods of the Egyptians, the Libyans, or the Greeks; as a philosopher he could not bow down to them nor serve them, they were so gross, so bad, and, many of them, at least, so vile withal. Hence, he preferred *the earth, the sea, and the nature of all things!* These be thy gods, O Strabo! The heathen, as Grotius observes, worshipped evil spirits *as such;* also human beings departed, as a drunken Bacchus, an effeminate Hercules, a Romulus, unnatural to his brother, and a Jupiter as unnatural to his father. They worshipped the stars and elements; and various kinds of brutes, reptiles, and serpents. Also things that have no being, such as virtues and vices; yea, and diseases, such as fever, &c. Tully and Livy tell us of temples being dedicated to *honor.* "Perhaps," says Le Clerc, "some may explain this worship of the heathen in this manner; as to say, that it was not so much the things which were commonly signified by those words that they worshipped, as a certain divine power, from which they flowed, or certain ideas in the divine understanding." . . . "But the heathen themselves never interpreted this matter thus." And what better are they who in the present day recognize no God but nature. "Nature," say they, "is God, and God is nature." And with them *nature* is everything, and everything is *nature,* except the religion of the Bible: that, of course, is quite *unnatural!* And as to dedicating temples, we imitate the heathen in that particular also: I myself was present when a certain temple was dedicated "To Universal Benevolence," here in Michigan. True we have not, as far as I know, dedicated temples to *vices* and *diseases;* but what we may do in the future is, of course, an open question. "At the present day," says Mr. Watson, "not merely a few speculative philosophers in the heathen world, but the many millions of the human race who profess the religion of *Budhu,* not only deny a Supreme First Cause, but dispute with subtilty and vehemence against the doctrine." "The Buddhists," says Dr. Davy, as quoted by Mr. Watson, "do not believe in the existence of a Supreme Being, self-existent and eternal, the creator and preserver of the universe: indeed, it is doubtful if they believe in the existence and operation of any cause beside fate and necessity, to which they seem to refer all changes in the moral and physical world. They appear to be materialists in the strictest sense of the term, and to have no notion of pure spirit or mind. *Prane* and *hitta*, life and intelligence, the most learned of them appear to consider identical;—seated in the heart, radiating from thence to different parts of the body, like heat from a fire, —uncreated, without beginning, at least that they know of; capable of being modified by a variety of circumstances, like the breath in different musical instruments;—and, like a vapor, capable of passing from one body to another;—and like a flame liable to be extinguished and totally annihilated. Gods, demons, men, reptiles, even the minutest and most imperfect animalcules, they consider as similar beings, formed of the four elements—heat, air, water, and that which is tangible, and animated by *praue* and *hitta*. They believe that a man may become a god or a demon; or that a god may become a man or an animalcule; that ordinary death is merely a change of form; and that this change is almost infinite, and bounded only by annihilation, which they esteem the acme of happiness!"

Men who had such erroneous views of God and of "the origin of all things," were, as might be expected, equally in the dark as to their nature, and as to a future state. "The Greeks," says Grotius, "who derived their learning from the Chaldeans and Egyptians, and who had some hope of another life after this, spoke very doubtfully concerning it, as is evident from the disputes of Socrates, and from the writings of Tully, Seneca, and others. And though they searched diligently for arguments to prove it, they could offer nothing of certainty. For those which they allege hold generally as strong for beasts as they do for men. Which when some of them considered, it is no wonder that they imagined that souls passed out of men into beasts, and out of beasts into men." In proof of this he gives us numerous testimonies, not from the ignorant and uninstructed masses, but from the brightest lights among the ancient heathen. The following are a few out of many: "Now I would have you understand," says Plato in his Phædon, "that I hope to go amongst good men; but I will not be too positive in affirming it." . . . "If those things I am speaking of should prove true, it is very well to be thus persuaded concerning them; but if there be nothing after death, yet I shall always be the less concerned for the present things of this life; and this my ignorance will not continue long, for that would be bad, but will shortly vanish." The following mournful words of Tully, as found in his first Tusculan question, indicate a painful uncertainty of mind. He says: "I know not what mighty thing they have got by it, who teach that, when the time of death comes, they shall entirely perish; which if it should be (for I do not say anything to the contrary), what ground of joy or glorying does it afford?" Again: "Now suppose the soul should perish with the body, can there be any pain, or can there be any sense at all, in the body after death? Nobody will say so." It is evident that, after the utmost effort, and the most painful exercises of mind, this great man, like many others, had to leave it an undecided question, whether "the soul should perish with the body." These testimonies prove the truth of that remark of Justin Martyr, which occurs in his dialogue with Trypho, and is quoted by Grotius: "The philosophers knew nothing of these things, nor can they tell what the soul is." Such are a few specimens of "the intuitions of pure reason," and such are "the primitive judgments" of those great men, when they attempted to explore the spiritual and the eternal world by the light of nature. But their taper was so feeble, and the darkness so dense, that they finally gave up the search in despair, and mournfully waited the coming of death to decide the great question. In the mean time, they placed the chief good and end of man in sensual pleasure. But this conclusion, too, was far from being satisfactory; hence they finally reached that conclusion, recorded by Pliny, in his natural history, "that no mortal man is happy." No, not while ignorant of himself, of God, and a future state. For a man to be happy in such a state, is simply impossible. But "This is life eternal, that they might know thee the only true God, and Jesus Christ whom thou hast sent." "I am come," says Jesus, "that they might have life." And again, "Happy are the pure in heart for they shall see God." Life and happiness come by the *supernatural*, not by the *natural;* "Life and immortality are brought to light by the gospel." That thing called *nature* has no salvation for fallen man; hence those who reject the *supernatural*, as we have shown the philosophers did, must, like them, remain in ignorance and misery. To turn from the *supernatural* to the *natural*, is to leave "the fountain of living waters," for the purpose of manufacturing "cisterns, broken cisterns, that can hold no water."

The following quotation from Calmet is well worthy a place just here; in it we discover the fact that the *intuitions* of the *natural man* in Judea are not much different from those of the *natural man* in Greece. We see, too, the importance of the apostolic warning, "Beware lest any man spoil you through philosophy and vain deceit, after the tradition of men, after the rudiments [or elements] of this world, and not after Christ. For in him dwelleth all the fulness of the godhead bodily. And ye are complete in him." Observe, Christ and *this* philosophy lead in opposite directions, so that he who follows the one does not follow the other. Observe, too, that when Paul connects with this caution the assertion, "ye are complete in him," he thereby intimates that the advocates of this philosophy recognize Christianity as incomplete, and that they come with their philosophy to perfect what is lacking in the Christian system. Of this we have a striking example in the teachings which have called forth this defence. Now, then, "beware" of this error, *for ye are complete* in Christ! Christianity is a perfect system. It is perfect, as we have shown, both in its teachings and in the evidence by which it proves these teachings to be from God. It is no new thing for error to be introduced and propagated under the name of philosophy; therefore, "Beware lest any man spoil you through philosophy and vain deceit." And your only safety is in holding to the great truth, that *ye are complete in Christ!* I am quite aware that by thus enforcing the apostolic warning I shall, no doubt, be represented by a certain class as an enemy to philosophy, as Watson has been, and as Paul was by the philosophers of his day, who even called him a "babbler," and so shall I be called, in all probability; but that is a matter of little consequence. I am thoroughly convinced of the error which I oppose, and of the truth which I defend, and have made up my mind to oppose the one and defend the other at the risk of all consequences. Calmet says:

"About the time that the several sects of philosophers were formed among the Greeks, as the Academics, the Peripatetics, and the Stoics, there also arose among the Jews several sects, as the Essenes, the Pharisees, and the Sadducees. The Pharisees had some resemblance to the Stoics, the Sadducees to the Epicureans, and the Essenes to the Academics. The Pharisees were proud, vain, and boasting, like the Stoics; the Sadducees, who denied the immortality of the soul, and the existence of spirits, freed themselves at once, like the Epicureans, from all solicitude about futurity; the Essenes were more moderate, more simple and religious, and, therefore, approached nearer to the Academics. The philosophers against whom Paul inveighs in his epistle to the Romans boasted the extent of their knowledge, the purity of their morality, the eloquence of their writings, the strength of their reasonings, and the subtilty of their arguments. Their weaknesses were pride, curiosity, presumption, hypocrisy, ambition. *They ascribed everything to human reason*, and would be thought superior in all things. Although their lives were disorderly, shameful, and even injurious to human nature, yet they would pass on the world for good men. To them the apostle opposed the humility of the cross of Christ, the force of his miracles, the purity of his moral doctrines, the depth of his mysteries, and the evident proofs of his mission."

What a terrible picture is here given of those philosophers! "They ascribed everything to human reason." And what was the result? What did "the intuitions of pure reason" do for them? Did they in this way become wise and good? Just the reverse. They were *proud, vain, foolish, sceptical*, if not *atheists*, and *immoral* in the last degree. What Calmet says of them is fully confirmed by Cicero in the following words, quoted by Watson. Speaking of their teachings, he says: "Do you think that these things had any influence upon the men (a very few excepted) who thought, and wrote, and disputed about them? Who is there of all the philosophers whose mind, life, and manners were conformable to right reason? Who ever made his philosophy the law and rule of his life, and not a mere show of his wit and parts? Who observed his own instructions, and lived in obedience to his own precepts? On the contrary, many of them were slaves to filthy lusts, many to pride, covetousness," &c. The testimony of Origen is to the same effect. "I know," says that father, "of but one Phaedo and one Polemon throughout all Greece who were ever made better by their philosophy." Such was *the natural man*, and such his *natural reason*, in philosophical Greece; nor was he any better even in the land of Israel. Despite Moses and the prophets, and right in the face of Jesus and the apostles, the Sadducees were gross materialists. "The Sadducees," says Josephus, "argue that the soul perishes with the body." And again, "They deny the soul's immortality, and rewards and punishments in another life." Jerome, too, as quoted by Grotius, bears testimony to the same fact; he says: "They believed the soul perishes with the body." And a higher authority than either says: "The Sadducees say that there is no resurrection, neither angel, nor spirit." Yet in the face of all these facts of human history it is confidently asserted that "The human intelligence is configured and correlated to eternal principles of order, and right, and good as they exist in the Infinite Intelligence." That "God has imposed upon his intelligence such laws of thought as determine him to form the idea of God, of right and wrong, of duty, and of accountability." That "the idea of God, the belief in God, may be justly represented as NATIVE to man." That "it springs up spontaneously, as a plant from its germ; it will well up from the depths of his soul." That, "accompanying this perception of the immutable distinction between virtue and vice, we have the consciousness of its being our DUTY to avoid the one and perform the other. We have also an abiding conviction that moral good is *rewardable*, and that vice merits *punishment*. And, finally, we have a conscious apprehension of a future *retribution*." Such, it is asserted, are *the mental and moral intuitions of universal mankind. All this is native to man; it springs up spontaneously from the depths of his soul, as a plant from its germ!* Thus, while Gentile and Jewish philosophers are denying the being of a God, the existence of angels and spirits, the resurrection of the human body, future rewards and punishments, and asserting the eternity of matter, Christian philosophers are asserting as above, of universal mankind! And they are equally regardless of the fact that all around them men are asserting that they have no souls, and going to and fro throughout the length and breadth of the land preaching *nosoulism*. And because Watson does not unite with them in these marvellous assertions, does not ignore but assert *the facts of human history*, these philosophers are highly displeased, and *can ill conceal their regrets*. Such are philosophers, such is philosophy, such is human nature, such the natural man. And in view of the whole I certainly feel increasingly thankful for the Bible, and for Watson's Institutes.

To the numerous facts of human history already given we will add the experience of Mr. Wesley, as recorded by himself, in his sermon, entitled, "The Case of Reason Impartially Considered." Speaking of what reason can *not* do, he says it cannot produce satisfactory conviction "of an invisible eternal world." And amongst other proofs of this, he adduces his own experience thus:

"Many years ago I found the truth of this by sad experience. After carefully heaping up the strongest arguments which I could find, either in ancient or modern authors, for the very being of a God, and (which is nearly connected with it) the existence of an invisible world; I have wandered up and down, musing with myself: What if all these things which I see around me, this earth and heaven, this universal frame, has existed from eternity? What if that melancholy supposition of the old poet be the real case?

Οἵη περ φυλλων γενεη, τοιηδε και ἀνδρων.

What if the generation of men be exactly parallel with the generation of leaves? If the earth drops its successive inhabitants, just as the tree drops its leaves? What if that saying of a great man be really true—

'Death is nothing, and nothing is after death'?

How am I sure that this is not the case; that I have not followed cunningly devised fables? And I have pursued the thought, till there was no spirit in me; and I was ready to choose strangling rather than life.

"But in a point of such unspeakable importance do not depend upon the word of another; but retire for a while from the busy world, and make the experiment yourself. Try whether *your* reason will give you a clear, satisfactory evidence of the invisible world. After the prejudices of education are laid aside, produce your strong reasons for the existence of this. Set them all in array; silence all objections, and put your doubts to flight. Alas! you cannot, with all your understanding. You may repress them for a season. But how quickly will they rally again, and attack you with redoubled violence! And what can poor reason do for your deliverance? The more vehemently you struggle, the more deeply you are entangled in the toils; and you find no way to escape.

"How was the case with that great admirer of reason, the author of the maxim above recited? I mean the famous Mr. Hobbes. None will deny that he had a strong understanding. But did it produce in him a full and satisfactory conviction of an invisible world? Did it open the eyes of his understanding to see

'Beyond the bounds of this diurnal sphere'?

Oh, no! Far from it! His dying words are never to be forgotten. 'Where are you going, sir,' said one of his friends. He answered, 'I am taking a leap in the dark!' and died. Just such an evidence of the invisible world can bare reason give to the wisest of men!"

It is worthy of remark that what Mr. Wesley here says of himself, is precisely what Grotius says of the ancient philosophers. Speaking "of another life after this," he says: "And though they searched diligently for arguments to prove it, they could offer nothing of certainty. For those which they allege hold generally as strong for beasts as they do for men, which when some of them considered, it is no wonder that they imagined that souls passed out of men into beasts, and out of beasts into men." The following argument of Socrates is given as a specimen: "That which moves of itself is eternal." According to this argument eternal beings are very numerous!

A certain missionary gives us the following account of the aborigines of New Zealand. He says: "War is all their glory; they kill and eat their prisoners, and consider the Supreme Being as an invisible man-eater, and regard him with a mixture of hatred and fear." See the tract quoted above. Here is another proof that "the human intelligence is configured and correlated to eternal principles of order, and right, and good as they exist in the Infinite Intelligence," and that "the idea of God, the belief in God, is native to man;" that "it springs up spontaneously as a plant from its germ," so perfectly *natural* is it! Thus we add fact to fact, knowing the obstinacy, not to say fanaticism, that characterizes the error which we oppose. We wish, also, to keep before the mind the fact that the *natural man* gets no better, only so far as the *supernatural* remedy is applied and accepted. Despite all the laws of nature, despite all your *systems* of *natural theology*, he gets worse instead of better, till the *supernatural* remedy is applied and accepted. *All the facts within the whole range of observation are with us in this matter, and not one with our opponents!* The heathen are not only as bad now as they were thousands of years ago, but worse, and becoming worse; the god, of the New Zealander is "an invisible man-eater," and though those poor wretches worship this imaginary monster god, they both fear and hate him. Here is another specimen of the "deductions from the mind's own first principles," which, we are told, "constitute *à priori* reasoning." It is a painful fact, however, that those poor wretches, with all "the facts of the universe" and their own "mental intuitions" to assist them, never reason themselves any wiser till the supernatural remedy dissipates the darkness and quickens them into life!

The fact is, it has been the great error of philosophers, both ancient and modern, to ignore or reject the *supernatural*, and attempt to account for and explain all the phenomena that are discoverable, whether in mind or matter, by what are called *natural laws*, and to rely upon reason alone in their investigations, as though it were beneath the philosopher to accept of the help offered by revelation. Hence many of their efforts have been perfectly abortive, and worse than abortive; not only because the work which they assigned to reason was beyond the power of reason, but also, because much of the phenomena which they undertook to explain upon *natural* principles was the work of *supernatural* power. Suppose, for instance, a man should recognize as natural phenomena the budding of Aaron's rod, and its bearing fruit the same night; the falling of the manna; Christ feeding the five thousand at one time, and seven thousand at another; his stilling the winds and the waves by the utterance of a word; and by a word giving sight to the blind, health to the leper, and life to the dead; and impose upon his reason the task of explaining all this by what are called *natural laws;* who does not see the result of such mistakes? That which he recognized as *natural* was *supernatural*, and the work which he assigned to reason was absolutely beyond the power of reason. Hence his efforts would not only be a failure, but would be puerile and even ridiculous. And just such have been the efforts of philosophers in reference to other matters equally *supernatural*, though recognized as *natural.* And theologians, as well as philosophers, have fallen into the same mistakes, and both philosophy and religion have suffered in consequence. A careful examination of the teachings which we oppose in this defence, and of the objections raised against the teachings of Richard Watson, will convince any one that they are characterized by these mistakes, viz., the not discriminating between the *natural* and the *supernatural*, between what *is*, and what *is not*, the work of reason. It is by the *supernatural* that fallen man is raised, from first to last, as we formerly showed. It is by the *supernatural* that his dead soul is quickened, and his blind eyes opened. And it is by the *supernatural* that the spirtual and the eternal worlds are revealed to him. Hence, all attempts to account for and explain these and similar *supernatural* phenomena by what are called *natural laws*, must ever prove an utter failure. For the same reason, whoever expects these *supernatural* and mighty works to be accomplished by what are called *natural laws*, will surely be disappointed. The whole system of grace which has been introduced for the salvation of fallen man is *supernatural:* there was no *natural* law by which forfeited life could be restored to fallen man. Hence St. Paul says: "If there had been a law given which could have given life, verily righteousness should have been by the law." It is for want of recognizing this great truth that men become infidels, who, it is well known, are always talking about *nature*, and will see nothing beyond, above, or superior to, *nature*. While Paul is saying, "I determined to know nothing among you, save Jesus Christ, and him crucified," they seem to say, "We are determined to know nothing among you but nature." It is a striking and very important characteristic of Mr. Watson that he carefully distinguishes between the *natural* and the *supernatural*, between what *is* and what *is not* the legitimate work of reason; and in these particulars also his writings and those of his opponents present a very striking contrast.

As the error of ignoring, or denying, the *supernatural*, and recognizing the *natural* only, has been a great error in all ages, and is now, it seems to us, a growing error, we will dwell upon it yet a little longer; especially as those who fall into this error are almost sure to fall into the other errors which we have specified.

We have an illustration and confirmation of these statements in the writings of modern geologists; they seem determined to account for and explain all the phenomena which come under their notice, by what are called *natural laws*. In this also their writings are a perfect contrast to those of Moses and Watson, both of whom recognize and specify a *supernatural* power as the cause of much of the phenomena referred to.

We have already seen how the ancient philosophers attempted to tell us how the earth was formed, and how its inhabitants originated. They all commenced with chaos,—

> "All things that are sprang from chaos vast."

As to living creatures, whether *mice* or *men*, some traced their origin to a maggot, and some to an egg, while others were satisfied to give us a less specific account, thus:

> "Heaven and earth were at first of one form,
> But when their different parts were separate,
> Thence sprang beasts, fowls, and all the shoals of fish,
> Nay, even men themselves."

Again: "Nature first formed all sorts of animals perfect; and then ordained, by a perpetual law, that their succession should be continued by procreation."

Diodorus Siculus, as quoted by Grotius, gives us, as his own views and those of preceding philosophers, the following: "In the beginning of the creation of all things, the heavens and the earth had the same form and appearance, their natures being mixed together; but afterward, the parts separating from one another, the world received that form in which we now behold it, and the air a continual motion. The fiery part ascended highest, because the lightness of its nature caused it to tend upward, for which reason the sun and multitude of stars go in a continual round; the muddy and grosser part, together with the fluid, sunk down, by reason of its heaviness. And this, rolling and turning itself continually round, from its moisture, produced the sea, and from the more solid parts produced the earth, as yet very soft and miry; but when the sun began to shine upon it, it grew firm and hard ; and the warmth causing the superficies of it to ferment, the moisture, in many places swelling, put forth certain putrid substances, covered with skins, such as we now see in the fenny moorish grounds, when, the earth being cool, the air happens to grow warm, not by a gradual change, but on a sudden. Afterward the forementioned substances, in the moist places, having received life from the heat in that manner, were nourished in the night by what fell from the clouds surrounding them, and in the day they were strengthened by the heat. Lastly, when these fœtuses were come to their full growth, and the membranes by which they were enclosed broke by the heat, all sorts of creatures immediately appeared; those that were of a hotter nature became birds, and mounted up high ; those that were of a grosser and earthy nature, became creeping things, and such like creatures, which are confined to the earth; and those which were of a watery nature immediately betook themselves to a place of the like quality, and were called fish."

Euripides, whom we quoted formerly, gives us a similar account of the origin of animals, only in his specification he very wisely includes "men themselves"! and closes by saying, "This, therefore, is the account we have received of the original of things." And after adducing the facts of observation in proof of all this, such as those already adduced, he closes thus: "Now, if after the earth has been thus hardened, and the air does not preserve its original temperature, yet some animals are notwithstanding produced; from hence, they say, it is manifest that in the beginning all sorts of living creatures were produced out of the earth in this manner."

Now we could easily show, as Grotius, Le Clerc, Watson, and others have already shown, that all these accounts of "the origin of all things" are gross perversions of the Mosaic account; but our purpose just here is to call attention to a single fact, namely this, that in all these accounts there is no recognition of the *supernatural*—all is *natural;* that is, everything was produced, "in the beginning," by what are called natural laws, as now understood. In a word, there is no God recognized from first to last—all is NATURE! So much for the geological theories, or what you please to call them, of olden times. Now we are going to show that the theories of many modern geologists are not a whit better; and we are strongly inclined to believe that they have many of their ideas from those ancient philosphers, though they have not acknowledged their indebtedness to them.

After examining the ancient theories, we are more than ever convinced of the correctness of the following remarks of Paley, which we introduce here, not only because they express our own views, and that better than we could ourselves, but also because Watson makes them his own, and quotes them as "just remarks on some modern schemes of atheism."

"I much doubt," says the doctor, "whether the new schemes have advanced anything upon the old, or done more than changed the terms of the nomenclature. For instance, I could never see the difference between the antiquated system of atoms and Buffon's organic molecules. This philosopher, having made a planet by knocking off from the sun a piece of melted glass, in consequence of the stroke of a comet, and having set it in motion by the same stroke, both round its own axis and the sun, finds his next difficulty to be, how to bring plants and animals upon it. In order to solve this difficulty, we are to suppose the universe replenished with particles endowed with life, but without organization or senses of their own; and endowed also with a tendency to marshal themselves into organized forms. The concourse of these particles, by virtue of this tendency, but without intelligence, will, or direction (for I do not find that any of these qualities are ascribed to them), has produced the living forms which we now see." Now we only ask the reader to compare this theory of Buffon with that of Diodorus, given above, and we are sure he will find that the former has not improved upon the latter, no, not in the least. Buffon supposes the universe replenished with particles endowed with life, but does not attempt to tell us where the particles came from, or how the life was produced. Diodorus represents the sun as producing fermentation, and then putrid substances in the muddy and marshy places on the earth's surface; and, finally, by the process described, "all sorts of creatures immediately appeared." We doubt not that the reader will give the preference to the ancient over the modern philosopher. This much, however, must be admitted: there is no God in either system, nor are we told where the sun and the earth came from in the one case, nor where the comet and the sun came from in the other, nor need we inquire: we know they believed in the eternity of matter!

But the doctor goes on: "Very few of the conjectures which philosophers hazard upon these subjects, have more of pretension in them than the challenging you to show the direct impossibility of the hypothesis. In the present example there seemed to be a positive objection to the whole scheme upon the very face of it; which was, that if the case were as here represented, *new* combinations ought to be perpetually taking place; new plants and animals, or organized bodies which are neither, ought to be starting up before our eyes every day. For this, however, our philosopher has an answer. While so many plants and animals are already in existence, and consequently, so many 'internal moulds,' as he calls them, are prepared and at hand, the organic particles run into these moulds, and are employed in supplying an accession of substance to them, as well for their growth as for their propagation; by which means things keep their ancient course. But, says the same philosopher, should any general loss or destruction of the present constitution of organized bodies take place, the particles, for want of 'moulds' into which they might enter, would run into different combinations, and replenish the waste with new species of organized substances.

"But these wonder-working instruments, these 'internal moulds,' what are they, after all? What, when examined, but a name without signification? Unintelligible, if not self-contradictory; at best differing in nothing from the 'essential forms' of the Greek philosophy? One short sentence of Buffon's works exhibits his scheme as follows: 'When this nutritious and prolific matter, which is diffused throughout all nature, passes through the *internal moulds* of an animal or vegetable, and finds a proper matrix or receptacle, it gives rise to an animal or vegetable of the same species'!" In all this there is no God, and, consequently, no common sense. Such are the teachings of the philosopher who was so much admired by Rousseau, that the latter, on entering the study of the former, bowed down and kissed the threshold of the door. They were true worshippers of nature and each other, but could not admire the Bible or worship its Author!

"Another system," continues the doctor, "which has lately been brought forward, and with much ingenuity, is that of *appetencies*. The principle, and the short account of the theory, is this: pieces of soft, ductile matter, being endued with propensities or appetencies for particular actions, would, by continual endeavors, carried on through a long series of generations, work themselves gradually into suitable forms; and at length acquire, though perhaps by obscure and almost imperceptible improvements, an organization fitted to the action which their respective propensities led them to exert. A piece of animated matter, for example, that was endued with a propensity to *fly*, though ever so shapeless, though no other we will suppose than a round ball, to begin with, would in a course of ages, if not in a million of years, perhaps in a hundred million of years (for our theorists, having eternity to dispose of, are never sparing in time), acquire *wings*. The same tendency to locomotion in an aquatic animal, or rather in an animated lump which might happen to be surrounded with water, would end in the production of *fins;* in a living substance, confined to the solid earth, would put out *legs* and *feet;* or if it took a different turn, would break the body into ringlets, and conclude by crawling upon the ground."

The reader is requested to notice that as yet no God is recognized, still the *supernatural* is excluded, all is *natural*, or, more properly speaking, all is *unnatural*. Observe, too, all these philosophers commence with *mere* matter, and, of course, *continue and end in mere matter;* for the stream could not rise above its source. But though they all commence with matter, they differ considerably as to the form in which they found that matter "in the beginning." Some commenced with a sun and a comet, the latter striking the earth from the former in the shape of a huge mass of molten glass. Others tell us "the earth existed originally as a thin vapor or nebula, like that of which comets are composed;" then "it cooled down to a fluid form, as steam condenses to water," and "the process of cooling continued," we are told, "until a crust formed upon the surface of the fluid sphere, as ice forms upon water;" and "as the cooling still proceeded, the water which had before existed as steam, condensed and covered the whole earth." We have neither time nor patience to follow our geological savans through the all but interminable process that followed; the heating, cooling, swelling, contracting, boiling, steaming, condensing, and thundering process was long as well as terrific, but the process which followed this, it is presumed, was still longer. This, however, is a matter of no moment, for "our theorists," as Paley observes, "having eternity to dispose of, are never sparing in time." It is acknowledged that "the process of deposition must, from the nature of the case, have proceeded with extreme slowness, and it is obvious that very long periods of time, amounting to hundreds of thousands of years, must have been required for its completion." And we are very gravely told that "no human beings existed during the immense periods which these formations represent." Surely it was not necessary to tell us that human beings did not exist on the earth while it was *a sphere of liquid fire*, nor yet, while it was enveloped in a body of steam so great that when it was condensed, that which before was a sphere of liquid fire was lost in a shoreless ocean! Nor do we see how such a body of *fire* or *water* could, with any propriety, be called "the earth," though Moses, let it be remembered, calls it "the earth," from the time it was created; not only after, but before, and during the work of the six days!" Nor do we think it could, with any propriety, be called "the earth" while it existed "as a thin vapor or nebula," as others say it did; nor need we be told that human beings did not exist during that period; nor do we see how there could be vegetable or animal life of any kind during these periods; so that all these changes, and others, which we are told occupied countless millions of years, must have taken place before what Moses calls the third day, for on that day the earth brought forth *grass*, *herb*, and *fruit tree*. Now these changes, which our theorists say occupied unknown and inconceivable periods of time, Moses says occupied six days! Those of our modern geologists who have not completely thrown off the authority of the Scriptures, are very much annoyed by this Moses; they try hard to get him to accept of their numerous and contradictory theories, but it is to no purpose; he remains unchanged and unchangeable. It is no use contending with him; what he says is LAW! Pharaoh found that out, and so will all that contend with him, rest assured of it. However, they try hard to persuade him to change his six days into countless millions of years, and his Sabbath into a period of corresponding length; but he seems to have no sympathy with their theories, for although it is essential to their geological systems, he will not grant them this single request, though they try hard to persuade him that it would be quite consistent with his system to do so; but he does not see it so; though they have used many arguments like the following: "How is the great age of the world before man was created, which geology requires, consistent with the Bible account that the work of creation was begun and completed in six days? The days of the Mosaic account should probably be regarded as long 'periods' (an interpretation which the original language of the Bible admits), and the evenings and mornings as the beginnings and endings of these periods." Moses, however, contends that he is giving a simple narrative, and that he means what he says. Moreover, he commands men to work six days, and rest one in every seven, and so do the sacred writers who follow him, and they will not be understood to command us to work several millions of years without stopping, and then rest, say, one million years, and enjoin this upon us by all the sanctions of the law, while, at the same time, they tell us that the average length of human life is threescore years and ten; nor will Moses admit that he uses the word day in the narrative of the creation in a sense different from that in which he uses it in the law of the Sabbath. And as to the plea that "geology requires" the word to be thus understood, Moses contends that his geology requires nothing of the sort, for *God spake, and it was done; he commanded, and it stood fast.* Moreover he says, that both his common sense and his honesty require that he should be understood to mean just what he says, and that he cannot involve himself simply to give sanction to their geological theories, which he knows are not true! Thus, not only Moses, but all the inspired writers, are unalterably opposed to all those geological whims.

But to return: we were speaking of the different shapes or states in which different geologists have assumed the earth to be when they commenced their different theories of its future formation. Many of them, like the ancient heathen, commence with a chaotic ocean containing the elements of all things. To this, too, we must object the *fact* that Moses calls our globe "the earth" from the moment it was created. But various interpretations have been given to the original Hebrew words, which in the common version are rendered *without form and void.* "The Seventy," says Watson, "render the phrase *tohu vabohu*, ἀορατος, και ἀκατασκευαστος, *invisible and unfurnished.*" Invisible, because God had not yet said, "*Let there be light;*" and *unfurnished*, because he had not yet said, "Let the earth bring forth grass, the herb yielding seed, and the fruit tree yielding fruit after his kind, whose seed is in itself, upon the earth." Nor had he yet created any living being. Hence the earth, as yet, was both *invisible and unfurnished.* "It is wonderful," says Rosenmuller, as quoted by Mr. Watson, "how so many interpreters could imagine that a chaos was described in the words *tohu vabohu.* This notion unquestionably took its origin from the fictions of the Greek and Latin poets, which were transferred by those interpreters to Moses." "Those fictions ground themselves," observes Mr. Watson, "upon traditions received from the earliest times; but the *additions* of poetic fancy are not to be applied to interpret the Scriptures." Mr. Watson observes further, after objecting to various geological notions: "If such interpretations of the Mosaic account cannot be allowed, the decisions of Scripture and some of the modern speculations in geology must be left directly to oppose each other, and their hostility on this point cannot be softened by the advocates of accommodation."

But that to which more especially we desire to call attention just here, is the notion that this shoreless ocean, holding in solution the materials of the future earth, if not of the universe, was left to sport in the fields of space, rolling and tossing its waves with terrific fury, till by the slow process of *deposition*, *stratification*, *crystallization*, and *petrification*, our earth was produced and left as it is, and all this by the wonderful power of that indefinable thing, *the infidel god*, NATURE. In all this process, observe, the *supernatural* is excluded, and God is not recognized at all! For all these geologists can get along very well without God, and still better without Moses!

The following quotation from "The London Encyclopædia" will show where Dr. Hutton and his followers commence their geological theory; it will also show how they also can construct a world without any power but that of *nature:* "Dr. Hutton does not go back to chaos to lay the foundation of his habitable world, nor does he borrow much assistance in constructing his fabric from chemical attractions. He rests upon a pre-existing continent, out of the ruins of which our present dry land was formed and arranged principally by mechanical means. The portion of the globe which we now possess was, according to his hypothesis, the bottom of the sea when the older continent was decaying to form it; this older continent was then, of course, immersed; and, lest we should be alarmed at the recurrence of a similar catastrophe to this scene of our interests, we are told that it will be followed by a similar renovation. Thus, as one continent descends another rises, like the opposite scales of a balance; and in the resources of this system that order of organic nature is supposed to be traced by which the continued existence of the different races is secured, not by the perpetuity of the individual, but by the successive reproduction of the kind. Our present world is thus one in an indefinite series of worlds which have existed in times past, and which are destined in future to appear; and all the less obvious or more striking changes which we witness are steps in the progress of mighty revolutions, to which the imagination can set no limits, either with regard to duration or magnitude." Still no God is recognized, nothing *supernatural* is admitted, all is as *natural* as the flowing of a river, or the crumbling of its banks, or the growth of a plant. And it is more than intimated that thus it has been in all time or eternity past, and will be in eternity to come!

The Neptunian or Wernerian system commences with

chaos, or a vast ocean with the materials of the future earth in solution, and proceeds on the principle of *deposition* and *formation*, as described above, till "the waters subsided and left the dry land for the support of animals and vegetables." The waters, however, "from some inscrutable causes, again rose and resumed their former bed, and a second time a chaotic fluid invested the crust of the earth. And, in the words of Thomson,

> 'A shoreless ocean tumbled round the globe.'

This rise of the waters Werner finds necessary to account for the position and structure of the secondary trap formations, so strangely attending or overlying the other secondary strata." As there is nothing in the processes here described very different from some previously given, it will suffice to add the following quotations: "When the waters had retired so much as to permit the formation of this class of rocks, and had ceased to cover them, the crust of the earth was prepared for supporting animal and vegetable life, and received from the hand of nature families of both in abundance." See "London Encylopædia," article Geology. Still there is nothing *supernatural ;* God is not recognized in all this—*Nature* does all!

Watson's reviewer gives us, on page 202 of the Review, the following quotation from Hugh Miller: "The globe itself was once a molten mass of liquid fire. There was not one spore, or monad, or atom of life through all its dark domains. Creation, from its centre to its circumference, was a creation of dead, inorganic matter." The reviewer adds: "The history of the globe, as written in fossil hieroglyphics on tables of stone, teaches us that there have been many successive and independent creations." Thus Hugh Miller is one of those who commence their geological process with "a molten mass of liquid fire," and the reviewer, it is presumed, is one of the same class, but he believes also in "many successive and independent creations." This he finds written "on tables of stone."

Such are a few of the geological notions that are scattered all over the land by newspapers, lecturers, and book-makers. Some commence to tinker up a world out of a mass of liquid fire, some out of a vast and shoreless ocean, and some out of a continent that strangely sprang up out of a vast ocean; while others, very fortunately, and not less strangely, obtain a huge mass of molten glass, struck off from the sun, and by great industry and the help of *nature*, of course, tinker up a world out of that. And when, in their imagination, they have succeeded in making a world without God, they proceed to furnish it without God! In doing this, as in constructing the earth, they have different beginnings. In originating living beings, some commence with a *maggot*, some with an *egg*, some with *molecules*, some with *appetencies*, *internal moulds*, or *prolific matter*. And from these, by the power of nature, they produce all that is!

The reader is no doubt weary of these godless theories, but not more so than we are ourselves. We will therefore dismiss them with a single quotation from the "London Encylopædia." Speaking of this class of geological theorists, the writer says: "The theories or dreams which they formed must therefore be viewed merely in the light of philosophical romances, or ingenious works of fancy, and would apply to any other planet as well as to ours. Nineteen of them may be found in the introduction to Mr. Accum's 'Chemistry.' They bear the same relation to the state and appearances of the earth as the Oceana or the Utopia bear to actually existing governments; and can no more account for its phenomena than the fictions of enchantment can explain the events of history."

Speaking of various geological conjectures, many of which are far in advance of those which we have given above, Mr. Watson says: "To all these suppositions, though not unsupported by the authority of some great critics, there are considerable objections; and if the difficulty of reconciling geological phenomena with the Mosaic chronology were greater than it appears, none of them ought hastily to be admitted. That creation, in the first verse of Genesis, signifies production out of thing, and not out of pre-existent matter, though the original word may be used in both senses, is made a matter of faith by the Apostle Paul, who tells us, '*that the things which are seen, were not made of things which do appear;*' which is sufficient to settle that point. By the same important passage it is also determined, that the worlds were produced in their *form,* as well as *substance,* instantly out of nothing; or it would not be true, that they were not made of things which do appear." "The apostle states," says Dr. Adam Clarke on the place, "that these things were *not made* out of a *pre-existent matter;* for, if they were, that matter, however extended or modified, must *appear* in that thing into which it is compounded and modified; therefore it could not be said, that the things which are *seen,* are not made of things that *appear;* and he shows us also, by these words, that the present mundane fabric was not formed or reformed from one anterior, as some suppose." This text, as here understood, and we do not see how it can be understood otherwise, settles these two grand points, namely, that the worlds had their origin in the creative act of the Almighty, and that, of course, *instantaneously.* Second, that they had their *form* by the *fiat* of the same Almighty Being, and that of course instantaneously. These two truths of revelation sweep away at a stroke all the geological tinkerings of philosophers, both ancient and modern! And all this is confirmed by the plain and unmistakable words of Moses in his narrative of the *creation* and *formation* of the worlds, and of the origin of all things. In proof of this we simply call attention to the following quotations, which we think are decisive of the points at issue: "In the beginning God created the heavens and the earth." "And God said, Let there be light: and there was light." "And God said, Let the waters under the heaven be gathered together unto one place, and let the dry land appear: and it was so." "And God said, Let the earth bring forth grass, the herb yielding seed, and the fruit tree yielding fruit after his kind, whose seed is in itself, upon the earth: and it was so." "And God said, Let the waters bring forth abundantly the moving creature that hath life, and fowl *that* may fly above the earth in the open firmament of heaven. And God created great whales, AND EVERY LIVING CREATURE THAT MOVETH, which the waters brought forth abundantly after their kind, and every winged fowl after his kind: and God saw that it was good. And God blessed them, saying, Be fruitful, and multiply, and fill the waters in the seas, and let fowl multiply in the earth." "And God made the beast of the earth after his kind, and cattle after their kind, and everything that creepeth upon the earth after his kind." "And God said, Let us make man in our image, after our likeness." "So God created man in his own image, in the image of God created he him; male and female created he them. And God blessed them, and God said unto them, Be fruitful, and multiply." Now, we simply call the attention of the reader to the two facts asserted in the above quotations. First, that the *existence* of the worlds, and of *men*, *animals*, and *vegetables*, is the instant result of God's *act*, or *word*. Second, that when *men*, *animals*, and *vegetables* produce their own species, the original power to do so is from that same God that gave them their existence. Had he not given the power and uttered the command, no being would have *multiplied*. When by *nature* philosophers mean this, we have no dispute, for according to this showing *nature itself* is God's creature! On these points Moses is still more specific, if that can be, in the second chapter of Genesis, where he recapitulates what "God *created* and *made*," or *created to make*, as it is in the margin. In evidence of this we will give yet another quotation: "These are the generations of the heavens and of the earth when they were *created*, in the day that the LORD God *made* the earth and the heavens, and every plant of the field *before it was in the earth*, and every herb of the field *before it grew*: for the LORD God had not caused it to rain upon the earth." Before the ordinary process of vegetation had commenced, God produced every *plant* and every *herb perfect*, and *instantaneous*, *with the seed in itself*. And, in short, everything, every creature, *was perfect*, *was complete in that very day on which it was created or made*. Here all is *supernatural*; the *being*, and the *original character* and *form* of *every creature* are attributed to the *immediate act* or *fiat* of the LORD God! When the geological dreams, specimens of which we have given above, are contrasted with these sublime teachings of Moses, on the same subject, they sink into drivelling nonsense, and appear supremely contemptible. That heathen philosophers should teach as they have done, is strange; but that Christian philosophers, with the Bible in their hand, should do so, is at once unaccountable and intolerable! And it has long appeared to us strange, passing strange, that a certain class of geologists, when attempting to account for the various geological phenomena, utterly ignore, not only the *creative* and *formative* acts of the Almighty, as recorded by Moses, but also *the original gathering together of the waters into one place*, and the general deluge; which, if they do not account for all the phenomena, will certainly account for much of them.

"An able work," says Mr. Watson, "has been recently published on the subject by Mr. Granville Penn, who has at once reproved the bold philosophy which excludes the operation of God, and employs itself only among second causes; and has unfolded the Mosaic account of two great revolutions of the earth, one of which took place when 'the waters were gathered into one place,' and the other at the deluge, 'when the fountains of the great deep were broken up,' and has applied them to account for those phenomena which have been made to require a theory not to be reconciled with the sacred historian. A scientific journal of great reputation, edited at the Royal Institution, has made an honorable disclaimer of those theories which contradicted the Scriptures, and speaks in commendation of Mr. Penn." We subjoin the quotation which Mr. Watson gives from the "scientific journal" referred to.

"We are not inclined, even if we had time, to enter into the comparative merits of the fire and water fancies, miscalled theories; but we have certain old-fashioned prejudices, which, in these *enlightened* days of *scepticism* and infidelity, will no doubt be set down as mightily ridiculous, but which, nevertheless, induce us to pause before we acquiesce either in the one or the other. There is another mode of accounting for the present state of the earth's structure, on principles at least as rational, in a philosophical light, as either the Plutonian or Neptunian; and inasmuch as it is more consistent with, and founded on, sacred history, incomparably superior. (See Mr. Granville Penn's 'Comparative Estimate of the Mineral and Mosaical Geologies.')"

It may well be said that the "fire and water fancies" are "miscalled theories;" and it is with equal propriety that they are referred to "scepticism and infidelity."

CHAPTER VIII.

To chapter xx, of his "Theological Institutes," entitled, "Miscellaneous Objections Answered," Mr. Watson appends an extract from Mr. Penn's work on geology; it commences on p. 259 of vol. i. As the "Institutes" are not much read, save by theological students, and Mr. Penn's work on geology is little known, we have concluded to introduce the entire extract just here. We do so the more readily because it may be viewed as embodying Mr. Watson's views, as far as it goes, and because, while others seem determined to exclude the Scriptures from their geological investigations, we are fully convinced that it is only in the light of Scripture teaching that this subject can be safely and satisfactorily investigated. With the torch of revelation in his hand, and receiving that torch as from the hand of God, the man of science will investigate geological phenomena both with pleasure and profit, to himself and to others.

Mr. Watson introduces the extract thus: "Mr. Penn first controverts the notion of those geologists who think that the earth was originally a fluid mass; and as they plead the authority of Sir Isaac Newton, who is said to have concluded from its figure (an *obtuse spheroid*), that it was originally a yielding mass, Mr. Penn shows that this was only put hypothetically by him; and that he has laid it down expressly as his belief, not that there was first a chaotic ocean, and then a gradual process of first formations, but that 'God at the beginning formed all material things of such figures and properties as most conduced to the end for which he formed them;' and that he judged it to be unphilosophical to ascribe them to any mediate or secondary cause, such as laws of nature operating in chaos. Mr. Penn then proceeds to show, that, though what geologists call first formations may have the appearance of having been produced by a *process*, say of crystallization, or any other, that is no proof that they were not formed by the immediate act of God, as we are taught in the Scriptures; and he confirms this by examples from the *first formations* in the animal and vegetable kingdom, and contends that the first formations of the mineral kingdom must come under the same rule."

The fact is, minerals, vegetables, and animals are, alike, the work of God, whether he produces them instantly by his creative act, or gradually according to what are called the laws of nature. As for law, whether human or divine, *it produces nothing, it does nothing!* It is merely the rule by which the *producing* or *doing* agent is pleased to act. And when God produces anything according to the laws of nature, we have no reason to suppose that he makes it essentially different from what he made that same thing when he produced it by his creative act; on the contrary, we have reason to suppose that what is produced by the creative act is the *pattern*, and that what is produced according to the laws of nature is made like *that pattern.* For instance, when God produced almonds upon Aaron's rod in one night, and that while it lay in the tabernacle, without either sun or rain, they were similar, doubtless, to those which he produced in the course of the season according to what are called the laws of nature: and if a naturalist, ignorant of the fact that they were produced as above, had examined them, he would, doubtless, have decided that they were produced in the course of the season according to the known laws of nature. It is certain, however, that he would have been mistaken. Just so it is with those things which God *now* produces according to what are called the laws of nature; they are doubtless the same as those which he originally produced by his creative act, so much so that the naturalist would not discover any difference. And it is equally true that it is God that produces in the one case as really as in the other. The almond tree that grows in the most fertile garden in Judea could no more produce almonds without God than could the rods that were deposited in the tabernacle. And what is true of the almond, is equally true of anything, and everything, that God produced by his creative act originally; they were similar to the same genera and species as now produced according to the laws of nature. So that arguments drawn from the present *appearance* of minerals, vegetables, and animals, do not prove that they were produced *originally by a slow process.* All such arguments are built upon a mere hypothesis which has no foundation in truth, and are, consequently, without foundation. And as all the geological systems to which we object are built upon this hypothesis, it follows that they are all without foundation. The Scriptures teach us that God *created* and *formed* the originals by his fiat, *instantly*, not by a long, slow process, and that what he afterward produced, and now produces, by what are called the laws of nature, are similar to the originals, and that the instantly created and slowly formed productions are alike the work of God.

The following is the extract which Mr. Watson furnishes from Mr. Penn's geological work referred to above:

"If a bone of the *first created man* now remained, and were mingled with other bones pertaining to a *generated race*, and if it were to be submitted to the inspection and examination of an anatomist, what opinion and judgment would its *sensible phenomena* suggest respecting *the mode* of its *first formation*, and what would be his conclusion? If he were unapprized of its true origin, his mind would *see nothing* in its *sensible phenomena* but the laws of *ossification;* just as the mineral geologist '*sees nothing* in the *details* of the formation of minerals, but *precipitations, crystallizations*, and *dissolutions*.' (D'Aubuisson, i, pp. 326–7.) He would, therefore, naturally pronounce of this bone, as of all other bones, that its '*fibres were originally soft*,' until, in the shelter of the maternal womb, it acquired '*the hardness of a cartilage and then of a bone;* that this effect '*was not produced at once, or in a very short time*,' but '*by degrees;*' that, after birth, it increased in hardness '*by the continual addition of ossifying matter, until it ceased to grow at all*.'

"*Physically true* as this reasoning would appear, it would nevertheless be *morally* and *really false*. Why would it be false? Because it concluded, from *mere sensible phenomena*, to the *certainty of a fact* which would not be established by the evidence of sensible phenomena *alone;* namely, *the mode* of the first formation of the substance of created bone.

"Let us proceed from animal to *vegetable matter;* and let us consider the *first created tree*, under which the created man first reposed, and from which he gathered his first fruit. That tree must have had a *stem* or *trunk* through which the juices were conveyed from the root to the fruit, and by which it was able to sustain the branches upon which the fruit grew.

"If a portion of this *created tree* now remained, and if a section of its wood were to be mingled with other sections of *propagated trees*, and submitted to the inspection and examination of a naturalist, what opinion and judgment would its *sensible phenomena* suggest to him respecting *the mode* of its *first formation;* and what would be his conclusion? If he were unapprized of its true origin, his mind would *see nothing* in its *sensible phenomena* but laws of *lignification;* just as the mineral geologist '*sees nothing* in the *details* of the formations of primitive rock, but *precipitations, crystallizations*, and *dissolutions*.' He would, therefore naturally pronounce of it as of all other sections of wood, that its '*fibres*,' when they first issued from the seed, '*were soft and herbaceous;*' that they '*did not suddenly pass to the hardness of perfect wood*,' but '*after many years;*' that the hardness of their folds, '*which indicate the growth of each year*,' was therefore effected only '*by degrees;*' and that, 'since *nature* does nothing but by a progressive course, it is not surprising that its substance acquired its hardness *only by little and little*.'

"*Physically true* as the naturalist would here appear to reason, yet his reasoning, like that of the anatomist, would be *morally and really false*. And why would it be false? For the same reason, because he concluded from *mere sensible phenomena* to the *certainty of a fact* which could not be established by the evidence of sensible phenomena *alone;* namely, *the mode* of the first formation of the substance of created wood.

"There only now remains to be considered the *third* or *mineral* kingdom of this terrestrial system; and it appears probable to reason and philosophy, by *prima facie* evidence, that the principle determining the mode of first formations, in *two parts* of this *threefold* division of matter, must have equal authority in this *third part.* And, indeed, after the closest investigation of the subject, we can discover no ground whatever for supposing that this *third* part is exempted from the authority of that *common principle;* or that *physics* are a whit more competent to dogmatize concerning the *mode* of first formations, from the evidence of phenomena alone, in the *mineral* kingdom, than they have been found to be in the *animal* or *vegetable;* or to affirm, from the *indications* of the former, that the mode of its first formations was more gradual and tardy than those of the other two.

"Let us try this point, by proceeding with our comparison; and let us consider the first created *rock*, as we have considered the first created *bone* and wood; and let us ask, *what is rock*, in its nature and composition?

"To this question mineralogy replies; 'By the word *rock* we mean every *mineral mass* of such bulk as to be regarded an *essential part* of the structure of the globe.' (D'Aubuisson, i, p. 272.) 'We understand by the word *mineral*, a natural body, inorganic, solid, homogeneous, that is, composed of integrant molecules of the same substance.' (D'Aubuisson, i, p. 271.) 'We may, perhaps, pronounce that a mass is *essential*, when its displacement would occasion the *downfall* of other masses which are placed upon it.' (D'Aubuisson, i, p. 272.) 'Such are those lofty and ancient mountains, *the first and most solid bones*, as it were of this globe—*les premiers, les plus solides ossemens*—which have merited the name of *primitive*, because, scorning all support and all foreign mixture, they repose always upon bases similar to themselves, and comprise within their substance no matter but of the same nature.' (Saussure,

'Voyages des Alps,' Disc. Prel. pp. 6, 7.) 'These are the primordial mountains which traverse our continents in various directions, rising above the clouds, separating the basins of rivers one from another; serving, by means of their eternal snows, as reservoirs for feeding the springs, and forming in some measure the *skeleton*, or, as it were, the *rough framework* of the earth.' (Cuvier, sec. 7, p. 39.) 'These primitive masses are stamped with the character of a formation altogether crystalline, as if they were really the product of a tranquil precipitation.' (D'Aubuisson, ii, p. 5.)

"Had the mineral geology contented itself with this simple mineralogical statement, we should have thus argued concerning the crystalline phenomena of the first mineral formations, conformably to the principles which we have recognized. As the bone of the first man, and the wood of the first tree, whose solidity was essential for 'giving shape, firmness, and support' to their respective systems, were not, and could not have been, formed by the gradual processes of *ossification* and *lignification*, of which they nevertheless must have exhibited the sensible phenomena, or apparent indications; so, reason directs us to conclude, that *primitive rock*, whose *solidity* was equally essential for giving shape, firmness, and support to the mineral system of the globe, was not, and could not have been, formed by the gradual process of *precipitation* and *crystallization*, notwithstanding any sensible phenomena, apparently indicative of those processes which it may exhibit; but that in the mineral kingdom, as in the animal and vegetable kingdoms, the creating agent *anticipated*, in his formations by an immediate act, *effects*, whose sensible phenomena could not determine the mode of their formation; because the real mode was in direct contradiction to the apparent indications of the phenomena.

"But the mineral geology has not contented itself with that simple mineralogical statement, nor drawn the conclusion which we have drawn in conformity with the principles and in observance of the rules of Newton's philosophy. It affirms 'that the *characters* by which geology is written in the book of nature, in which it is to be studied, are *minerals*' (D'Aubuisson, Disc. Prel., p. 29); and it '*sees nothing*' in the book of nature but '*precipitations*, *crystallizations*, and *dissolutions*;' and therefore, because it *sees nothing else*, it concludes, without hesitation, from *crystalline phenomena* to *actual crystallization*. Thus, by attempting the impossibility of deducing a *universal principle*, viz., *the mode of first formation* from the analysis of *a single individual*, viz., *mineral matter*, separate from coördinate *animal* and *vegetable matter*, and concluding from that defective analysis to the *general law* of first formations, it set out with inadequate light, and it is no wonder that it ended in absolute darkness, for such is its *elemental chaos*, and its *chemical precipitation of this globe:* a doctrine so nearly resembling the exploded *atomic philosophy* of the Epicurean school, that it requires a very close and laborious inspection to discover a single feature by which they may be distinguished from each other."

Here Mr. Watson observes: "This argument is largely supported and illustrated in the work; and thus by referring first formations of every kind to an immediate act of God, those immense periods of time which geology demands for its chemical process are rendered unnecessary. From *first formations* Mr. Penn proceeds to oppose the notion that the earth has undergone many general revolutions, and thinks that all geological phenomena may be better explained by the Mosaic record, which confines those general revolutions to two. Mr. Penn's course of observation will be seen by the following recapitulation of the second and third parts of his work." ("Institutes," vol. i, p. 261.)

Mr. Penn goes on to show, "That this globe, so constructed at its origin, has undergone *two* and *only two* general changes or revolutions of its substance, each of which was caused by the immediate will, intelligence, and power of God, exercised upon the work which he had formed, and directing the laws or agencies which he had ordained within it.

"That, by the FIRST change or revolution [that of gathering the waters into one place and making the dry land appear], one portion or division of the surface of the globe was suddenly and violently fractured and depressed, in order to form, in the first instance, a receptacle or bed for the waters [hitherto] universally diffused over the surface, and to expose the other portion, that it might become a dwelling for animal life; but yet with an ulterior design that this first bed of the waters should eventually become the chief theatre of animal existence, by the portion first exposed experiencing a similar fracture and depression, and thus becoming in its turn the receptacle of the same waters, which should then be transfused into it, leaving their former receptacle void and dry.

"That this FIRST revolution took place before the existence, that is, before the creation of any organized beings.

"That the sea, collected into this vast fractured cavity of the globe surface, continued to occupy it during 1656 years [from the creation to the deluge], during which long period of time its waters acted in various modes, *chemical* and *mechanical*, upon the several soils and fragments which formed its bed, and marine organic matter, animal and vegetable, was generated and accumulated in vast abundance.

"That, after the expiration of these 1656 years, it pleased God, in a SECOND revolution, to execute his ulterior design, by repeating the amazing operation by which he had exposed the first earth, and by the disruption and depression of the first earth below the level of the bed of the first sea, to produce a new bed, into which the waters descended from their former bed, leaving it to become the theatre of the future generation of mankind.

"That THIS PRESENT EARTH WAS THAT FORMER BED.

"That it must, therefore, necessarily exhibit manifest and universal evidence of the vicissitudes which it has undergone, viz., of the vast apparent ruin occasioned by its first violent disruption and depression; of the presence and operation of the marine fluid during the long interval which succeeded, and of the action and effects of that fluid in its ultimate retreat.

"Within the limits of this *general scheme* all speculation must be confined which would aspire to the quality of *sound geology;* yet vast and sublime is the field which it lays open to exercise the intelligence and experience of sober and philosophical mineralogy and chemistry. Upon this legitimate ground, those many valuable writers who have unwarily lent their science to uphold and propagate the vicious doctrine of a chaotic geogony, may geologize with full security, and may there concur to promote that true advancement of *natural* philosophy which Newton holds to be inseparable from a proportionate advancement of the *moral.* They must thus at length succeed in perfecting a *true philosophical geology*, which never can exist unless the principle of Newton form the *foundation*, and the relation of Moses the *working plan.*"

Our own views of the geological theory here given, are somewhat correctly expressed in the quotation furnished by

Mr. Watson from the "scientific journal of great reputation," which quotation we have given above. The reader will observe that Mr. Penn attributes geological phenomena to three distinct causes: first, the creative act of the Almighty; second, the gathering together of the waters in connection with the work of the six days; third, the general deluge. This view is unquestionably Scriptural, and, consequently, perfectly safe; and that these three events, or causes, specified by God himself, are adequate to the production of the geological phenomena under consideration will, we think, be admitted by all: nor can this view be considered unreasonable, especially if we recognize God as having in view the ultimate end, or ends, specified by Mr. Penn; and this we certainly must recognize, for God not only *created* and *made* all, but he did so with reference to *specific* and *wise* ends. "God," says Sir Isaac Newton, "at the beginning formed all material things of such figures and properties as most conduced to the end for which he formed them." Whether the present earth was, in part or in whole, the bed of the waters during the antediluvian period, we do not pretend to say; certainly the conjecture is not an unreasonable one, and, to say the least, it is perfectly harmless. As to those who recognize all geological phenomena as resulting from what are called natural laws, and see nothing, as Mr. Penn observes, but *precipitations*, *crystallizations*, *dissolutions*, &c., we must be permitted to say to them as Jesus Christ said to similar theorists: "Ye do err, not knowing the Scriptures, nor the power of God." (Matt. xxii, 29.) Indeed, by such theorists God is not recognized at all; their theories are amongst the most godless of which we know anything. Those who recognize the inspiration of the Scriptures, and yet adopt such theories, try to bend the Scriptures to them; hence they would have us understand the days of Moses to be periods of inconceivable length: an interpretation which the sacred narrative will never admit of, and which is as dangerous as it is forced; dangerous, because if such a mode of interpretation be allowed, the Scriptures may be made to mean anything or nothing, and a license will thus be given to errorists to bend the sacred text as their erroneous theories may seem to require; dangerous and forced, because it not only affects the law of the Sabbath, but is utterly inadmissible, as the following quotation will show: "Remember the Sabbath day to keep it holy. Six days shalt thou labor, and do all thy work: but the seventh day is the Sabbath of the LORD thy God: in it thou shalt not do any work, thou, nor thy son, nor thy daughter, nor thy man servant nor thy maid servant, nor thy cattle, nor thy stranger that is within thy gates: for in six days the LORD made heaven and earth, the sea and all that in them is, and rested the seventh day. wherefore the LORD blessed the Sabbath day and hallowed it." (Exodus xx, 8–11.) Now, it is quite obvious that the "six days" during which "the Lord made heaven and earth," and "the seventh day" upon which he is said to have rested, are of equal length with the "six days" during which he commands man to work, and "the seventh day," or "Sabbath of the LORD," during which he commands him to rest, and "not do any work." Hence, if the former are periods of inconceivable duration, so are the latter, and, if so, God commands man to work during six periods of inconceivable duration, and to rest during one period equally long; and this command is enforced by the sanction of the moral law. That is, God commands man, on pain of his displeasure, to work, say, six millions of years without resting, and then rest one million of years, and "not do any work" during all that period, and his servants and children, yea and his cattle too, are to rest with him all that time; and all this notwithstanding the fact, that he has limited man's life to threescore years and ten! Now, if our geological theorists shrink from this conclusion, as of course they will, then they must simply give up their whole theory, at least so far as we have objected to it, or give up the Bible; for they cannot possibly hold both, seeing their teachings and those of the Bible are utterly irreconcilable. We earnestly advise them to hold to the Bible and give up the geological speculations; we believe the world can get along very well without the latter, but we know it cannot get along without the former.

It will be seen that in geological as in other theories which have passed under review, the grand error, which is the fruitful source of numerous other errors, consists in ignoring or denying the *supernatural*, and attributing everything to what are called natural laws; but the Scriptures recognize both, and clearly distinguish the one from the other. "In six days the Lord made heaven and earth, the sea and all that in them is." (Genesis ii, 1.) "By the word of the Lord were the heavens made; and all the host of them by the breath of his mouth." (Psal. xxxiii, 6.) It is clear that the work here specified is the effect of a cause purely *supernatural*. But "the heavens and the earth, and all the host of them," being produced as here specified, God established what are called natural laws for man's guidance, so that he might confidently expect given results from given causes, without which he would not know how or when to act, or what to expect, as the result of his action. The geological phenomena which we now witness are partly *supernatural*, and partly *natural* in their cause. Some were produced by the original *fiat* of the Almighty, and by supernatural interposition since then; and some have been produced according to what are called natural laws; but as the *natural* and the *supernatural* productions are similar, it is sometimes impossible to distinguish them; hence geologists greatly err when they attribute to the slow process of natural laws everything that is similar to what are known to have been produced in that way. But while we recognize geological phenomena as being both *natural* and *supernatural* in their cause, we recognize the salvation of fallen man as being purely *supernatural in its cause from first to last.* "For if there had been a law given which could have given life [to fallen man], verily righteousness should have been by the law." But there was no such law revealed before the fall; the supernatural remedy was introduced after the fall, and it is declared to be the only remedy the case would admit of; and every contrary supposition, or assumption, is declared to be antagonistic to this scheme: hence the apostle says, "for if righteousness *come* by the law, then Christ is dead in vain," that is, he died to no purpose if life could have been restored to fallen man by previously existing laws. By attending to this distinction between the *natural* and the *supernatural*, we will avoid many of the mistakes into which theologians and philosophers have fallen. And we may safely affirm that, where this distinction is properly recognized, infidelity and the various rationalistic and kindred schemes can have no existence.

CHAPTER IX.

Having shown that the supernatural phenomena recorded in the Bible are God's seals affixed to its teachings, and that they prove those teachings to be what they profess to be, we here subjoin "Leslie's Method with Deists," which, as an argument to prove that those phenomena are *facts*, not *fiction*, is, we believe, conclusive beyond the possibility of successful contradiction. So that when this is taken in connection with what we have said in the preceding pages, we hope it will be seen that *the Bible is complete in itself, both in teaching and evidence.*

Leslie's Method with Deists: wherein the truth of the Christian religion is demonstrated, in a letter to a friend.

CHRISTIANITY DEMONSTRATED.

Dear Sir:—You are desirous, you inform me, to receive from me some one topic of reason which shall demonstrate the truth of the Christian religion, and at the same time distinguish it from the impostures of Mohammed and the heathen deities, that our deists may be brought to this test, and be obliged either to renounce their reason, and the common reason of mankind, or to admit the clear proof, from reason, of the revelation of Christ; which must be such a proof as no impostor can pretend to, otherwise it will not prove Christianity not to be an imposture. And you cannot but imagine, you add, that there must be such a proof, because every truth is in itself one: and therefore one reason for it, if it be a true reason, must be sufficient; and, if sufficient, better than many, because multiplicity creates confusion, especially in weak judgments.

Sir, you have imposed a hard task upon me: I wish I could perform it. For, though every truth be one, yet our sight is so feeble that we cannot always come to it directly, but by many inferences and layings of things together. But I think that in the case before us there is such a proof as you desire, and I will set it down as shortly and as plainly as I can.

I suppose, then, that the truth of the Christian doctrines will be sufficiently evinced if the matters of fact recorded of Christ in the gospels are proved to be true; for his miracles, if true, established the truth of what he delivered. The same may be said with regard to Moses. If he led the children of Israel through the Red Sea, and did such other wonderful things as are recorded of him in the book of Exodus, it must necessarily follow that he was sent by God; these being the strongest evidences we can require, and which every deist will confess he would admit if he himself had witnessed their performance. So that the stress of this cause will depend upon the proof of these matters of fact.

With a view, therefore, to this proof, I shall proceed,

I. To lay down such marks, as to the truth of matters of fact in general, that, where they all meet, such matters of fact cannot be false: and,

II. To show that they all do meet in the matters of fact of Moses and of Christ, and do not meet in those reported of Mohammed and of the heathen deities, nor can possibly meet in any imposture whatsoever.

I. The marks are these :—

1. That the fact be such as men's *outward senses* can judge of:

2. That it be performed *publicly*, in the presence of witnesses:

3. That there be *public monuments* and *actions* kept up in memory of it: and

4. That such monuments and actions shall be established, and commence, *at the time of the fact.*

The first two of these marks make it impossible for any false fact to be imposed upon men at the time when it was said to be done, because every man's senses would contradict it. For example: suppose I should pretend that, yesterday, I divided the Thames, in the presence of all the people of London, and led the whole city over to Southwark on dry land, the waters standing like walls on each side: it would be morally impossible for me to convince the people of London that this was true, when every man, woman, and child could contradict me, and affirm that they had not seen the Thames so divided, nor been led over to Southwark on dry land. I take it, then, for granted (and, I apprehend, with the allowance of all the deists in the world) that no such imposition could be put upon mankind at the time when such matter of fact was said to be done.

"But," it may be urged, "the fact might be invented when the men of that generation in which it was said to be done were all past and gone; and the credulity of after ages might be induced to believe that things had been performed in earlier times which had not!"

From this, the two latter marks secure us as much as the first two in the former case. For whenever such a fact was invented, if it was stated that not only public monuments of it remained, but likewise that public actions or observances had been kept up in memory of it ever since, the deceit must be detected by no such monuments appearing, and by the experience of every man, woman, and child, who must know that no such actions or observances had ever taken place. For example: suppose I should now fabricate a story of something done a thousand years ago. I might perhaps get a few persons to believe me; but if I were farther to add, that from that day to this every man, at the age of twelve years, had a joint of his little finger cut off in memory of it, and that ofcourse every man then living actually wanted a joint of that finger, and vouched this institution in confirmation of its truth—it would be morally impossible for me to gain credit in such a case, because every man then living would contradict me as to the circumstance of cutting off a joint of the finger; and that, being an essential part of my original matter of fact, must prove the whole to be false.

II. Let us now come to the second point, and show that all these marks do meet in the matters of fact of Moses and of Christ, and do not meet in those reported of Mohammed and of the heathen deities, nor can possibly meet in any imposture whatsoever.

As to Moses, he, I take it for granted, could not have persuaded six hundred thousand men that he had brought them out of Egypt by the Red Sea, fed them forty years with miraculous manna, &c., if it had not been true: because the senses of every man who was then alive would have contradicted him. So that here are the first two marks.

For the same reason it would have been equally impossible for him to have made them receive his five books as true which related all these as done before their eyes, if they had not been so done. Observe how positively he speaks to them: "And know you this day, for I speak not with your children, which have not known, and which have not seen the chastisement of the Lord your God, his greatness, his mighty hand, and his stretched-out arm, and his miracles; but your eyes have seen all the great acts of the Lord which he did." (Deut. xi, 2–7.) Hence we must admit it to be impossible that these books, if written by Moses in support of an imposture, could have been put upon the people who were alive at the time when such things were said to be done.

"But they might have been written," it may be urged, "in some age after Moses, and published as his!"

To this I reply that, if it were so, it was impossible they should have been received as such; because they speak of themselves as delivered by Moses, and kept in the ark from his time (Deut. xxxi, 24–26), and state that a copy of them was likewise deposited in the hands of the king, "that he might learn to fear the Lord his God, to keep all the words of this law and these statutes, to do them." (Deut. xvii, 19.) Here these books expressly represent themselves as being not only the civil history, but also the established municipal law of the Jews, binding the king as well as the people. In whatever age, therefore, after Moses they might have been forged it was impossible they should have gained any credit, because they could not then have been found either in the ark, or with the king, or anywhere else: and, when they were first published, every body must know that they had never heard of them before.

And they could still less receive them as their book of statutes, and the standing law of the land, by which they had all along been governed. Could any man, at this day, invent a set of acts of parliament for England, and make it pass upon the nation as the only book of statutes which they had ever known? As impossible was it for these books, if written in any age after Moses, to have been received for what they declare themselves to be, that is, the municipal law of the *Jews;* and for any man to have persuaded that people that they had owned them as their code of statutes from the time of Moses, that is, before they had ever heard of them! Nay, more: they must instantly have forgotten their former laws if they could receive these books as such; and as such only could they receive them, because such they vouched themselves to be. Let me ask the deists but one short question: "Was a book of sham laws ever palmed upon any nation since the world began?" If not, with what face can they say this of the law books of the Jews? Why will they affirm that of them which they admit never to have happened in any other instance?

But they must be still more unreasonable, for the books of Moses have an ampler demonstration of their truth than even other law books have; as they not only contain the laws themselves, but give an historical account of their institution and regular fulfilment: of the passover, for instance, in memory of their supernatural protection upon the slaying of the first-born of Egypt; the dedication of the first-born of Israel, both of man and beast; the preservation of Aaron's rod, which budded, of the pot of manna, and of the brazen serpent, which remained till the days of Hezekiah. (2 Kings, xviii, 4, &c.) And, besides these memorials of particular occurrences, there were other solemn observances, in general memory of their deliverance out of Egypt, &c., as their annual expiations, their new moons, their sabbaths, and their ordinary sacrifices; so that there were yearly, monthly, weekly, and daily recognitions of these things. The same books likewise farther inform us that the tribe of Levi were appointed and consecrated by God as his ministers, by whom alone these institutions were to be celebrated: that it was death for any others to approach the altar; that their high priest wore a brilliant mitre and magnificent robes, with the miraculous Urim and Thummim in his breastplate; that at his word all the people were to go out, and to come in; that these Levites were also their judges, even in all civil causes, &c.

Hence, too, therefore, in whatever age after Moses they might have been forged, it was impossible they should have gained any credit, unless indeed the fabricators could have made the whole nation believe, *in spite of their invariable experience to the contrary*, that they had received these books long before from their fathers; had been taught them when they were children, and had taught them to their own children; that they had been circumcised themselves, and had circumcised their families, and uniformly observed their whole minute detail of sacrifices and ceremonies; that they had never eaten any swine's flesh, or other prohibited meats; that they had a splendid tabernacle, with a regular priesthood to administer in it, confined to one particular tribe, and a superintendent high priest, whose death alone could deliver those that had fled to the cities of refuge; that these priests were their ordinary judges, even in civil matters, &c. But this would surely have been impossible if none of these things had been practised; and it would consequently have been impossible to circulate as true a set of books which affirmed that they had practised them, and upon that practice rested their own pretensions to acceptance. So that here are the two latter marks.

"But," to advance to the utmost degree of supposition,

it may be urged, "These things might have been practised prior to this alleged forgery; and those books only deceived the nation by making them believe that they were practised in memory of such and such occurrences as were then invented!"

In this hypothesis, however groundless, the same impossibilities press upon our notice as before: for it implies that the Jews had previously kept these observances in memory of nothing, or without knowing why they kept them; whereas, in all their particulars, they strikingly express their original; as the passover, instituted in memory of God's passing over the children of the Israelites when he slew the first-born of Egypt, &c.

Let us admit, however contrary both to probability and to matter of fact, that they did not know why they kept these observances; yet was it possible to persuade them that they were kept in memory of something which they had never heard of before? For example: suppose I should now forge some romantic story of strange things done a long while ago; and, in confirmation of this, should endeavor to convince the Christian world that they had regularly, from that period to this, kept holy the first day of the week in memory of such or such a man: a Cæsar, or a Mohammed; and had all been baptized in his name, and sworn by it upon the very book which I had then fabricated, and which of course they had never seen before in their public courts of judicature; that this book likewise contained their law, civil and ecclesiastical, which they had ever since his time acknowledged, and no other:—I ask any deist whether he thinks it possible that such a cheat could be received as the gospel of Christians, or not? The same reason holds with regard to the books of Moses, and must hold with regard to every book which contains matters of fact accompanied by the abovementioned four marks: for these marks, together, secure mankind from imposition, with regard to any false fact, as well in after ages as at the time when it was said to be done.

Let me produce, as another and a familiar illustration, the *Stonehenge* of Salisbury Plain. Almost everybody has seen or heard of it; and yet nobody knows by whom or in memory of what it was set up.

Now, suppose I should write a book to-morrow, and state in it that these huge stones were erected by a Cæsar or a Mohammed, in memory of such and such of their actions; and should further add, that this book was written at the time when those actions were performed, and by the doers themselves, or by eye-witnesses; and had been constantly received as true, and quoted by authors of the greatest credit in regular succession ever since; that it was well known in England, and even enjoined by act of parliament to be taught our children, and that we accordingly did teach it our children, and had been taught it ourselves when we were children;—would this, I demand of any deist, pass current in England? Or, rather, should not I, or any other person who might insist upon its reception, instead of being believed, be considered insane?

Let us compare, then, this rude structure with the Stonehenge, as I may call it, or "twelve stones" set up at Gilgal, Josh. iv. 6. It is there said that the reason why they were set up was, that when the children of the Jews, in after ages, should ask their meaning, it should be told them, chap. iv, 20–22. And the thing in memory of which they were set up, the passage over Jordan, was such as could not possibly have been imposed upon that people at the time when it was said to be done: it was not less miraculous, and from the previous notice, preparations, and other striking circumstances of its performance, chap. iii, 5, 15, still more unassailable by the petty cavils of infidel sophistry, than their passage through the Red Sea.

Now, to form our argument, let us suppose that there never was any such thing as that passage over Jordan; that these stones at Gilgal had been set up on some unknown occasion; and that some designing man, in an after age, invented this book of Joshua; affirmed that it was written at the time of that imaginary event by Joshua himself, and adduced this pile of stones as a testimony of its truth:—would not everybody say to him, "We know this pile very well, but we never before heard of this reason for it, nor of this book of Joshua. Where has it lain concealed all this while? and where and how came you, after so long a period, to find it? Besides, it informs us that this passage over Jordan was solemnly directed to be taught our children from age to age; and, to that end, that they were always to be instructed in the meaning of this particular monument; but we were never taught it ourselves when we were children, nor did we ever teach it to our children. And it is in the highest degree improbable that such an emphatic ordinance should have been forgotten during the continuance of so remarkable a pile of stones, set up expressly for the purpose of preserving its remembrance."

If, then, for these reasons, no such fabrication could be put upon us as to the stones in Salisbury Plain, how much less could it succeed as to the stonage at Gilgal? If, where we are ignorant of the true origin of a mere naked monument, such a sham origin cannot be imposed, how much less practicable would it be to impose upon us in actions and observances which we celebrate in memory of what we actually know; to make us forget what we have regularly commemorated; and to persuade us that we have constantly kept such and such institutions with reference to something which we never heard of before; that is, that we knew something before we knew it! And if we find it thus impossible to practise deceit, even in cases which have not the above four marks, how much more impossible must it be that any deceit should be practised in cases in which all these four marks meet!

In the matters of fact of Christ likewise, as well as in those of Moses, these four marks are to be found. The reasoning, indeed, which has already been advanced with respect to the Old Testament, is generally applicable to the New. The miracles of Christ, like those of Moses, were such as men's *outward senses* could judge of, and were performed *publicly*, in the presence of those to whom the history of them, contained in the gospel, was addressed. And it is related that "about three thousand" at one time, Acts ii, 41, and about "five thousand" at another, iv, 4, were converted in consequence of what they themselves saw and heard, in matters where it was impossible that they should have been deceived. Here, therefore, were the first two marks.

And with regard to the latter two, baptism and the Lord's supper were instituted as memorials of certain things, not in after ages, but *at the time* when these things were said to be done; and have been strictly observed, *from that time to this*, without interruption. Christ himself also ordained apostles, &c., to preach and administer his ordinances, and to govern his church, "even unto the end of the world." Now the Christian ministry is as notorious a matter of fact among us as the setting apart of the tribe of Levi was among the Jews; and as the era and object of their appointment are part of the gospel narrative, if that narrative had been a fiction of some subsequent age at the time of its fabrication no such order of men could have been found, which would have effectually given the lie to the whole story. And the truth of the matters of fact of Christ being no otherwise asserted than as there were at the time (whenever the deist will suppose the gospel to have been fabricated) public ordinances and a public ministry of his institution to dispense them, and it being impossible, upon this hypothesis, that there could be any such things then in existence, we must admit it to be equally impossible that the forgery should have been successful. Hence it was as impossible to deceive mankind, in respect to these matters of fact, by inventing them in after ages, as at the time when they were said to be done.

The matters of fact reported of Mohammed and of the heathen deities do all want some of these four marks, by which the certainty of facts is established. Mohammed himself, as he tells us in his Koran (vi, &c.), pretended to no miracles; and those which are commonly related of him pass, even among his followers, for ridiculous legends, and as such are rejected by their scholars and philosophers. They have not either of the first two marks; for his converse with the moon, his night journey from Mecca to Jerusalem, and thence to heaven, &c., were not performed before any witnesses, nor was the tour indeed of a nature to admit human attestation; and to the two latter they do not even affect to advance any claim.

The same may be affirmed, with little variation, of the stories of the heathen deities: of Mercury's stealing sheep, Jupiter's transforming himself into a bull, &c., besides the absurdity of such degrading and profligate adventures. And accordingly we find that the more enlightened pagans themselves considered them as fables involving a mystical meaning, of which several of their writers have endeavored to give us the explication. It is true these gods had their priests, their feasts, their games, and other public ceremonies; but all these want the fourth mark, of commencing *at the time* when the things which they commemorate were said to have been done. Hence they cannot secure mankind in subsequent ages from imposture, as they furnish no internal means of detection at the period of the forgery. The *Bacchanalia*, for example, and other heathen festivals, were established long after the events to which they refer; and the priests of Juno, Mars, &c., were not ordained by those imaginary deities, but appointed by others in some after age, and are therefore no evidence to the truth of their preternatural achievements.

To apply what has been said:

We may challenge all the deists in the world to show any fabulous action accompanied by these four marks. The thing is impossible. The histories of the Old and New Testaments never could have been received if they had not been true; because the priesthoods of Levi and of Christ, the observance of the Sabbath, the passover, and circumcision, and the ordinances of baptism and the Lord's supper, &c., are there represented as descending uninterruptedly from the times of their respective institution. And it would have been as impossible to persuade men in after ages that they had been circumcised or baptized, and celebrated passovers, Sabbaths, and other ordinances, under the ministration of a certain order of priests, if they had done none of those things, as to make them believe at the time, without any real foundation, that they had gone through seas on dry land, seen the dead raised, &c. But without such a persuasion it was impossible that either the law or the gospel could have been received. And the truth of the matters of fact of each being no otherwise asserted than as such public ceremonies had been previously practised, their certainty is established upon the FULL CONVICTION OF THE SENSES OF MANKIND.

I do not say that everything which wants these four marks is false; but that everything which has them all must be true.

I can have no doubt that there was such a man as Julius Cæsar; that he conquered at Pharsalia, and was killed in the senate house, though neither his actions nor his assassination be commemorated by any public observances. But this shows that the matters of fact of Moses and of Christ have come down to us better certified than any other whatsoever. And yet our deists, who would consider any one as hopelessly irrational that should offer to deny the existence of Cæsar, value themselves as the only men of profound sense and judgment for ridiculing the histories of Moses and of Christ, though guarded by infallible marks, which that of Cæsar wants.

Besides, the nature of the subject would of itself lead to a more minute examination of the one than of the other: for of what consequence is it to me, or to the world, whether there ever was such a man as Cæsar: whether he conquered at Pharsalia, and was killed in the senate house, or not? But our eternal welfare is concerned in the truth of what is recorded in the Scriptures; whence they would naturally be more narrowly scrutinized when proposed for acceptance.

How unreasonable, then, is it to reject matters of fact so important, so sifted, and so attested; and yet to think it absurd, even to madness, to deny other matters of fact, which have not the thousandth part of their evidence, have had comparatively little investigation, and are of no consequence at all!

THE TRUTH OF CHRISTIANITY DEMONSTRATED.

To the preceding four marks, which are common to the matters of fact of Moses and of Christ, I now proceed to subjoin four additional marks; the three last of which, no matter of fact, how true soever, either has had, or can have, except that of Christ.

This will obviously appear if it be considered,

5. That the book which relates the facts *contains likewise the laws* of the people to whom it belongs:

6. That Christ was previously announced, for that very period, by a long train of *prophecies;* and,

7. Still more peculiarly prefigured by *types*, both of a circumstantial and personal nature, from the earliest ages; and,

8. That the facts of Christianity are such as to make it impossible for either their relaters or hearers to believe them, if false, without supposing a *universal deception of the senses of mankind.*

The *fifth mark*, which has been subordinately discussed in the former part of this tract in such a manner as to supersede the necessity of dwelling upon it in this, renders it impossible for any one to have imposed such a book upon any people. For example: suppose I should forge a code of laws for Great Britain, and publish it next term; could I hope to persuade the judges, lawyers, and people, that this was their genuine statute book, by which all their causes had been determined in the public courts for so many centuries past? Before they could be brought to this, they must totally forget their established laws, which they had so laboriously committed to memory, and so familiarly quoted in every day's practice, and believe that this new book, which they had never seen before, was that old book which had been pleaded so long in Westminster Hall, which had been so often printed, and of which the originals are now so carefully preserved in the Tower.

This applies strongly to the books of Moses, in which, not only the history of the Jews, but likewise their whole law, secular and ecclesiastical, was contained. And though, from the early extension and destined universality of the Christian system, it could not, without unnecessary confusion, furnish a uniform civil code to all its various followers, who were already under the government of laws in some degree adapted to their respective climates and characters, yet was it intended as the spiritual guide of the new church. And in this respect this mark is still stronger with regard to the gospel than even to the books of Moses; inasmuch as it is easier (however hard) to imagine the substitution of an entire statute-book in one particular nation, than that all the nations of Christendom should have unanimously conspired in the forgery. But without such a conspiracy such a forgery could never have succeeded, as the gospel universally formed a regular part of their daily public offices.

But I hasten to the *sixth mark*, namely, *prophecy*.

The great fact of Christ's coming was previously announced to the *Jews*, in the Old Testament, "by all the holy prophets which have been since the world began," Luke i, 70.

The first promise upon the subject was made to Adam immediately after the fall, Gen. iii, 15. Compare Col. ii, 15, and Heb. ii. 14.

He was again repeatedly promised to Abraham, Gen. xii, 3; xviii, 18, and xxii, 18; Gal. iii, 16; to Isaac, Gen. xxvi, 4; and to Jacob, Gen. xxviii, 14.

Jacob expressly prophesied of him under the appellation of "Shiloh," or *Him that was to be sent*, Gen. xlix. 10.

Balaam, also, with the voice of inspiration, pronounced him "the Star of Jacob and the sceptre of Israel," Num. xxiv, 17. Moses spoke of him as One "greater than himself," Deut. xviii, 15, 18, 19; Acts iii, 22; and Daniel hailed his arrival under the name of "Messiah the Prince," chap. ix, 25.

It was foretold that he should be born of a virgin, Isa. vii, 14; in the city of Bethlehem, Micah v, 2; of the seed of Jesse, Isa. xi, 1, 10; that he should lead a life of poverty and suffering, Psa. xxii; inflicted upon him, "not for himself," Dan. ix, 26, but for the sins of others, Isa. liii; and, after a short confinement in the grave, should rise again, Psa. xvi, 10; Acts ii, 27, 31, and xiii, 35, 37; that he "should sit upon the throne of David forever," and be called "the mighty God," Isa. ix, 6, 7; "the Lord our righteousness," Jer. xxxiii, 16; "Immanuel, that is, God with us," Isa. vii. 14; Matt. i, 23; and by David himself, whose son he was according to the flesh, "Lord," Psa. cx, 1; applied to Christ by himself, Matt. xxii, 44, and by Peter, Acts ii, 34.

The time of his incarnation was to be before "the sceptre should depart from Judah," Gen. xlix, 10; during the continuance of the second temple, Hag. ii, 7, 9, and within seventy weeks, or 490 days, that is, according to the constant interpretation of prophecy, 490 years from its erection, Dan. ix, 24.

From these, and many other predictions, the coming of Christ was at all times the general expectation of the Jews, and fully matured at the time of his actual advent, as may be inferred from the number of false messiahs who appeared about that period.

That he was likewise the expectation of the Gentiles (in conformity to the prophecies of Gen. xxix, 10, and Hag. ii,

7, where the terms "people" and "nations" denote the heathen world), is evinced by the coming of the wise men from the East, &c.; a story which would, of course, have been contradicted by some of the individuals so disgracefully concerned in it, if the fact of their arrival, and the consequent massacre of the infants in and about Bethlehem had not been fresh in every one's memory: by them, for instance, who afterward suborned false witnesses against Christ, and gave large money to the soldiers to conceal, if possible, the event of his resurrection; or them who, in still later days, everywhere zealously "spake against" the tenets and practices of his rising church.

All over the East, indeed, there was a general tradition, that *about that time a king of the* Jews *would be born, who should govern the whole earth.* This prevailed so strongly at Rome, a few months before the birth of Augustus, that the senate made a decree to expose all the children born that year; but the execution of it was eluded by a trick of some of the senators, who, from the pregnancy of their wives, were led to hope that they might be the fathers of the promised prince. Its currency is also recorded with a remarkable identity of phrase, by the pens of Suetonius and Tacitus. Now, that in this there was no collusion between the Chaldeans, Romans, and Jews, is sufficiently proved by the desperate methods suggested, or carried into effect, for its discomfiture. Nor, in fact, is it practicable for whole nations of contemporary (and still less, if possible, for those of successive) generations to concert a story perfectly harmonious in all its minute accompaniments of time, place, manner, and other circumstances.

In addition to the above general predictions of the coming, life, death, and resurrection of Christ, there are others which foretell still more strikingly several particular incidents of the gospel narrative; instances unparalleled in the whole range of history, and which could have been foreseen by God alone. They were certainly not foreseen by the human agents concerned in their execution, or they would never have contributed to the fulfilment of prophecies referred even by themselves to the Messiah, and therefore verifying the divine mission of him whom they crucified as an impostor.

Observe, then, how literally many of these predictions were fulfilled. For example: read Psa. lxix, 21, "They gave me gall to eat, and vinegar to drink;" and compare Matt. xxvii, 34, "They gave him vinegar to drink, mingled with gall." Again, it is said, Psa. xxii, 16–18, "They pierced my hands and my feet. They part my garments among them, and cast lots upon my vesture;" * as if it had

* The soldiers did not tear his coat, because it was *without seam, woven from the top throughout*, and therefore they *cast lots for it*. But this was entirely accidental. With the passage in the Psalms, as Romans, they were not likely to be acquainted. The same remark applies to the next instance, from Zechariah.

And here it may be suggested (in reply to those who insidiously magnify "the power of chance, the ingenuity of accommodation, and the industry of research," as chiefly supporting the credit of obscure prophecy), that greater plainness would have enabled wicked men, as free agents, to prevent its accomplishment, when obviously directed against themselves. The Jews not understanding what Christ meant by his "lifting up," John viii, 28; xii, 32, 33; and not knowing that he had foretold his crucifixion to his apostles, Matt. xx, 19, instead of finally stoning him,—the death appointed by their law, Lev. xxiv, 16, for blasphemy, Matt. xxvi, 65; more than once menaced against the Saviour, John viii, 59; x, 33; and actually inflicted upon Stephen, Acts vii, 58, for that offence,—unconsciously delivered him to the predicted Roman cross. Again: the piercing of his side was no part of the Roman sentence, but merely to ascertain his being dead, previously to taking him down from the cross; "that the body might not remain there on the Sabbath day," which commenced that been written *after*, John xix, 23, 24. It is predicted, likewise, Zech. xii, 10, "They shall look upon me whom they have pierced;" and we are told, John xix, 34, that "one of the soldiers with a spear pierced his side."

Compare also Psa. xxii, 7, 8, "All they that see me laugh me to scorn: they shoot out their lips, and shake their heads, saying, He trusted in God that he would deliver him: let him deliver him if he will have him," with Matt. xxvii, 39, 41, 43, "And they that passed by reviled him, wagging their heads, and saying, Come down from the cross. Likewise also the chief priests, mocking him, with the scribes and elders, said, He trusted in God; let him deliver him now, if he will have him; for he said, I am the Son of God." His very price, and the mode of laying out the money, previously specified, Zech. ix, 13, are historically stated by Matthew, in perfect correspondence with the prophet, chap. xxvii, 6, 7. And his riding into Jerusalem upon an ass, predicted, Zech. ix, 9, and referred by one of the most learned of the Jewish rabbis to the Messiah, is recorded by the same inspired historian, chap. xxi, 9. Lastly, it was foretold that "he should make his grave with the wicked, and with the rich in his death," Isa. liii, 9; or, as Dr. Lowth translates the passage, "His grave was appointed with the wicked, but with the rich man was his tomb;" which prediction was precisely verified by the very improbable incidents of his being crucified *between two thieves*, Matt. xxvii, 38, and afterward *laid in the tomb of the rich man of* Arimathea, Matt. xxvii, 57, 60.

Thus do the prophecies of the Old Testament, without variation or ambiguity, refer to the person and character

evening, a few hours after the crucifixion. From his early *giving up the ghost*, however, it was not necessary that "a bone of him should be broken," Exod. xii, 46; Num. ix, 12; Psa. xxxiv, 20; like those of the two thieves, his fellow sufferers, John xix, 32, 36.

of Christ. His own predictions in the New demand a few brief observations.

Those relating to the destruction of Jerusalem, which specified that it should be "laid even with the ground," and "not one stone be left upon another," Luke ix, 44, "before that generation passed," Matt. xxiv, 34, were fulfilled in a most surprisingly literal manner, the very foundations of the temple being ploughed up by Turnus Rufus. In another remarkable prophecy he announced the many false messiahs that should come after him, and the ruin in which their followers should be involved, Matt. xxvi, 25, 26. That great numbers actually assumed that holy character before the final fall of the city, and led the people into the wilderness to their destruction, we learn from Josephus, Antiq. Jud. xviii, 12 ; xx, 6, and B. J. viii, 31. Nay, such was their wretched infatuation, that under this delusion they rejected the offers of Titus, who courted them to peace, Id. B. J. vii, 12.

It will be sufficient barely to mention his foretelling the dispersion of that unhappy nation, and the triumph of his gospel over *the gates of hell*, under every possible disadvantage,—himself low and despised, his immediate associates only twelve, and those illiterate and unpolished, and his adversaries the allied powers, prejudices, habits, interests, and appetites of mankind.

But the *seventh mark* is still more peculiar, if possible, to Christ than even that of prophecy. For whatever may be weakly pretended with regard to the oracular predictions of Delphi or Dodona, the heathens never affected to prefigure any future event by *types* or resemblances of the fact, consisting of analogies either in individuals, or in sensible institutions directed to be continued, till the antitype itself should make its appearance.

These types, in the instance of Christ, were of a twofold nature, *circumstantial* and *personal.*

Of the *former* kind (not to notice the general rite of sacrifice) may be produced, as examples, 1. *The passover*, appointed in memory of that great night when the destroying angel, who slew all "the first-born of Egypt," passed over those houses upon whose door-posts the blood of the paschal lamb was sprinkled, and directed to be eaten with what the apostle, 1 Cor. v, 7, 8, calls "the unleavened bread of sincerity and truth." 2. *The annual expiation*, in two respects: first, as the high-priest entered into the holy of holies (representing heaven, Exod. xxv, 40; Heb. ix, 24) with the blood of the sacrifice, whose body was burned without the camp; "wherefore Jesus also, that he might sanctify the people with his own blood, suffered without the gate," Heb. xiii, 12; and "after he had offered one sacrifice for sin, for ever sat down at the right hand of God," Heb. x, 12; and, secondly, as "all the iniquity of the children of Israel was put upon the head" of the scape goat, Lev. xvi, 21. 3. *The brazen serpent*, by looking up to which the people were cured of the stings of the fiery serpents; and whose "lifting up" was, by Christ himself, interpreted as emblematical of his being lifted up on the cross, John iii, 14. 4. *The manna*, which represented "the bread of life, that came down from heaven," John vi, 31–35. 5. *The rock*, whence the waters flowed, to supply drink in the wilderness; "and that rock was Christ," 1 Cor. x, 4. 6. *The Sabbath*, "a shadow of Christ," Col. ii, 16, 17: and, as a figure of his eternal rest, denominated "a sign of the perpetual covenant," Exod. xxxi, 16, 17; Ezek. xx, 12, 20. And, lastly, to omit others, *the temple*, where alone the shadowy sacrifices were to be offered, because Christ, "the body," was to be offered there himself.

Of *personal types*, likewise, I shall confine myself to such as are so considered in the New Testament.

1. *Adam*, between whom and Christ a striking series of relations is remarked, Rom. v, 12–21, and 1 Cor. xv, 45–49. 2. *Noah*, who was "saved by water; the like figure whereunto, even baptism, doth now save us, by the resurrection of Jesus Christ," 1 Pet. iii, 20, 21. 3. *Melchisedek*, king of Salem, who was made "like unto the Son of God, a priest continually," Heb. vii, 3. 4. *Abraham*, "the heir of the world," Rom. iv, 13, "in whom all the nations of the earth are blessed," Gen. xviii, 18. 5. *Isaac*, in his birth and intended sacrifice, whence also his father received him in a figure, Heb. xi, 19, that is, of the resurrection of Christ. He, too, was the promised seed, Gen. xxi, 12, and Gal. iii, 16, in whom all the nations of the earth were to be blessed, Gen. xxii, 18. 6. *Jacob*, in his vision of the ladder, Gen. xxviii, 12, and John 1, 51, and his wrestling with the angel; whence he, and after him the church, obtained the name of Israel, Gen. xxxii, 24, and Matt. xi, 21. The *Gentile* world also, like Jacob, gained the blessing and heirship from their elder brethren, the Jews. 7. *Moses*, Deut. xviii, 18, and John i, 45, in redeeming the children of Israel out of Egypt. 8. *Joshua*, called also Jesus, Heb. iv, 8, in acquiring for them the possession of the Holy Land, and as lieutenant to the "captain of the host of the Lord," Josh. v. 14. 9. *David*, Psa. xvi, 10, and Acts ii, 25–35, upon whose throne Christ is said to sit, Isa. ix, 7, and by whose name he is frequently designated, Hos. iii, 5 &c., in his pastoral, regal, and prophetical capacity. 10. *Jonah*, in his dark imprisonment of three days, applied by Christ to himself, Matt. xii, 40.

The eighth *mark* is, that the facts of Christianity are such as to make it impossible for either the relaters or the hearers to believe them, if false, without supposing a universal deception of the senses of mankind.

For they were related by the doers, or by eye-witnesses, to those who themselves likewise either were or might have been present, and undoubtedly knew many that were present, at their performance. To this circumstance, indeed, both Christ and his apostles both often appeal. And they were of such a nature as wholly to exclude every chance of imposition. What juggler could have given sight to him "that was born blind;" have fed five thousand hungry guests with "five loaves and two fishes;" or have raised one, who had been "four days buried," from his grave?

When, then, we add to this, that none of the Jewish or Roman persecutors of Christianity, to whom its first teachers frequently referred as witnesses of those facts, ever ventured to deny them; that no apostate disciple, under the fear of punishment, or the hope of reward, not even the artful and accomplished Julian himself, ever pretended to detect them; that neither learning nor ingenuity, in the long lapse of so many years, has been able to show their falsehood; though for the first three centuries after their promulgation the civil government strongly stimulated hostile inquiry; and that their original relaters, after lives of uninterrupted hardship, joyfully incurred death in defence of their truth,—we cannot imagine the possibility of a more perfect or abundant demonstration.

It now rests with the deists, if they would vindicate their claim to the self-bestowed title of "*men of reason*," to adduce some matters of fact of former ages, which they allow to be true, possessing evidence superior, or even similar, to those of Christ. This, however, it must at the same time be observed, would be far from proving the matters of fact respecting Christ to be false; but certainly without this they cannot reasonably assert that their own facts alone, so much less powerfully attested, are true.

Let them produce their Cæsar, or Mohammed,

1. Performing a fact, of which men's *outward senses* can judge:

2. *Publicly*, in the presence of witnesses:

3. In memory of which *public monuments and actions* are kept up:

4. Instituted and commencing *at the time of the fact:*

5. Recorded likewise in a set of books, addressed to the identical people before whom it was performed, and containing their *whole code of civil and ecclesiastical laws:*

6. As the work of one previously announced for that very period by a long train of *prophecies:*

7. And still more peculiarly prefigured by *types*, both of a circumstantial and personal nature, from the earliest ages: and,

8. Of such a character as made it impossible for either the relaters or hearers to believe it, if false, without supposing a *universal deception of the senses of mankind.*

Farther: let them display, in its *professed* eye-witnesses, similar *proofs of veracity;* in some *doctrines* founded upon it, and *unaided by force or intrigue*, a like *triumph* over the *prejudices* and *passions* of mankind: among its *believers*, equal *skill* and equal *diligence* in *scrutinizing* its evidences, OR LET THEM SUBMIT TO THE IRRESISTIBLE CERTAINTY OF THE CHRISTIAN RELIGION.

And now, reader, *solemnly consider* what that religion *is*, the truth of which is proved by so many decisive marks. It is a declared revelation from God; pronounces all men guilty in his sight; proclaims pardon as his free gift through the meritorious righteousness, sacrifice, and intercession of his only Son, to all who trust alone in his mercy and grace, cordially repenting and forsaking their sins; requires fervent love, ardent zeal, and cordial submission toward himself, and the highest degree of personal purity and temperance, with rectitude and benevolence toward others; and offers the aid of the Holy Spirit for these purposes to all who sincerely ask it. *Consider*, this religion is the *only true* one, and this is *tremendously true*:—while it promises peace on earth and eternal happiness to all who *do* receive and obey it, it denounces everlasting destruction against all who *do not*. It is in vain for you to admit its truth unless you receive it as *your* confidence, and obey it as *your* rule. O study, O embrace it *for yourself;* and may the God of love and peace be with you! Amen.

THE END.

www.ingramcontent.com/pod-product-compliance
Lightning Source LLC
LaVergne TN
LVHW010230110826
845151LV00004B/1245

9781425526429